Transdisciplinary Impulses towards
Socio-Ecological Transformation

Publication Series
"Ecology and Education"
of GERA's Subdivision
Education for Sustainable Development

Schriftenreihe
„Ökologie und Erziehungswissenschaft"
der Kommission
Bildung für nachhaltige Entwicklung
der Deutschen Gesellschaft für
Erziehungswissenschaft (DGfE)

Helge Kminek
Anna Geyer
Markus B. Siewert (eds.)

Transdisciplinary Impulses towards
Socio-Ecological Transformation

Engaged Reflections – Reflected Engagements

Verlag Barbara Budrich
Opladen • Berlin • Toronto 2022

All rights reserved. No part of this publication may be reproduced, stored in or introduced into a retrieval system, or transmitted, in any form, or by any means (electronic, mechanical, photocopying, recording or otherwise) without the prior written permission of Barbara Budrich Publishers. Any person who does any unauthorized act in relation to this publication may be liable to criminal prosecution and civil claims for damages.

You must not circulate this book in any other binding or cover and you must impose this same condition on any acquirer.

A CIP catalogue record for this book is available from
Die Deutsche Bibliothek (The German Library)

© 2022 by Verlag Barbara Budrich GmbH, Opladen, Berlin & Toronto
www.budrich.eu

    ISBN 978-3-8474-2569-4
    eISBN 978-3-8474-1721-7 (PDF)
    eISBN 978-3-8474-1800-9 (EPUB)
    DOI   10.3224/84742569

Das Werk einschließlich aller seiner Teile ist urheberrechtlich geschützt. Jede Verwertung außerhalb der engen Grenzen des Urheberrechtsgesetzes ist ohne Zustimmung des Verlages unzulässig und strafbar. Das gilt insbesondere für Vervielfältigungen, Übersetzungen, Mikroverfilmungen und die Einspeicherung und Verarbeitung in elektronischen Systemen.

Die Deutsche Bibliothek – CIP-Einheitsaufnahme
Ein Titeldatensatz für die Publikation ist bei der Deutschen Bibliothek erhältlich.

Verlag Barbara Budrich GmbH
Stauffenbergstr. 7. D-51379 Leverkusen Opladen, Germany

86 Delma Drive. Toronto, ON M8W 4P6 Canada
www.barbara-budrich.net

Jacket illustration by Bettina Lehfeldt, Kleinmachnow –
   www.lehfeldtgraphic.de
Typographical editing by Anja Borkam, Jena – kontakt@lektorat-borkam.de
Printed in Europe on acid-free paper by docupoint GmbH, Barleben

Contents

Helge Kminek, Anna Geyer and Markus B. Siewert
Engaged Reflections – Reflected Engagements
Introduction to the Topic and the Contributions 7

Jonathan Maskit
Urban Mobility – Urban Discovery:
A Phenomenological Aesthetics for Urban Environments 13

Diana Hummel
Population Dynamics and Sustainable Development
in the Anthropocene 31

Christian Stache
Education for Sustainability as a Critical Theory of the Social
Relationship to Nature 51

Helge Kminek
A Contribution from the Philosophy of Science for Education for
Sustainable Development 69

Beer Albers
Autonomy and Second Nature: A Hegelian Account of Education for
Sustainable Development 91

Franz Rauch, Günther Pfaffenwimmer and Renate Hübner
Networking for Sustainability in Education 115

Leon Fuchs, Christina Höfling and Lena Theiler
ESD in the Museum: The Project BioKompass. A Practical View from
the Senckenberg Natural History Museum Frankfurt 139

Anna Geyer
Sustainable Development at Institutions of Higher Education –
The Example of Goethe University 157

Georg Ehring
Reports on Climate Change 175

List of Authors 183

Index 187

Engaged Reflections – Reflected Engagements
Introduction to the Topic and the Contributions

Helge Kminek, Anna Geyer and Markus B. Siewert

According to Goethe's *Faust* (1987), the task of science is to recognise what holds the world together at its innermost core. This task is to be expanded today. Against the backdrop of the realisation that science and research are not and cannot be value-free, an awareness of their ethical responsibility for society is forming. This is all the more accurate in light of the fact that humankind – above all the Western industrial societies of the Global North – is working towards the destruction of its own basis of life. We call this the *environmental question*. The latest IPCC report does not give us the all-clear but rather, in this context, scientists and researchers are increasingly making it their explicit task to co-operate in handling this problem.

Furthermore, there is an increasing awareness that interdisciplinary as well as transdisciplinary boundaries between science and practice must be bridged for the purpose of progress in knowledge production and problem solving. This requirement arises in connection with the environmental question. Due to its multidimensional nature, science and research will only be able to contribute systematically to solving the problem if it engages with the practical complexities which are otherwise reduced for the sake of knowledge generation.

This means that for successfully dealing with the environmental question, (i) science and practice, viewed dichotomously, are separate but dependent on each other. Yet, if one thinks dialectically, (ii) science and practice cannot be completely differentiated. (i) In dichotomous thinking, science is characterised by the fact that, freed from the pressure to act, it can reflect on practice in an unbiased way, point out its blind spots and develop proposals for solutions. Hence, science is not and cannot be practice. On the other hand, practice faces responsibility for its actions, although it can only ever justify its decision afterwards. After all, every practice of action must always be justified and justified in retrospect. This is the case even if one announces a certain action and justification in advance. (ii) Considered dialectically, science is itself a form of practice, namely when it faces its responsibility and strives to contribute to solving problems. Conversely, practice is science when the actors, within the scope of their possibilities, systematically reflect on their practice and consciously incorporate research results into their actions.

This kind of science is engaged reflection and this form of practice is reflective engagement. It is this dialectic self-understanding that the transdisciplinary contributions of this anthology have in common. *Transdisciplinary Impulses towards Socio-Ecological Transformation* is the product of a lecture series, which took place at Goethe University Frankfurt during the winter term of 2019/2020. It was part of a teaching project by the editors on Education for Sustainable Development within the framework of the quality teaching fund at Goethe University.

The volume starts with a contribution by *Jonathan Maskit* which is located in the tradition of phenomenological aesthetics. He descriptively explores whether possibilities of movement in cities enables or prevents different experiences. If one relates the contribution to the various questions concerning the design of transport infrastructure in terms of sustainability, then his philosophical contribution opens up numerous perspectives and occasions for reflection. At the same time, it indicates what philosophical reflections can contribute to the question of transformation to sustainable societies.

The humanities approach is followed by a social science contribution. *Diana Hummel* examines the significance of global population dynamics for sustainable development in the Anthropocene. She reconstructs different positions in this highly controversial scientific debate and exposes the "Social Ecology" approach which tries to overcome the separation of nature and the social. Her reflection leads to the question of the responsibility of science and normativity. She concludes by invoking six principles for inter- and transdisciplinary research.

In the third contribution to the anthology, *Christian Stache* puts forward his central thesis that a return to Marx's critique of capitalism is necessary. For this, a critique of Donna Haraway's approach takes on a central argumentation of demarcation. The approach is accused of putting nature and society in one, which is objectively wrong, as well as a strict dichotomy of nature and society. Only a Marxist-dialectical understanding of nature and society is appropriate. Furthermore, Christian Stache criticises the concepts of Education for Sustainable Development (ESD), arguing that they lack an adequate theory of society and description of the problem, for which a return to the work of Marx is decisive. Through his critique

Introduction to the Topic and the Contributions   9

of ESD, Christian Stache's contribution leads to the genuine contributions of educational science.

In the next contribution *Helge Kminek* combines issues of the Philosophy of Science and ESD. Underlying his contribution is the thesis that for the systematic further development of the debates on ESD, a science-theory informed ordering of these debates is necessary. To this end, he develops the first formal model that relates structural cornerstones to each other. The other contributions in the volume can be systematically located within this model.

Beer Albers presents a contribution to the philosophy of education and addresses whether ESD should pursue the goal of educating subjects to become mature and make autonomous reflective decisions (*Bildung*), or whether it should educate them to behave in a sustainable manner. Albers argues, following Hegel's theory of education, that the tension between education and autonomy on the one hand and education and conditioning on the other hand should be dialectically mediated and resolved at a higher level.

The contribution by *Franz Rauch, Günther Pfaffenwimmer* and *Renate Hübner* proposes that communication is a central dimension for educational processes in the context of Education for Sustainable Development. This thesis is substantiated by giving an insight into the development of a network of schools, in the sense of ESD, with reference to further background theories. The article thus highlights the importance of organisational development of schools and educational institutions that want to establish, consolidate and further develop ESD.

Leon Fuchs, Christina Höfling and *Lena Theiler* reflect on a participatory special exhibition at the Senckenberg Naturmuseum Frankfurt with regard to the question of how museums can contribute to social change processes as places of learning for Education for Sustainable Development. For this purpose, they outline the special features of (natural history) museums as extracurricular places of learning in relation to ESD, present the practical implementation of the project and conclude with a summary of the main insights gained by the project.

Examining how sustainability can be implemented at institutions of higher education, *Anna Geyer* describes the onset of a sustainable transformation at Goethe University, Frankfurt. She touches upon relevant actors, initiatives and projects, thereby underlining the importance of cooperation between academic, administrative and technical staff, political bodies and students. As critical barriers are highlighted and a first-hand account on the intricacies of pushing for sustainable transformations is provided, this approach may be valuable especially to sustainability actors at other institutions of higher education.

The anthology ends with a contribution by *Georg Ehring*. Ehring is head of the economy and environment editorial department of the radio station *Deutschlandfunk*. He reports on his experiences of journalistic work on climate change and reflects on the question of what good journalism should look like in view of the dangers posed by unrestrained climate change.

The environmental question is *the* question of our time. At the last G20 meeting and COP26 conference in Glasgow, it must have become obvious to all participants – policymakers, non-governmental organizations and activists, business representatives, scientists – that a response is overdue, and that we are in dire need of action. Even though (almost) all agree on the problem, it is still heavily contested how to define, negotiate and implement the necessary solutions. In the meantime, the possibilities for successful counter-actions are shrinking. The contributions collected in this anthology address the environmental question from very different angles but share a common core: a call for engaged reflections and reflected engagement at various levels of society. In doing so, it is our hope that the collected essays help us towards a better understanding of the underlying structural intricacies, shed light on its tensions, point towards valuable lessons and even propose solutions to address the environmental question.

Writing a book is always a team effort, and we are grateful for all the support and help we received. We would like to thank Goethe University Frankfurt for the financial support through its teaching grant scheme which allowed us to organise a module on "Education for Sustainable Development by and at the Goethe University," which this lecture series was part of. A special thanks goes to all the wonderful colleagues who participated in the lecture series and then continued their work as authors for this anthology. Holding the book in your hands, we hope that you see it as we do: as the fruit of a very productive and collegial collaboration. Our gratitude also goes to all the students and the wider public who participated in the events of the lecture series in the winter term of 2019/2020 – the last pre-Covid semester where lectures in person were still taken for granted. Finally, a very big thank you to Simone Blandford for her final proofreading of the book manuscript and to Franziska Deller for her support from the publisher Barbara Budrich. And last but not least,

Introduction to the Topic and the Contributions

Markus B. Siewert and Anna Geyer would like to express their gratitude to Helge Kminek who put the anthology together. And Helge Kminek thanks Anna Geyer very much for finding last formal errors and corrections in the bibliographies. Our project started in 2019 driven by the motivation to engage in deeper reflections and reflect on our engagement with how to work and live more sustainable at Goethe University in Frankfurt. This book is the product of this truly interdisciplinary journey.

Frankfurt & Munich, January 2022
Helge Kminek, Anna Geyer and Markus B. Siewert

Goethe, Johann W. von (1987 [1808]): Faust, part one. Translated by
   Nicholas Boyle. Cambridge: Cambridge Univ. Press.

Urban Mobility – Urban Discovery: A Phenomenological Aesthetics for Urban Environments[1]

Jonathan Maskit

1. Introduction

In "Can Cities be Both Natural and Successful?" W. S. K. Cameron argues that the "contemporary [environmental] challenge is not to renounce [cities], but to redeem them" (Cameron 2012: 42). This paper follows Cameron's lead, although I take things in a rather different direction. Cameron's paper reflects recent trends in environmental philosophy, particularly in environmental aesthetics and environmental justice. After several decades focused largely on nature, many scholars have shown a growing concern for what we might call human environments (Lawson 1995; Carlson & Berleant 2007; Menser 2013; Maskit 2016). While I recognize that both "natural" and "human" are contested terms, I wish only to distinguish here between the sorts of environments that people unreflectively treat as natural, e.g., wilderness areas, and those we treat unreflectively as human, e.g., cities (Stefanovic & Scharper 2012 explicitly problematizes this distinction). Whether there are or are not ontological, metaphysical, or other significant differences between natural and human environments is not my concern in this paper; my focus is how we experience an environment. My method is thus phenomenological or aesthetic, or, to be more accurate, phenomenologically aesthetic.

In order to avoid the apparently unsolvable puzzles posed by Cartesian scepticism, Husserl famously invoked the *epochē*, the phenomenological reduction, setting aside both the world's ontological status and questions thereabout. One might imagine that I am doing something similar here,

---

[1] The article first appeared in the Journal Environmental Philosophy in spring 2018: "Urban Mobility—Urban Discovery: A Phenomenological Aesthetics for Urban Environments". Environmental Philosophy 15, 1, pp. 43-58.
We would like to thank the editors of Environmental Philosophy for their permission to republish the article. The article has been slightly modified for this anthology.

although not, as Husserl had, to open up the space of transcendental consciousness for investigation. Rather, I wish to proceed in a more embodied way, following the method developed by Alfred Schütz, investigating how we, as embodied beings, can encounter a particular sort of environment: the city (Schutz & Luckmann 1973 and 1989; Maskit 2017). In particular, I investigate how different transportation technologies can foster or hinder our experiences of the city. In brief, this paper offers a phenomenological aesthetic account of our technologically mediated experiences of the urban environment. While there is a continuing interest in phenomenology as a method in environmental philosophy, most work in this area has concerned itself with natural environments (Bannon 2016, Donohoe 2017). Amongst environmental and everyday aestheticians, there is an ongoing interest in built environments, although most of the work in this field has not been particularly phenomenological (some exceptions: Berleant 2007; Sepänmaa 2007; Bonsdorff 2007).

Inspired by Kant's Copernican turn, although with narrower ambitions, I will pursue a phenomenology of human bodies in motion. I make no claims about introducing a second Copernican turn in philosophy or even in phenomenology. I hope only to provide an account of how being in motion, and being in motion in different ways, shapes our experience of the environment through which we move.

The goal of this paper is not, as might seem to be the case, merely descriptive. While description, phenomenological or otherwise, is certainly valuable, it is here put in service of a larger argument about the aesthetics of urban life. That argument, although more implied than developed in this paper, forms part of a larger investigation into the aesthetics of sustainable living, whose goal is to argue that a less energy- and resource-intensive form of life can, at least in certain circumstances, be both ecologically more sustainable and more humanly fulfilling. This larger project reflects an issue Cameron briefly took up in his paper on natural cities, where he argued that a city such as Bonn, Germany is liveable precisely because it is a dense, walkable city with a robust public transit network (Cameron 2012: 45).

The paper begins (II) with a framework for considering mobility from the standpoint of phenomenological everyday aesthetics. This framework suggests a tetrad of triads, in each of which the third term is a sort of *Aufhebung* of the first two. I then (III) suggest a typology of different forms of urban mobility. This typology distinguishes between private and public forms of transportation as well as between faster and slower modes. I next (IV) suggest a trio of factors that play into how we experience an urban environment while moving through it. This begins my application of the framework developed in (II) to the typology developed in (III). Next (V) I continue to apply the framework of experience and the trio of factors to the typology of transportation modes to show the ways in which each of them can foster or hinder an aesthetic experience of the urban environment. I conclude (VI) with some reflections on what has been left out or overlooked in this analysis.

2. Mobility and Phenomenological Everyday Aesthetics

What constitutes an aesthetically fulfilling daily life? This would seem to be a question beyond answer. When dealing with art or the beauty of nature, practicing aestheticians may insist that there's something to Kant's antinomy of taste: judgments of taste occupy some peculiar middle ground between pure subjectivity (*de gustibus non disputandum est*) and pure objectivity. Yet, when it comes to the everyday we are likely to lean more towards the former pole of the antinomy than the latter. It seems difficult to say that people ought to enjoy the sorts of food, drink, sporting events, style of clothing, or even style of life that I do. Subjective preference and culture seem to play overwhelming roles in these cases (Saito 2007; Light & Smith 2005; Leddy 2012).

Perhaps the problem could be phrased more formally: rather than ask what particular experiences constitute an aesthetically fulfilling everyday life, we should ask whether aesthetics matters in everyday life at all and, if so, if there are non-aesthetic aspects to life that shape its aesthetic possibilities. It seems strange to insist that a fulfilling life must include opera, landscape paintings, formal dance, or *haute cuisine*. It is equally strange to insist upon folk music, street art, line dancing, or tacos. Preference for any of these things seems at minimum culturally specific and may even be entirely subjective. Yet cultures and individuals do have preferences for these sorts of things and these preferences seem largely aesthetic. If a life is pursued, at least in part, for aesthetic reasons, then we must say that aesthetics matters even when no art is involved. That is, it seems that aesthetic experience is important to many people, although perhaps not all, at least if we have a sufficiently broad understanding of aesthetics.

How then ought we account for these everyday aesthetic possibilities and experiences? One possible answer is to provide a sweeping theory of everyday aesthetics with the goal of accounting for all possible everyday aesthetic experiences. Such is not my goal. I will instead seek to make sense of the far narrower domain of everyday experience in which I am interested: the domain of urban transportation as a "medium" of urban discovery. To do so, I propose some categories or types of experience. In a Kantian spirit, my proposed characteristics are organised into a tetrad of triads. Like Kant's table of the categories in the *Critique of Pure Reason*, my four tetrads could be grouped into two dyads, the first "spatial" (A and B) the second "temporal" (C and D). I have scare-quoted these terms to highlight (a) that my analysis is in no way transcendental and (b) that the spatial has to do as well with human bodies arrayed in a social space, whose fabric is partially constituted out of relationships, while the temporal in this instance concerns both cognition and affect.

It is important to note that there are no claims made as to any of these categories being preferable to others. Some people are more social than others. Similarly, some prefer the familiar and the safe, while others seek out the novel and even the dangerous. One might even seek what Gilles Deleuze called a degree zero of all these things: a meditative life, perhaps (Deleuze 2004: 186).

I have left out many aspects of what we might term a fulfilling life. I have made no mention of political engagement, of service, of ethics, or of duty. I make no claim that aesthetics is all that matters in life nor even that it is the most important thing. Rather, I take it to be one important part of human life. Further, while one might think that one can analytically disentangle, say, the social from the aesthetic, in practice these two are likely to be intertwined, as we see if we consider the role of food in social interaction. Perhaps it is even analytically impossible to disentangle the social from the aesthetic. Indeed, one might say that the pleasure we take in our friends is similar in kind to that we take in art or literature. Figuring out whom to invite to a party or dinner is, we might say, a sort of curatorship.

A Framework for an Everyday Phenomenological Aesthetics of Mobility (Source: own illustration.)

A.
Social Character of Experience
A.1. Being alone or being with family and friends (private life)
A.2. Being with strangers (public life)
A.3. Being in a group (communal life)

B.
Somatic Character of Experience
B.1. Moving (walking, cycling)
B.2. Being moved (jostling, avoiding)
B.3. Moving with others (social dancing, queuing)

C.
Temporal-Epistemic Character of Experience
C.1. Familiarity (the known)
C.2. Novelty (the unknown)
C.3. Serendipity (the [pleasantly] unexpected)

D.
Affective Character of Experience
D.1. Feeling of safety
D.2. Feeling of danger
D.3. Excitement (sublimity)

3. Modalities of Urban Mobility

If we consider the twelve categories I've suggested, we can see that each of them could be favoured or hindered by different material conditions. Being with family or friends requires spatial proximity. Today's world, in which so many of us, at least of a certain class, have dispersed across the globe, often lends itself to technically mediated friendships better than to embodied encounters. On the other hand, if one is interested in the novelty of being with others, then today's world affords us countless opportunities, again, given sufficient personal resources and opportunities.

These opportunities require both sufficient economic resources and a well-functioning technological system of travel, not to mention advances in global security and law. Rather than looking at global travel, my focus is on cities. How do different forms of urban organization, different forms of transportation, etc. shape the possibilities for everyday experience? What effect will urban planning, transportation modalities, density of building, etc. play in shaping the social, somatic, temporal-epistemic and affective character of experience? Or, to turn the question around, if there are certain characters of experience that are valued, either individually, or, more importantly, socially or even societally, how can choices about infrastructure make the lives lived in a place more likely to have more (or better) of the desired values? To put the question most broadly, what might a phenomenological investigation of the aesthetics of everyday life have to add to discussions about urban planning? To answer these questions, I propose thinking of transportation modes as follows:

Private Modalities

Low-speed: walking, cycling, skateboarding, pedicabs, Segways, etc.

High-speed: cars, scooters, motorcycles, taxis, etc.

Public Modalities

Low-speed: trams, buses, etc.

High-speed: subways, trains, etc.

I must make several comments before proceeding. First, my distinction between public and private is about accessibility rather than ownership. It makes no difference whether a bus is privately or publicly owned, so long as it is available to all. Similarly, a rented or borrowed car or bicycle is no less private than is one that the user owns. Second, I have assumed a city with few needs for traversing water other than by bridge or tunnel. One can easily treat ferries as an additional form of low-speed public transit, but other than those committed to kayaking and the like (low-speed private) or with access to an owned or rented motorboat (high-speed private), most of us simply won't cross water in a vehicle to which we have exclusive access. Third, my distinction between high- and low-speed is as much phenomenological as measured. Perceived velocity is, like perceived time, highly variable. Bicycling feels much faster than driving, even though it is, in terms of distance covered, usually markedly slower, except perhaps during rush hour. My categorization combines both measured and perceived speed and has to do as much with how far one is traveling and how fast one perceives the mode to be as it does with how fast one actually gets from A to B. Finally, several of these transportation modes could be either high- or low-speed (or even in-between) depending upon the layout of the city, how many other users there are and other factors. As mentioned above, walking can, in some instances, be faster than driving. Subways could be faster or slower, depending upon how far apart stations are and other factors. Subways also have the peculiar feature of leaving us with no perceivable clues as to how far we've travelled. Unless one can see some of the same features – buildings, recognizable natural landmarks, etc. both from the point of origin and the point of arrival – just how far one has travelled is difficult to know without consulting a map, whether paper or electronic.

4. Factors Affecting Our Experience of the Urban Environment

The speed of a transportation mode matters for other reasons than how quickly it gets us where we're going. While we usually use transportation simply to get from one place to another, transportation itself can be experienced aesthetically in at least two ways.

First, the experience of mobility can be, as I've argued elsewhere, boring, thrilling, enlivening, or otherwise aesthetically engaging. The degree to which mobility is engaging depends greatly on how intentional we need to be in piloting or controlling the technology. Active forms of transportation such as cycling or driving are more likely to be thrilling or otherwise engaging. Passive forms of mobility in which we are passengers tend to be more boring. These differences, however, are situational and depend to a degree on the individual. By and large, public transit does not require much attention from us, freeing us up to work, sleep, chat, or otherwise engage with others and our surroundings. By contrast, we might find cycling to work to be an entirely pleasurable experience, even if nothing particularly exciting happens on any particular day (Maskit 2017).

Second, and this is where the focus of this paper lies, different modes of transportation offer different aesthetic possibilities for encountering the city through which we move. Transportation can open a city up to us, a phenomenon we might term, after Heidegger, techno-unconcealment, or it can hide that city from us in techno-concealment. Three factors matter to make these possibilities real: (1) speed, (2) the ability to survey one's surroundings and (3) ease of interruption. In discussing these three aspects, I will keep in mind what I above termed the *temporal-epistemic character of experience*. That is, I take it that speed, the ability to survey one's surroundings and ease of interruption all play roles in whether and how we are able to experience the environment through which we move as familiar or novel. In particular, I am interested in how these three factors make possible the discovery and exploration of novelty.

Speed. I sorted various transportation modalities above by how quickly they get us from one place to another, although I also suggested that this notion of speed is intended to capture both measured velocity and the experience of speed. While speed is often associated with efficiency, to do so emphasizes the teleological aspects of transportation over the experiential. It is certainly true that if one's only goal is to get someplace, then getting there faster is probably, all-in-all, a good thing. However, if one's goal is to discover where one is – to experience the place or see what it has to offer – then speed is not necessarily an ally. Whether from the windows of a car or the windows of a train, our surroundings pass us by (a strange turn of phrase – we are the ones who are in motion) so quickly that we often have a hard time discerning what we're seeing. If we add to this velocity the need to pay attention that accompanies many private transportation modes, then our ability to perceive our surroundings, at least if we are driving rather than being a passenger, may well be sharply reduced.

By contrast, slower modes of transport move one more slowly (obviously!), thus providing more time to look around. Trams move more slowly than trains and stop more often, providing riders more time to figure out what they are seeing or even where they are. Walking, cycling and the like, although they require one to pay attention to where one is going, because they happen more slowly, permit one also to look around, even while moving. While a bicyclist may not be able to look away from the road for any longer than a driver, because they are moving more slowly they can survey their surroundings more carefully.

Ability to survey one's surroundings. Speed, it turns out, is of import primarily for how it affects our ability to survey the urban fabric as we traverse it. There are, however, other factors at work. All modes of enclosed transportation – cars, buses, trains, trams, etc. – provide only a limited view of one's surroundings. Only from the front seats, if even there, can one see one's surroundings "as they develop". Passengers seated further back have, at best, views to right and left, meaning that the amount of time they have to figure out what they're seeing is limited. Things become more complicated when the car or bus is on a highway, the train is on an elevated track, or, most starkly, the subway is in a tunnel. From these vantage points, one may get a view onto things one wouldn't otherwise have: the view from a bridge or elevated railway line may let one see a park or waterfront one might have missed from street level, but more often than not one feels oneself removed from the city, perhaps unsure of where one is, and mostly unable really to *see* one's surroundings. This situation is clearest with subways, which, by definition, run below the streets, through tunnels. One can see nothing as one travels, other than perhaps the occasional light or flash of electricity. Upon leaving, we often find ourselves disoriented as to where we are and what direction we are facing. Coming out of the subway, unless one already knows the station and the neighbourhood, almost always require some sort of re-orientation. Taken together, these factors lead to a disjointed or incoherent form of experience, i.e., one may not be fully aware of what one is seeing, where one is, etc.

By contrast, non-enclosed transportation modes, walking, cycling and the like, permit one to survey one's surroundings more coherently. One can scan in all directions without one's vision being fragmented by window frames, a roof, etc. Our other senses too, can play a larger role with these transportation modes. We can hear what is going on around us, rather than what is happening inside the vehicle; we can smell where we are; we can feel the temperature of the air. This sensory connectedness to one's environment is only possible if one is *outside*, which is to say *in* the place where one is, rather than *in* a vehicle.

The ability to sense where one is, is itself part of the aesthetics of urban life. To pass through in a metal box leaves one always a bit disconnected from where one is. We might term this phenomenon transportation mediation. Counter-intuitively, my experience has been that motorized forms of urban transportation also give one a warped sense of how far it is from one place to another. The simple fact of getting in a car or taking a bus or train makes things seem further away than they are. (This phenomenon is even clearer with airplanes.) It is only when one bikes or walks that one may discover how close by something is that had seemed like it was more of a journey. Just as one does not have a sense of how much work is required to, say, make mayonnaise, until one has done it oneself, one's sense of time, space and distance only becomes clear when one moves oneself.

Ease of interruption. An additional factor to be considered is how easy it is to interrupt one's journey if one's interest is piqued. We see something, perhaps we don't yet know what, from our seat on the bus or the saddle of our bicycle and, time permitting (which all too often it isn't), we may wish to stop to investigate. Here again users of slower modes of transportation have an advantage. Pedestrians can simply stop, turn around, go back, cross the street, etc. if they see, hear, or smell something of interest. Riders of trams and buses too, can interrupt their journeys if they should happen to see a storefront, statue, or street performer they'd like to investigate further. Unlike the pedestrian, the public transit user may have to reckon with buying another ticket or waiting for the next tram or bus. These temporal or financial exigencies may be enough to discourage some exploration.

Other forms of low-speed private transportation – cycling, skateboarding, etc. – lend themselves as well, or almost as well, to interruption as does walking. Skateboarding requires only picking up the board, at which point one becomes a pedestrian. Cycling can be slightly more complicated. One can walk the bike, which may not permit access to museums, shops, or restaurants. Alternatively, one can search for someplace to lock the bicycle, which is a commitment of time, but unlike with public transit, not usually of money.

Train and subway riders, although they are, as we saw above, less likely to have reason to interrupt their journeys, can do so under the same sorts of conditions as tram and bus riders: they may have to wait or pay an additional fare. Drivers of cars, however, are particularly disadvantaged in this regard. We saw above that they are less likely to have reason to stop – they simply can't both watch the road and visually catch novelties. If a driver does decide to stop, they now must deal with their car. Unlike the skateboard, which can simply be carried, or the bicycle, that can be walked or (often) relatively easily parked, the car often becomes all-too-present-at-hand when one decides to stop. The denser the city, the harder or more expensive it will be to park a car. The opportunity costs, whether in time or money, involved in stopping to investigate something that looked like it might be interesting are most often too high to be overcome. That is, unless there is low-cost or free parking adjacent to what one wishes to investigate, most of us simply won't bother stopping. Unlike pedestrians, cyclists and users of public transit, drivers, it turns out, are uniquely disadvantaged in their ability to explore the space through which they travel.

5. The Aesthetics of Urban Mobility

In the preceding section I discussed the ways in which different transportation modalities provide different access to the aesthetic possibilities of the city. I did so by looking at the speed of different transportation modes, the ability to survey one's surroundings they provide, and the ease with which they could be interrupted. That is, I investigated the *temporal-epistemic character of experience* fostered or hindered by different forms of transportation. I argued that pedestrians, cyclists and users of other low-speed forms of private transportation are particularly well positioned to explore the city. Next come tram and bus passengers, who may, in some cases, have certain advantages, for example, in a sprawling city or one with particularly inhospitable weather. One thing I have left out of my account has been the possibility of hybrid mobility in which one combines two or more transportation modes. Public transit in many places is built to accommodate bicycles or other forms of low-speed private transportation, thus making possible a form of low-then-high-then-low speed travel. Similarly, one could set out to explore a particular neighbourhood on foot, but arrive there by public transit. Cars too can be used in this way, although one must still deal with parking as discussed above. Only in those cities that are built low to the ground and truly sprawling does a car or motorcycle make sense as a viable form of urban exploration, although it must be noted that this is possible in part because such sprawl is usually unable to support much in the way of public transit, leaving private motorized transportation as perhaps the best (or only) option. In other words, questions concerning the effectiveness of a form of transportation cannot be fully addressed without also addressing urban density and planning. Unfortunately, such issues cannot be addressed here (see section VI).

What I have not yet discussed, except in passing, are the ways in which getting around the city can *itself* be aesthetic. I have argued elsewhere that a complete phenomenology of mobility would need to account for both a multiplicity of transportation modes (as above), but also for a multiplicity of differences between users of transportation along axes such as age, sex, sexuality, physical ability and the like. Overlapping these two matrices I looked at experiences of safety, excitement, autonomy and the like as elements of lived experience (Maskit 2017). To give a complete account of the aesthetics of transport would require something similar. One cannot expect all transportation users to have the same aesthetic possibilities or experiences. I will here give only an abbreviated account of the aesthetics of mobility using two further triads from the framework for an aesthetics of mobility I developed in section II.

Social Character of Experience. All forms of public transit entail being with strangers. One must share the space of the bus, tram, or train with those one does not know. Such public life offers aesthetic possibilities that are both positive – street performers, people-watching, the voyeuristic thrill of listening to others' conversations – and negative – aggression, poor bodily hygiene, unwelcome comments and the like. But public transit can also offer opportunities for being with family and friends that are, because of the situation, different from possibilities to be had outside the transit environment. Because the space is public, friends and family may hesitate to have the most intimate of conversations, perhaps out of fear of embarrassment. Unlike most forms of private transportation, public transit offers a form of communal life. For example, on the way to or from a sporting event one experiences being with the other supporters of one's team, even if they are all strangers. On the other hand, game day may well be one of the most alienating times to ride public transit for those who are indifferent or, even worse, for those who root for the visiting team.

Low-speed forms of private transportation also offer some interesting social-aesthetic possibilities. Unlike being in a car, where one is largely cut off from others and must rely on gestures and honking even to attempt communication, pedestrians, cyclists and the like share a social space with others and can, if both parties wish, engage with those others. One might set out alone and then become part of a group. But these forms of mobility are also well suited to groups made up of friends or family. While walking or riding with others may not permit the uninterrupted stretches of time that riding transit does, it provides a greater degree of intimacy, since one and one's companions are not in a mobile space, such as a tram, but are moving through space with a constantly changing cast of strangers, none of whom will be privy to more than a snippet of conversation. Like public transit, walking, cycling and the like require that we share space intimately (although more transiently) with those we don't know, again, for better or for worse. And, again like public transit, these forms of transportation lend themselves well to communal life. Indeed, the final approach to, or the initial exit from, a stadium, theatre, or festival is most likely to be on foot (or in a wheelchair) in a space intimately shared with those strangers with whom one will share, or will have shared, some communal experience.

The automobile (or taxi) stands out for its social insularity. If one drives alone, one has no social interaction while driving, other than those mediated by technology, say, by talking on the phone. Multiple occupants of a car share a space, but that space is both cut off from the space outside of it and rigidly structured. Unlike many modes of public transit, which permit people to sit facing each other or at least to move about, the car holds its passengers in place. All sit facing forward with one, the driver, never fully able to take part in social interaction. Because passengers cannot all see each other, the gestural aspects of communication are diminished, as is the ability to gauge others' reactions. On the other hand, because the car's interior is not shared with strangers and the time there mostly cannot be used for other activities, it lends itself to a particular sort of intimacy. Parents and children, for example, may find this the only time when they really talk to each other about substantive things (Vazquez 2017). This, at least, can be the case, although the proliferation of smart phones, video entertainment systems and the like may well make this intimacy less likely to occur.

Somatic Character of Experience. Here things become more complicated, as all forms of getting around are necessarily bodily. Here we might order the various forms of transportation along two different axes. The first assesses degree of *somatic activity*, the second assesses degree of *intentional engagement*. There is a degree of artificiality to this distinction, since somatic activity, other than that governed by the autonomous nervous system, cannot happen without intentional engagement. Nevertheless, the distinction is analytically useful, since it helps us see that an activity such as driving a car, which requires little physical exertion, is nevertheless intensely engaging, while walking may well require significantly more physical exertion, but significantly less intentional engagement. I do not, however, mean to limit somatic activity to mere physical exertion, which is partly why the distinction is artificial. Walking, cycling, driving and the like are all learned activities in which somatic activity and intentional engagement are, in practice, inseparable.

On the scale of somatic activity, walking and cycling are clearly the most somatically active modes of transportation, as they both require the (almost) constant use of our large muscles in order to succeed. Being a passenger on public transit, at least *while* one is a passenger (since one must get to, on and off the bus, tram, or train by walking or rolling) and *if* one has been lucky enough to find a seat, is, at least as far as locomotion is concerned, passive. Yes, one uses one's body to look around, but one's body provides none of the energy for forward motion. Standing on a moving bus or tram requires distinctly more somatic activity than does standing on a sidewalk, although less activity than one expends in walking or cycling. Driving a car may require more somatic engagement than sitting on public transit since driving requires almost constant, but subtle, movements of the head, hands and feet. Such movements are by and large less strenuous than those involved in standing on a bus or train in motion. Being a passenger in a car is more passive than being on public transit, since one is literally bound in place.

On the scale of intentional engagement, automobiles, bicycles and motorized forms of personal transportation lead the pack. All require near-constant attention to one's environment, since, as those who drive or ride know, something unexpected can always happen. Walking, because of its slower speed and more deeply embedded somatic character, requires less of our attention, at least so long as the pavement is level and not-too-crowded. As soon as we have to navigate surface irregularities, crowds, or interactions with other transportation modes, e.g., while crossing a street, walking too may require our full attention. Public transit, if we're seated, except insofar as we are unsure where we are going or need to change modes, requires little intentional bodily engagement, other than attempting not to crowd others or the like. Standing in a moving vehicle often turns out to be an intensely engaged form of somatic activity, one that is not merely muscular, but also intentional.

There are further elements to the somatic character of experience. Whether we find ourselves in a position where others may affect us in our bodies also varies with transportation mode. In cars, we are almost entirely isolated from anyone other than those with whom we have chosen to share the car's interior. Others affect our bodies, for the most part, only in traumatic ways, as in a collision. In public transit we are open to being bumped, jostled, stepped upon and the like. While walking too we are prone, especially in crowds, to these sorts of inadvertent contact with others. While cycling and the like, as with driving, we hope to avoid such contact, as it is often dangerous, or at least destabilizing.

No form of transportation, other than perhaps walking, seems easily to support the sort of sophisticated, coordinated movement of dancing and the like. Walking, and insofar as it is an extension of walking public transit, lends itself to holding hands, skipping and hugging. One might say that walking can even be dancing, at least in some circumstances. Bicycling and the like are less amenable, as is riding in a car, although for somewhat different reasons. While cycling, contact with others, even if planned, is hard to pull off, except for short spans of time or under controlled circumstances. Cars permit the holding of hands and the like, but the limited somatic mobility, and the need for the driver to use her hands to

Urban Mobility – Urban Discovery 27

steer or shift, means that any coordinated action must be rather limited in scope.

6. Summary and Outlook

There are a number of important topics that I have not discussed in this paper, although they have mostly been mentioned, at least in passing. I would like to address these briefly in closing as a more complete treatment of the aesthetics of mobility would need to take account of these issues.

First is the *affective character of experience*. I have passed over this topic in part because it is something I have discussed elsewhere (Maskit 2017). More importantly whether we feel safe or endangered, bored or excited, while moving about a city is much more a part of the experience of the particular mode of transportation we are using and much less about what we are able to discover about the city through which we move. However, taking account of safety and the perception thereof is certainly an important part of urban planning and certainly is worth analysis as part of the phenomenological aesthetics of transit.

Second are issues concerning *power*. If urban space is structured by power, as theorists such as Michel de Certeau have argued, then such structuration needs to be accounted for in an analysis of mobility (de Certeau 2011). It is not simply that some have greater access to the city than do others (although this is certainly part of it). It is rather that the very way in which space is structured is itself an instantiation of power that fosters or hinders different forms of life.

Third are the problems associated with *mobility and difference*. There are a number of problems that arise for a phenomenology of transportation if we consider age, sex/gender, sexuality, race, dis/ability, class and the like. I have been writing as if all of us were, in many regards, the same: equally in/vulnerable, equally able, etc. Yet we know that there are real differences that make a difference in how well one mode of transportation will or won't work for any given person. There are issues of safety (both real and perceived), autonomy, etc. (Maskit 2017).

Fourth are questions that arise around *technological mediation*. Seen one way, headphones and portable music, which have been with us since the 1980s, cut us off, at least partially, from the soundscape of the city. Seen another way, these technologies transform our experience of where we are, giving us a curated soundtrack that can enhance our experience, just as music does for a film. Either way, it is clear that this is a technological mediation of our experience that needs to be accounted for. Smartphones, which give us constant access to our work, our friends, our social media, etc. act simultaneously to mediate our experience of where we are, often by making us feel distant from that place because we are techno-mentally "somewhere else". The widespread use of mapping software has surely changed our sense of place as well. We now have a far more detailed sense of where we are and what's nearby, but this leaves far less of our experience up to chance, thus reducing the possibility of serendipity. Why, for example, go into a promising looking bar, café, or restaurant, when one can see what others have thought of it first? This may well save us from some disappointing experiences, but it means that the aesthetic evaluations of daily life are now crowd-sourced, which may lead, in some cases, to a sort of levelling down.

A different sort of technological mediation is likely to arise with self-driving vehicles. While such vehicles form a vanishingly minor part of the transportation world today, they are likely to be increasingly important and thus are in need of consideration.

Finally, there are issues concerning *spatial planning*. I have been discussing how we encounter a city without consideration of the city's transportation infrastructure. Poorly maintained public transit is a very different thing from that which is well maintained. Walking, cycling and the like can be difficult and more dangerous in a space shared with cars. Cyclists, if provided with their own system of bike paths, can pay less attention to traffic and more to the space they are navigating. By contrast, cyclists who must "share" the road with motorized vehicles are severely restricted in their ability to experience their environment. This issue lets us see that if we want to make it possible for people to experience our cities in the best possible way, those cities need to be built in a way to make such experiences possible.

Bibliography

Bannon, Bryan E. (2016): Nature and Experience: Phenomenology and the Environment. London: Rowman & Littlefield International.
Berleant, Arnold (2007): Cultivating an Urban Aesthetic. In: Carlson, Allen/Berleant, Arnold (ed.): The Aesthetics of Human Environments. Peterborough, ON: Broadview Press, pp. 79-91.
Bonsdorff, Pauline von (2007): Urban Richness and the Art of Building. In: Carlson, Allen/Berleant, Arnold (ed.): The Aesthetics of Human Environments. Peterborough, ON: Broadview Press, pp. 66-78.
Cameron, W. S. K. (2012): Can Cities be Both Natural and Successful? Reflections Grounding Two Apparently Oxymoronic Aspirations. In: Stefanovic, Ingrid

L./Scharper, Stephen B. (ed.): The Natural City: Re-Envisioning the Built Environment. ON: Univ. of Toronto Press, pp. 36-49.
Carlson, Allen/Berleant, Arnold (2007): The Aesthetics of Human Environments. Peterborough, ON: Broadview Press.
de Certeau, Michel (2011): The Practice of Everyday Life. 3rd edition. Translated by Steven F. Rendall. Berkeley: Univ. of California Press.
Deleuze, Gilles (2004): Desert Islands and Other Texts. Edited by David Lapoujade. Translated by Michael Taormina. Los Angeles: Semiotext(e).
Donohoe, Janet (2017): Place and Phenomenology. London: Rowman & Littlefield International.
Kenaan, Hagi (2016): Streetography: On Visual Resistance. In: Journal of Aesthetics and Phenomenology 3, pp. 147-166.
Lawson, Bill (1995): Living for the City: Urban United States and Environmental Justice. In: Lawson, Bill/Westra, Laura (ed.): Faces of Environmental Racism. Lanham, MD: Rowman & Littlefield, pp. 41-56.
Light, Andrew/Smith, Jonathan M. (2005): The Aesthetics of Everyday Life. NY: Columbia Univ. Press.
Leddy, Thomas (2012): The Extraordinary in the Ordinary: The Aesthetics of Everyday Life. Peterborough, ON: Broadview Press.
Maskit, Jonathan (2016): Urban Aesthetics. Special issue of The Journal of Aesthetics and Phenomenology 3.2.
Maskit, Jonathan (2017): Lifeworld Transit Difference. In: Donohoe, Janet (ed.): Place and Phenomenology. London: Rowman & Littlefield International, pp. 227-244.
Menser, Michael (2013): The Bioregion and Social Difference: Learning from Iris Young's Metropolitan Regionalism. In: Environmental Ethics 35, pp. 439-459.
Saito, Yuriko (2007): Everyday Aesthetics. Oxford: Oxford Univ. Press.
Schutz, Alfred/Luckmann, Thomas (1973): Structures of the Lifeworld. Volume One. Translated by Richard Zaner and H. Tristram Englehardt. Jr. Evanston, IL: Northwestern Univ. Press.
Schutz, Alfred/Luckmann, Thomas (1989): Structures of the Lifeworld. Volume Two. Translated by Richard Zaner and H. Tristram Englehardt. Jr. Evanston, IL: Northwestern Univ. Press.
Sepänmaa, Yrjö (2007): Multi-sensoriness and the City. In: Carlson, Allen/Berleant, Arnold (ed.): The Aesthetics of Human Environments. Peterborough, ON: Broadview Press, pp. 92-99.
Stefanovic, Ingrid L./Scharper, Stephen B. (2012): The Natural City: Re-Envisioning the Built Environment. Toronto, ON: Univ. of Toronto Press.
Vazquez, Raine (2017): Post-presentation discussion at Considerations in Urban Aesthetics: Planning, Mobilities, and Everyday Life (12th IIAA International Summer Conference on Environmental Aesthetics). Lahti/Helsinki, Finland.

Population Dynamics and Sustainable Development in the Anthropocene

Diana Hummel

1. Introduction

The impact of demographic changes on society and on natural life support systems is frequently the subject of intense and controversial debate, both within science and public discourse. The size and growth, spatial distribution, age structure and future development of the human population influence virtually all areas of society e.g., the demand for goods and services, political stability, economic development, utilization of natural resources and ecosystems. Demographic changes can thus pose considerable challenges for sustainable development and related policies. The current development of the human population has significant impacts on the distant future, while at the same time, estimates of future trends of the human population are characterized by considerable uncertainty and limited reliability. In addition, it is difficult to determine the connection between population dynamics and sustainability, since the problems associated with demographic changes are complex as a result of strong interactions of social, cultural, ecological, economic and political aspects at different temporal, spatial and social scales.

In the context of the diagnosis of the Anthropocene, the topic of human population dynamics has gained momentum. The Anthropocene – the "age of humankind" – signifies a new geological epoch, in which human activity is regarded as the dominant driver of planetary evolution, and from which human responsibility for the future of the planet is derived (Ellis 2018; Horn & Bergthaller 2019). Notwithstanding the various significations and rationales of the Anthropocene concept, it "has become a device for re-examining and discussing the role of humanity in the natural world, on timescales from the deep past to the far future, and on scales from the intimately reflective and personal to the planetary and geological" (Malhi 2017: 25.6).

The geoscientific hypothesis asserts that from at least the beginning of industrialization in the mid-18th century, "humankind" has left deep and visible traces on Earth, as serious as geophysical forces such as meteor strikes, the ice age or volcanic events. Since then, the concept has found its way beyond the Earth system sciences into other scientific discourses spanning across natural sciences, social sciences and the humanities, as well as extra-scientific realms such as the arts. Correspondingly, the concept can be employed for a range of diverse purposes. "As its broadest contemporary use it encompasses a notion that the relationship of humanity with the natural world has changed, (…) that therefore all of 'nature' is touched by the hand of humanity, and that realization of the implications of this change requires a new worldview" (Malhi 2017: 25.6f.). The concept of the Anthropocene can therefore be regarded both as a "boundary concept" at the interface of science, society and politics, and as a "scientific mindset" of diagnosing the times as a global social-ecological crisis. The latter points to new constellations of societal relations to nature and thus to the nexus of people, nature and politics (Jahn et al. 2016).

In the context of this debate, the topic of "human population dynamics" is gaining (renewed) significance. The numerical development of the world population seems to confirm the hypothesis of the Anthropocene. According to estimates of the United Nations, the world population, currently around 7.9 billion people, could grow to around 9.7 billion in 2050 and 10.9 billion at the end of this century (UN-DESA 2019a). The question then arises: What is the significance of human population dynamics for sustainable development in the Anthropocene? As will be illustrated in this chapter, the topic is considered and discussed – often very controversially – in academic and public debates, and the question can be answered very differently.

The chapter starts with a brief illustration of the major characteristics of global population changes. Subsequently, different narratives of population and development in the Anthropocene are outlined. After that, the approach of Social Ecology will be highlighted, which perceives the issue of population dynamics within the concept of societal relations to nature with a focus on the population's provisioning. The chapter concludes with some considerations on the role and contribution of science.

1.1   *Global Population Dynamics: Trends and Heterogeneity*

Over the last few centuries, the world has witnessed tremendous demographic transformations, and the 20th century recorded the fastest-ever changes in population size. Between 1800 and 1927, the number of human earth inhabitants doubled from one to two billion and in the 20th century it quadrupled in size, from 1.6 to 6.1 billion people. In 2021, the global population reached around 7.9 billion people. According to the recent revision of the World Population Prospects of the United Nations (UN-DESA 2019a), four demographic "megatrends" hold important implications for sustainable development: population growth, population ageing, migration and urbanization, as well as key trends in human fertility and mortality.

Population growth: At a global level, estimates assume continued population growth, albeit at a slowing rate. The growth rate of the world's population peaked between 1965 and 1970 by around 2.1 percent per year. Since then, the pace of global population growth has slowed by half, and is projected to continue to slow through the end of the 21st century. Future demographic development depends on specific assumptions underlying the projections, (e.g., the rate of fertility decline in a given world region or country), which are, however, characterized by inherent uncertainty. At the global level, uncertainty depends on the range of plausible future trends in fertility, mortality and international migration, which have been assessed by the UN demographers for each country or area using demographic and statistical methods. This analysis concludes that, with a certainty of 95 percent, the size of the global population will stand between 8.5 and 8.6 billion people in 2030, between 9.4 and 10.1 billion in 2050, and between 9.4 and 12.7 billion in 2100 (UN-DESA 2019a: 5).

Decreasing fertility rates and increasing life expectancy: Global population dynamics are driven largely by trends in fertility. On a global scale, the average number of live births per woman over a life time has dropped considerably over the past several decades. In 1990, the total fertility rate amounted to 3.2 children and decreased to 2.5 children per woman in 2019. Fortunately, global life expectancy is expected to keep on rising from the average of 72.6 years in 2019 to 77.1 years in 2050 (UN-DESA 2019a: 28).

Population ageing: Given the declining fertility rates and rising life expectancy, the future world population will grow older. It is projected that the number of people aged 65 or more will double between 2019 and 2050, while the number of children under five is projected to remain unchanged. According to the estimates of the UN Population Division, in 2050 there will be more than twice as many people 65 or older than children under five (UN-DESA 2019a).

Migration, international as well as national, has intensified during the last decades as a result of globalization and related social, economic, political, technological and environmental crises and transformations.

According to the International Organization for Migration (IOM 2020), the number of international migrants was estimated to be around 272 million people globally in 2019, which is over three times higher than the estimated number of 84 million people in 1970 (IOM 2020: 21). However, the majority of people move within their own countries, with an estimated 740 million internal migrants in 2009 (IOM 2020: 19). In addition, refugee movements must be considered, with a global refugee population of almost 29 million people in 2018. These are, however, only official numbers. In addition, displaced persons on a national level who moved due to violence and conflict must be added. Their number is estimated to be around 41.3 million (IOM 2020: 3f.).

Urbanization is a further demographic megatrend of great significance for sustainable development. Globally, there are already more people living in cities and urban areas than in rural regions, reaching 55 percent of the world's population in 2018. It is estimated that by 2050, around 68 percent of the world's population will live in urban areas (UN-DESA 2019b).

While these megatrends and transformations appear to be general demographic patterns on a global scale, population dynamics have produced unprecedented demographic diversity across regions and countries. In addition to the overall trends, it is the disparity and non-simultaneity that represent specific characteristics of global population dynamics, which can be detected between and within individual countries and regions i.e., with respect to alterations of the population's age structure or changes in fertility rates. For example, some groups of countries in the Global South still record high fertility rates, while others record low fertility rates which until recently were only found in high-income countries in the Global North. For example, in the period between 2015 and 2020, African sub-Sahara countries recorded on average 4.6 live births per woman, while Thailand and Brazil registered a total fertility rate (TFR) of 1.5 respectively with 1.7 live births per woman. France recorded a TFR of 1.9 and in Germany the number was 1.6 (UN-DESA 2019c).

Along with the growing heterogeneity of global demographic developments, scientific and public discourses and problem descriptions have changed (Hummel 2011; 2012). Until the 1990s, global population development and population growth in developing countries were the focus of attention. Already since the 1970s, when the world population grew exponentially and the doubling periods of world population size became increasingly shorter, the concern for the natural environment and the threat of overuse of finite natural resources has become increasingly articulated in academic and public discourse. Even today, in view of the global climate crisis, biodiversity loss and resource depletion, it is frequently argued that growing population numbers (particularly in the

Global South) will increase the demand for goods and services for basic needs satisfaction and will thus increase CO_2 emissions and exacerbate environmental destruction. At the same time, decreasing population numbers and fertility rates, as well as population ageing (particularly in the Global North) are often regarded as ecologically relieving (Livi Bacci 2017). These ideas are often driven by notions of simple causal connections: the fewer people, the less resource consumption and ecological destruction. But what significance is assigned to human population dynamics in the Anthropocene debate?

2. Narratives of Population and Development in the Anthropocene Debate

Points of view concerning the topic of population dynamics can be related to the following narratives that are characteristic of Anthropocene discourse: a) analytical-descriptive narratives, b) alarmistic-catastrophic narratives, c) optimistic-technocratic narratives and d) critical-relational narratives. Admittedly, these narratives comprise a broad spectrum of arguments and can be differently labelled; they can also vary and or overlap (for partially similar and different narratives see Dürbeck 2018; Bonneuil 2016; Jahn & Keil 2021). Although not all problem descriptions regarding population dynamics explicitly refer to the idea of an Anthropocene, the various narratives can serve to organise and structure the diverse discourses on demographic changes, global-ecological crises phenomena and sustainable development, as well as respective lines of reasoning.

2.1 Analytical-descriptive Narratives

Analytical-descriptive narratives see population dynamics as one essential driving force among other interconnected global drivers of planetary upheavals such as climate change, biodiversity loss or increasing scarcity and pollution of water resources. These narratives usually focus on the global scale and depict the massive, irremediable impact of human activity on the planet. Population dynamics – notably population growth – is habitually related to other factors such as the global gross domestic product (GDP), landcover changes and resource utilization by means of quantitative model calculations and simulations, without necessarily being associated with normative statements on demographic development. For example, in his high-profile article entitled "Geology of Mankind", the atmosphere chemist Paul Crutzen stated that,

> The rapid expansion of mankind in numbers and per capita exploitation of Earth' resources has continued apace. During the past three centuries, the human population has increased tenfold to more than 6 billion and is expected to reach 10 billion (Crutzen 2002: 23).

The author continues to point out the anthropogenic impacts on the global ecosystem such as the expansion of land use, destruction of tropical rainforests, overexploitation of fresh water resources and the increase in greenhouse gases. "So far, these effects have largely been caused by only 25% of the world population" (ibid.). This statement addresses the high resource consumption of the rich industrialized countries, but Crutzen remains prosaic and does not stoop to calls for curbing population growth.

Similarly, the analytical-descriptive narrative also applies to the hypothesis of the "Great Acceleration" which is closely related to the concept of "Planetary Boundaries". The latter defines thresholds or tipping points for a total of nine areas of the Earth system, with already exceeded threshold values in three areas: climate change, biodiversity and nitrogen input into the biosphere. Other areas with problematic tendencies are stratospheric ozone depletion, ocean acidification, global fresh water use, land use change, atmospheric aerosol loading and chemical pollution. These essential dimensions are intended to provide a "safe operating space for humanity" (Rockstroem et al. 2009).

With the concept of "Great Acceleration", Will Steffen and colleagues (Steffen et al. 2015) depicted the simultaneous acceleration of growth rates across twelve socio-economic trends. Among them were the population in general, urban population, water use and the GDP, as well as twelve Earth System trends (including carbon dioxide, methane, surface temperature, tropical forest loss) from 1750 until 2000, with an update in 2010 and a distinction between OECD (Organization for Economic Cooperation and Development) countries, BRICS countries (Brazil, Russia, India, China and South Africa) and the rest of the world. One of the most notable insights the study provides is the emphasis on the fact that most population growth has been in the non-OECD countries, while the world's economy (in terms of GDP) is still dominated by the OECD countries. Regarding the impacts of consumption, the largest share of the human imprint on the Earth System can be attributed to OECD countries. According to the authors, this finding is one of the most striking results, which "points to the profound scale of global inequality, which distorts the distribution of the benefits of the Great Acceleration and confounds efforts to deal with its impacts on the Earth System" (Steffen et al. 2015: 91).

A recent study dealing with the options of sustainable nutrition within the planetary boundaries reveals that food security for a world population of more than 10 billion people is feasible (Gerten et al. 2020). As the authors illustrate, today almost half of the current global agricultural food production depends on local to global transgressions of four interlinked planetary boundaries: biosphere integrity, land-system change, fresh water use and the nitrogen cycle. As the model reveals, respecting these boundaries could currently provide food security for only 3.4 billion people. However, as the simulations suggest, transformations towards more sustainable agriculture and consumption patterns could support the alimentation of 10.2 billion people with 2,355 kcal per capita per day within the respective planetary boundaries (ibid.: 201). Essential prerequisites are optimized water, nutrients and land management, reduction of food losses, spatial reallocation of cropland, as well as dietary changes towards less resource-demanding food consumption.

2.1.1 Alarmistic-catastrophic Narratives

Alarmistic-catastrophic narratives regard "humanity" as the major destructive force of life support systems. With its expansive way of living and its resource-exploiting economy, humankind destroys its own basis of development and that of all other life on earth.

Efforts to understand the relation between demographic, social and environmental changes have a long tradition, beginning with Thomas Malthus' concern regarding increasing populations that outstrip the food bases. In his "Essay on the Principle of Population" (Malthus 1798) he stated that given its exponential growth, the human population is basically growing faster than food production. Sooner or later, unchecked population growth would result in misery, famine and epidemics and would thus also lead to a reduction of the population.

In the Anthropocene discourse, a resurgence of neo-Malthusian ideologies can be observed, i.e., ideologies that primarily consider population growth and high birth rates in countries of the Global South as the central cause of ecological destruction, poverty and growing conflicts and call for measures to curb population growth. Warnings concerning the consequences of "overpopulation" or even of a "population explosion" frequently entered the debate decades ago, for instance with Paul Ehrlich's book *The Population Bomb* (Ehrlich 1968). In the report *The Limits to Growth* (Meadows et al. 1972), the Club of Rome predicted an "overshoot and collapse" of global carrying capacity over the next 100 years. Such scenarios of collapse are based on the assumption that the world population or the population in countries of the Global

South will grow too fast or even exponentially without population control, thus exceeding the limits of (global) carrying capacity.

With the debate on sustainable development from the 1980s onward, the ecological discourse became increasingly linked to the discourse on development and modernization, and the topic of 'population dynamics' was for a long time widely seen in connection with the population growth in developing countries. The World Commission on Environment and Development argued that "rapidly growing populations can increase the pressure on resources and slow any rise in living standards; thus sustainable development can only be pursued if population size and growth are in harmony with the changing productive potential of the ecosystem" (WECD 1987: 9). This argument implies a notion of an optimal population size and composition, however, without this being explicitly and more precisely elucidated. In light of global climate change, the neo-Malthusian assumption of population growth as a major driver is (re)emphasized. For example, in 2017, more than 15,000 scholars from all over the world signed the "World Scientists' Warning to Humanity" which states that, "We are jeopardizing our future by not reining in our intense but geographically and demographically uneven material consumption and by not perceiving continued rapid population growth as a primary driver behind many ecological and even societal threats" (Ripple et al. 2017: 1026). In addition to nature conservation, environmental education, the promotion of plant-based diets, green technologies and the reduction of birth rates through better access to family planning are called for in the declaration as urgent measures.

The British campaign "Population Matters", earlier named "Optimum Population Trust", has suggested even more drastic measures:

> We can and must ease the pressure on our world. As individuals and communities, we can take action such as buying less, reusing and recycling more, moving towards a plant-based diet and ensuring what we do use and consume is sustainable as possible. Above all, we can choose to have smaller families. As long as our numbers are growing, the value of every other action we take risks being cancelled out by the demands and needs of new people joining the population (see online: https://populationmatters.org/campaigns/anthropocene; accessed: 28.06.2021).

In these narratives of overshooting planetary carrying capacity due to unchecked population growth, the microcosm of individual lifestyles is linked to the macrocosm of global-ecological or even planetary crises. Solution strategies with reference to global threats bring about new critical scales for people's everyday actions. Similar to the use of plastic bags and cars or vegetarian lifestyles, the number of children of individual women and men is no longer a private matter, but becomes a matter of planetary importance. Thus, in these narratives, the curtailment of the birth rate in the Global South and the restriction of resource-wasting consumption in the Global North can apparently be easily offset against one another. Recently, the initiative "BirthStrike" has been set up by critical young women and men who, in the face of the climate crisis, publicly decide against bringing children into the word. However, this initiative explicitly distinguishes itself from anti-natalist movements and seeks to communicate the urgency of the global ecological crisis (see online: https://www.theguardian.com/lifeandstyle/2019/mar/12/birthstrikers-meet-the-women-who-refuse-to-have-children-until-climate-change-ends; accessed: 29.10.2021).

2.1.2 Optimistic-technocratic Narratives

In contrast, the optimistic-technocratic narratives regard humanity as a kind of "manager of the world". Here, the idea is that by means of scientific and technological progress, as well as through institutional transformations, the global-ecological threats, including demographic challenges could be countered.

Today, there is broad consensus in the scientific debate about population, (sustainable) development and environment that demographic developments depend on socio-cultural and economic conditions, and in turn affect societal and economic development as well as the use of natural resources and ecosystem services in each specific context. A report from the Royal Society (2012) published a decade ago, emphasized the diversity of demographic changes and their impact on sustainability, consumption and human wellbeing. The argument goes that it is not just population size that impacts people's contributions to ecosystem changes and sustainable development, but that demographic heterogeneity must also be taken into account, in particular differences in a population's age composition, as well as the density and distribution of the population. Optimistic-technocratic narratives often emphasize the "demographic divide" between high-fertility countries with strongly growing and young populations on the one side and low-fertility countries faced with a significantly "over-aged" population and population decline on the other, that are contributing very differently to environmental degradation and CO_2 emissions, but also to economic development (see for example UNFPA 2012). High birth rates in the Global South and resource-wasting consumption and production patterns in the Global North can thus be seen as two sides of the same coin, both jeopardizing sustainable development.

Explicitly referring to the Anthropocene and the Sustainable Development Goals (SDG), Barrett et al. (2020) examines the social dimensions of fertility behaviour in poor world regions, as well as consumption in the rich industrial states. From the perspective of ecological economics, they argue that people's attitudes and practices that are related in terms of reproduction of behaviour as well as consumption are socially embedded, and that a reduction of both would be feasible without curtailing people's wellbeing. The authors develop a specific impact equation that comprises of, among other variables, population, natural capital stocks, humanity's impact on the biosphere (the "global ecological footprint"), standard of living as measured by GDP per capita, improvements in technology (e.g., decarbonizing the energy sector or application of biotechnology in agriculture), as well as institutional measures (e.g., for reducing food waste or designation of protected areas). Focusing on Sub-Sahara Africa as a region of high fertility, the study points to the cultural attitudes towards large families and the notion of "children as wealth" (Barrett et al. 2020: 6034). But the authors emphasize that reproductive practices could be changed by improved access to family planning and modern contraceptives as well as media campaigns that spread information about alternative, less children-rich family models, without requiring "coercion, taxation or even education" (ibid.). According to the authors, social preferences also apply to the area of consumption. "To shift consumption patterns in the rich world and the aspiring consumption patterns of the poor world and those of emerging economies away from resource-intensive goods and services will require massive, coordinated actions" (ibid.: 6305); among them, as highlighted in the study, a reformation of market institutions and technological improvements such as fracking.

Some optimistic-technocratic narratives also stress the crucial role of education. For example, as the study of Abel et al. (2016) illustrates, future world population growth could be reduced by successfully implementing the SDG. By translating respective SDG goals and related targets, particularly in the fields of child mortality, reproductive health and (female) education into population scenarios, the results point in the direction of a lower population growth than that projected by the UN, reaching around 8.2-8.7 billion by the end of the 21st century. The authors stress that,

> demography is not destiny and that politics, particularly in the field of female education and reproductive health, can contribute greatly to reducing the world population growth […]. Given our assumptions, the SDG have a sizeable effect on global population growth, providing an additional rationale for vigorously pursuing their implementation (Abel et al. 2016: 14294).

2.1.3 Critical-relational Narratives

In critical-relational narratives, the topic "population" is seen in the context of complex, power-driven relations and interactions between individuals, society and nature.

Various critical assessments of the hegemonic discourses on global "overpopulation" have been expressed since the 1970s: on the one hand against the problem descriptions and rhetorical patterns, and on the other against racist, sexist and neo-colonial political practices of population control (Hartmann 1995; Angus & Butler 2011). Early attention was drawn to the repressive nature of anti-natalist population programmes in many countries of the Global South such as India, Bangladesh or Peru, that included forced sterilization, lack of information about the effects of long-term contraceptives such as hormonal implants, and subtle exploitation of poverty and social pressures by means of incentives such as cash rewards for women who agreed to sterilization. Critical scholars argue that such population programmes ignore cultural, social and economic conditions as well as prevailing gender and class asymmetries. Fixed on contraceptive technologies, they reduce complex issues of sexuality, reproduction and genealogy to a simplistic logic of supply and demand (Gottschlich & Schultz 2020: 135).

Much of the criticism of international population policies are directed against the prevailing interpretations of the "population problem", and rejects mono-causal explanations of population growth as a primary cause of hunger, poverty, migration movements and environmental degradation. Notably, feminist scholars have been repeatedly cautioned against the return of neo-Malthusian patterns of thought, in the context of climate crisis, that claim population growth as major cause. From these perspectives, calls for population control testify to authoritarian or technocratic notions of feasibility and reveal a continuity of colonial devaluations and upvaluations of populations (Hartmann & Barajas-Román 2009; Gottschlich & Schultz 2020; Schultz 2020).

> While in the Global South the existence of the people themselves becomes the object of bargaining, in the Global North it is consumption standards or per capita emissions. Absurdly, it is precisely those who are most excluded from resource consumption and who have contributed least to climate change who become the focus of climate protection and population policy (Gottschlich & Schultz 2020: 139).

Yet, even the critical-relational discourse cannot be regarded as unanimous, but instead encompasses a variety of perspectives. For example, feminist science researcher Donna Haraway regards "the acceleration in human numbers" (Haraway 2016: 6) definitely and explicitly as a problem. With her book *Staying with the Trouble. Making Kin in the Chtulucene* (2016) she sparked great controversy within the critical and feminist debate. While distancing herself from repressive population control, she nevertheless takes the position that the number of people living on earth is far too high. Haraway, therefore, argues for "multispecies ecojustice" and "action to unravel the ties of both genealogy and kin, and kin and species" (Haraway 2016: 102).

> Over a couple hundred years from now, maybe the human people of this planet can again be numbered 2 or 3 billion or so, while all along the way being part of increasing well-being for diverse human beings and other critters as means and not just ends. So make kin, not babies! (ibid.: 103).

With this view, Haraway opposes prevailing patriarchal models of family and consanguinity and outlines a vision of interspecies kinship. Other feminist authors fundamentally scrutinize the argument of "fewer people – less consumption – less environmental destruction" as an undue oversimplification; the search for integrated and inclusive societal solutions is replaced by a simplistic causal relationship, and the population growth rate is regarded as an isolated natural constant. Several critical scholars have introduced the term "demographisation" in order to analyse the increasing significance of demographic rationalities (Hummel & Lux 2006; Schultz 2020). In the discourse about global crises, manifestations of demographic changes are increasingly regarded as a "problem" that needs to be intensively studied in terms of its causes and consequences, but apparently also requires political interventions. This results in a demographisation of societal and political problems. More and more problems are brought into a (causal) connection with population dynamics – from the threat to social security, too high or too low birth rates, shrinking or growth of cities up to the overexploitation of natural resources. Essentially, all of these issues could be framed differently: as a lack of opportunities to reconcile family and occupation, as misguided economic and development policies or as a lack of distributive justice. As Susanne Schultz (2020) stresses, an important effect of demographisation is its ignorance with respect to relations:

> complex and alterable (re)production relations, consumption relations, distribution relations, or societal relations to nature, but about isolable statistical variables that, once isolated from each other, can be linked mathematically as factors – be it resources, jobs, or CO_2 emissions (Schultz 2020: 29).

Strategies of demographisation, i.e., translating social crises and conflicts into questions of "population" are therefore regarded as inherently incompatible with emancipatory projects oriented towards reproductive justice and the broader social-ecological transformations.

The approach of Social Ecology can be assigned to the critical-relational narratives. From this theoretical perspective, the growth dynamics of population and causal connections, as described in alarmistic-catastrophic narratives, and to some extent also in the optimistic-technocratic narratives illustrated above, turn out to be an expression of a crisis of societal *relations to nature* (Becker & Jahn 2006; Jahn et al. 2016; Hummel et al. 2017). The explicit claim of Social Ecology is to develop alternative starting-points for societal shaping towards more sustainable social-ecological transformations. Since it promises a way out of the impasses of the discourse centred on the dynamics of human population and the apparent necessity of its control, this approach shall be considered in more detail below.

2.2 Population Dynamics and Social-ecological Transformations

From the perspective of Social Ecology, the Anthropocene represents a "scientifically minded diagnosis of crisis", pointing "to a new understanding of the relationship between nature and society: societal action and natural processes are so closely intertwined that they can no longer be examined independently of each other" (Jahn et al. 2016: 4). This implies that science must pursue a systemic view and an inter- and transdisciplinary approach that integrates natural science, engineering, social science and humanities, but also extra-scientific, practical knowledge of various societal actors. Furthermore, "science must not only raise questions about 'planetary boundaries'; it must also go beyond the definition of the 'anthropos' and determine what social, cultural and political boundaries (and potentials) there are, thus casting a more discriminating look at production, gender and power relations" (ibid.: 7).

2.2.1 Crisis of Societal Relations to Nature

The diagnosis of a global "crisis of societal natural relations" points to the fact that the manifold global crisis phenomena, such as climate change, the overexploitation and pollution of natural resources, the decline of biological diversity and the spread of pandemics, do not represent disturbances of the "environment" or of "nature", but rather crisis-driven disturbances of the relations between individuals, society and nature in their interaction. Societal relations to nature emerge from the culturally and historically specific forms and practices with which individuals and societies shape and regulate their relations with nature. Thus, they must be considered in their plurality, and with their context-dependent material and cultural-symbolic features (Hummel et al. 2017; Becker et al. 2011).

Attention is thus focused on complex *patterns of relations* at different spatial, temporal and social scales. The core question is: How do crisis-prone societal relations to nature take shape in a global context?

From a normative perspective, the concept refers to the idea of basic needs: Societal relations should be regulated in such a way that the needs satisfaction for all human beings will be ensured. This perspective explicitly refers to ideas of justice, equality and sustainable development. The focus is on basic societal relations to nature such as land use and nutrition, shelter and housing, production and consumption, and also sexuality and reproduction. These are areas where social-ecological problems intensify when they are regulated in manners that reinforce crises (Hummel et al. 2017; Becker et al. 2011), and they refer to basic issues of sustainable development, as they are addressed in the 2030 Agenda for Sustainable Development and the concrete goals of the SDGs.

In terms of population dynamics, Social Ecology emphasizes that demographic changes not only include quantitative processes such as changing fertility and mortality rates or the number of habitants in a given area, but also qualitative phenomena such as changing household and family structures, lifestyles, income, social status and consumption patterns. From this vantage point, demographic changes are embedded in broader social-ecological transformations. Urbanization is a good example: as a world-wide social and demographic phenomenon, it is linked to changing needs and lifestyles, higher incomes and rising living standards, as well as changing individual values, preferences and demands. Western lifestyles are becoming more attractive around the globe, which in turn alters consumption behaviour and subsequently brings about increasing pressure on ecosystems.

2.2.2 *A Systemic View: Provisioning the Population*

Every society needs to address the task of providing its members with food, energy, water, housing, education and health services in such a way that basic human needs and rights are met. A decent quality of life can be realized, while at the same time the sustainability of natural life support systems are ensured. The basic assumption of the social-ecological approach is that demographic changes are connected to social-ecological problems that cannot be assigned to a fixed category of either 'society' or 'nature'. Thus this approach attempts to avoid both a naturalist and a socio-centric perspective (Hummel et al. 2008; Hummel et al. 2017). So, the epistemic interest is not restricted to the effects of demographic changes on either the environment or society. Population changes rely on bio-physical conditions as well as on social, cultural and economic settings, and in turn influence these factors. This means that demographic changes such as migration, urbanization and population growth or decline (to name a few) indicate transformations of societal relations to nature.

By systematically relating population dynamics to the issue of provisioning the population with goods and services that are based on natural resources and ecosystems such as food, water supply and sanitation, housing and energy supply, this approach allows for a problem-oriented analysis of social-ecological challenges in the context of demographic changes. Provisioning systems include bio-physical and material-energetic dimensions (e.g., agricultural land and soils, or wells and bridges), as well as cultural-symbolic dimensions (e.g., social norms, values, institutions, knowledge systems), and they consist of different groups of societal actors (e.g., the population of a given area, but also agriculture, water authorities, politics and administration). Given these attributes, provisioning systems can be conceptualized as social-ecological systems (Hummel et al. 2013; Hummel 2012; Hummel et al. 2008). In this way, population dynamics are de-centred to a certain extent. The starting point is the issue of sustainable provisioning contrary to the problem of a supposedly "sustainable demographic development". The basic assumption is that the number and distribution of people in a given society implies specific regulation requirements for provisioning systems, which can result in specific social-ecological problems. This is associated with the normative premise that it is not population dynamics or absolute population numbers as such that generate these problems, but rather the adaptive capacity of provisioning structures to cope with demographic changes (Hummel 2012).

2.2.3 Shaping Social-ecological Transformations in the Anthropocene

The designation of the Anthropocene exhibits profound implications for the relationship between society and nature, as well as the relationship between society and science. Science itself must change its structures and has to pursue an integrated view that provides system knowledge for a deeper understanding of the complex crisis phenomena, in conjunction with critical orientation and transformation knowledge for supporting sustainable development (Jahn et al. 2016). Considering demographic changes in the Anthropocene, it must be concluded that there are no simple and globally applicable solutions for a supposed balance between population, natural resources and sustainable development. In addition, there is no global "we" when it comes to the question of what defines a "good life". Consequently, issues of shaping societal relations to nature should come to the fore, in the sense of a continuous process of negotiating the numerous and diverse notions of a "good life" by means of "a collective, cooperative, and experimental activity for a different today" (Jahn et al. 2020: 6).

With respect to issues of population dynamics and sustainable development, a set of principles for shaping social-ecological transformations as developed by Jahn et al. (2020) provide a meaningful orientation for an inter- and transdisciplinary research approach:

1) *Focusing on relations between society and nature* (contrary to the notion of "nature as resource") reveals that population dynamics do not simply influence environmental conditions but are themselves embedded in historically and culturally specific societal relations to nature.
2) *Enabling coexistence* of different social groups, but also of human and non-human subjects, takes complex issues of power, control and domination into account.
3) *Defining and reflecting on limits* implies the recognition of interactions at different temporal, spatial and social scales, but also a reflexive and self-critical stance with respect to the limitations of the adopted research approach. This includes the reflection on normative ideas and a biopolitics in which the boundaries between the "natural" and the "societal" are shifted or dissolved and social conditions are naturalized.
4) *Dealing with complexity* includes a reflective and transparent approach to uncertainty, ignorance, but also contested knowledge with respect to the scientific analysis and normative assessments of population dynamics, as well as the acceptance of a limited degree of control.
5) *Strengthening resilience* refers to the functionality, adaptivity and transformability of provisioning systems to cope with demographic changes.
6) *Ensuring participation of all actors* means recognizing all relevant societal stakeholders and knowledge holders, i.e., different parts of the population, but also practitioners, political decision-makers and scientific disciplines with diverse claims, interests and capabilities for action.

3. Conclusion

It is striking that the Anthropocene debate frequently invokes the "human population", "humankind" or "humanity" as an entirety and as a species. This appears highly problematic, since such perspectives run the risk of levelling out issues of social inequality and multiple forms of power relations and domination. As Erle Ellis has aptly put it, it seems more than questionable "to understand the Anthropocene as a 'species history' of the 'Anthropos', lumping every person on Earth into a single undifferentiated mass […]. It should be clear that there is no one 'human' way of transforming the Earth. Different people use and transform environments differently, producing different consequences, and different people experience these consequences differently" (Ellis 2018: 132f.). Moreover, feminist criticism points to the reductionism and limitations of a hegemonic, masculinist frame of the Anthropocene, which "inevitably culminates in *Man* as the master creation, the Master of the Universe, and now its destroyer and, possibly its saviour" (Di Chiro 2017: 489). The reference to humanity as a whole can also lead to de-politization and the negation of concrete responsibility: "if 'we' (humans) are *all* to blame for the climate crisis, then *no one* is to blame and, therefore, *no one* is responsible, so we're all left to our own devices to become more resilient" (ibid.).

Population is not a purely discursive construct, but rather a societally shaped and at the same time scientifically constructed object, which in turn shapes social reality. In this dual form it influences scientific and political thinking, which in turn is integrated into discourses and practices that intervene in the reality of people grouped into a population. Population is therefore both a political and a scientific category (Hummel 2000). Population dynamics cannot be considered independently of social, economic and ecological conditions, but neither can it be considered independently of the scientific methods and models used for its analysis. What is considered to be too high, too low or to be an ideal population development is always determined as a function of theories, measurements, quantifications and simulations – there is no objective measure for it (Hummel & Lux 2006). Societal, ecological, and demographic developments are strongly interdependent, yet they remain undetermined and open. Demographic changes alone do not determine societal development and its natural basis because societies can actively shape the impacts of demographic changes. In contrast to the prevailing views of population dynamics as major cause for crisis-prone transformations illustrated in some narratives described above, population dynamics can then be regarded as critical drivers for more sustainable development paths.

Bibliography

Abel, Guy J./Barakat, Bilal/KC, Samir/Lutz, Wolfgang (2016): Meeting the Sustainable Development Goals leads to lower world population growth. In: Proc Natl Acad Sci U S A 113, 50, pp. 14294-14299.
Angus, Ian/Butler, Simone (2011): Too Many People? Population, Immigration, and the Environmental Crisis. Chicago, Illinois: Haymarket Books.
Barrett, Scott/Dasgupta, Aisha/Dasgupta, Partha/Adger, W. Neil/Anderies, John/van den Bergh, Jeroen/Blesoe, Caroline/Bongaarts, John/Carpenter, Stephen/ Chapin III, F. Stuart/Crépin, Anne-Sophie/Daily, Gretchen/Ehrlich, Paul/Folke, Carl/Kautsky, Nils/Lambin, Eric F./Levin, Simon A./Mäler, Karl-Göran/Naylor, Rosamond/Nyborg, Karine/Polasky, Stephen/Scheffer, Marten/Shogren, Jason/Jørgensen, Peter S./Walker, Brian/Wilen, James (2020): Social dimensions of fertility behavior and consumption patterns in the Anthropocene. In: Proc Natl Acad Sci U S A 117, 12, pp. 6300-6307.
Becker, Egon/Jahn, Thomas (2006): Soziale Ökologie. Grundzüge einer Wissenschaft von den gesellschaftlichen Naturverhältnissen. Frankfurt/New York: Campus.
Becker, Egon/Hummel, Diana/Jahn, Thomas (2011): Gesellschaftliche Naturverhältnisse als Rahmenkonzept. In: Groß, Matthias (ed.): Handbuch Umweltsoziologie. Heidelberg: VS Verlag, pp. 75-96.
Bonneuil, Christophe (2016): The Geological Turn. Narratives of the Anthropocene. In: Hamilton, Clive/Gemenne, François/Bonneuil, Christophe (ed.): The Anthropocene and the Global Environmental Crisis: Rethinking Modernity. London: Routledge, pp. 15-31.
Crutzen, Paul (2002): Geology of mankind. In: Nature 415, 23.
Di Chiro, Giovanna (2017): Welcome to the White (M)Anthropocene? A feminist critique. In: MacGregor, Sherilyn (ed.): Routledge Handbook of Gender and Environment. New York: Routledge, pp. 487-505.
Dürbeck, Gabriele (2018): Narrative des Anthropozäns. Systematisierung eines interdisziplinären Diskurses. In: Aus Politik und Zeitgeschichte 68, 21-23, pp. 11-17.
Ehrlich, Paul (1968): The Population Bomb. New York: Ballantine Books.
Ellis, Erle C. (2018): Anthropocene. A Very Short Introduction. Oxford: Oxford Univ. Press.
Gerten, Dieter/Heck, Vera/Jägermeyr, Jonas/Bodirsky, Benjamin L./Fetzer, Ingo/Jalava, Mika/Kummu, Matti/Lucht, Wolfgang/Rockström, Johan/Schaphoff, Sibyll/Schellnhuber, Hans J. (2020): Feeding ten billion people is possible within four terrestrial planetary boundaries. In: Nature Sustainability 3, 3, pp. 200-208.
Gottschlich, Daniela/Schultz, Susanne (2020): Weniger Klimawandel durch weniger Menschen? Feministische Kritik am neomalthusianischen Revival. In: Mölders, Tanja/Thiem, Anja/Katz, Christine (ed.): Nachhaltigkeit (re)produktiv denken. Pfade kritischer sozial-ökologischer Wissenschaft. Opladen/Berlin/Toronto: Barbara Budrich, pp. 134-140.

Haraway, Donna (2016): Staying with the Trouble. Making Kin in the Chtulucene. Durham/London: Duke Univ. Press.
Hartmann, Betsy/Barajas-Roman, Elizabeth (2009): The Population Bomb is Back – with a Global Warming Twist. In: Women in Action 2, pp. 70-78.
Hartmann, Betsy (1995): Reproductive Rights and Wrongs. The Global Politics of Population Control. Boston/Massachusetts: South End Press.
Horn, Eva/Bergthaller, Hannes (2019): Anthropozän zur Einführung. Hamburg: Junius.
Hummel, Diana (2000): Der Bevölkerungsdiskurs. Demographisches Wissen und politische Macht. Opladen: Leske & Budrich.
Hummel, Diana (2012): Population dynamics and adaptive capacity of supply systems. In: Glaser, Marion/Krause, Gesche/Ratter, Beate/Welp, Martin (ed.): Human nature interactions in the anthropocene. London: Routledge, pp. 181-210.
Hummel, Diana/Jahn, Thomas/Keil, Florian/Liehr, Stefan/Stieß, Immanuel (2017): Social Ecology as Critical, Transdisciplinary Science – Conceptualizing, Analyzing and Shaping Societal Relations to Nature. In: Sustainability 9, 7, pp. 1050.
Hummel, Diana/Adamo, Susana/de Sherbinin, Alex/Murphy, Laura/Aggarwal, Rimjhim/Zulu, Leo/Liu, Jianguo/Knight, Kyle (2013): Inter- and transdisciplinary approaches to population-environment research for sustainability aims: a review and appraisal. In: Population & Environment 34, 4, pp. 481-509.
Hummel, Diana/Hertler, Christine/Niemann, Steffen/Lux, Alexandra/Janowicz, Cedric (2008): The analytical framework. In: Hummel, Diana (ed.): Population dynamics and supply systems. A transdisciplinary approach. Frankfurt/New York: Campus, pp. 11-69.
Hummel, Diana/Lux, Alexandra (2006): Bevölkerungsentwicklung. In: Becker, Egon/Jahn, Thomas (ed.): Soziale Ökologie. Grundzüge einer Wissenschaft von den gesellschaftlichen Naturverhältnissen. Frankfurt/New York: Campus, pp. 409-422.
International Organization for Migration (IOM) (2020): World Migration Report 2020. Geneva: IOM.
Jahn, Thomas/Keil, Florian (2021): Sozial-ökologische Gestaltung im Anthropozän. Abschlussbericht zum institutseigenen Projekt "Kognitive Integration und Innovation" (KI3). Frankfurt a. M.: ISOE – Institut für sozial-ökologische Forschung.
Jahn, Thomas/Hummel, Diana/Drees, Lukas/Liehr, Stefan/Lux, Alexandra/Mehring, Marion/Stieß, Immanuel/Völker, Carolin/Winker, Martina/Zimmermann, Martin (2020): Shaping social-ecological transformations in the Anthropocene. Frankfurt a. M.: ISOE-Diskussionspapiere 45.
Jahn, Thomas/Hummel, Diana/Schramm, Engelbert (2016): Sustainable Science in the Anthropocene. Frankfurt a. M.: ISOE-Diskussionspapiere 40.
Livi Bacci, Massimo (2017): Planet und Mensch. Bevölkerungswachstum im 21. Jahrhundert. Berlin: Wagenbach.

Malhi, Yadvinder (2017): The Concept of the Anthropocene. In: Annual Review of Environment and Resources 42, 1, pp. 25.1-25.28.
Malthus, Thomas R. (1798): An Essay on the Principle of Population. London: J. Johnson. Library of Economics and Liberty. Online: http://www.econlib.org/library/Mathus/malPop1.html (accessed: 10.06.2021).
Meadows, Donella/Meadows, Dennis L./Randers, Jørgen/Behrens III, William W. (1972): The Limits to Growth. A Report for the Club of Rome's Project on the Predicament of Mankind. New York: Universe Books.
Ripple, William J./Wolf, Christopher/Newsome, Thomas M./Galetti, Mauro/Alamgir, Mohammed/Christ, Eileen/Mahmoud, Mahmoud I./Laurance, William F. (2017): World Scientists' Warning to Humanity: A Second Note. In: BioSciene 67, 12, pp. 1026-1028.
Rockström, Johan/Steffen, Will/Noone, Kevin/Persson, Åsa/Chapin III, F. Stuart/Lambin, Eric/Lenton, Timothy M./Scheffer, Marten/Folke, Carl/Schellnhuber, Hans J./Nykvist, Björn/de Wit, Cynthia A./Hughes, Terry/van der Leeuw, Sander/Rodhe, Henning/Sörlin, Sverker/Snyder, Peter K./Costanza, Robert/Svedin, Uno/Falkenmark, Malin/Karlberg, Louise/Corell, Robert W./Fabry, Victoria J./Hansen, James/Walker, Brian/Liverman, Diana/Richardson, Katherine/Crutzen, Paul/Foley, Jonathan (2009): Planetary Boundaries. Exploring the Safe Operating Space for Humanity. In: Ecology and Society 14, 2, pp. 32.
Schultz, Susanne (2020): Der gefährliche Geist der 'Bevölkerung' in der Klimadebatte. In: Femina Politica 2, pp. 23-36.
Steffen, Will/Broadgate, Wendy/Deutsch, Lisa/Gaffney, Owen/Ludwig, Cornelia (2015): The trajectory of the Anthropocene: The Great Acceleration. In: The Anthropocene Review 2, 1, pp. 81-98.
The Royal Society (2012): People and the Planet. London: The Royal Society Science Policy.
United Nations, Department of Economic and Social Affairs, Population Division (UN-DESA) (2019a): World Population Prospects 2019: Highlights (ST/ESA/SER.A/423). Online: https://population.un.org/wpp/Publications/Files/WPP2019_Highlights.pdf (accessed: 10.06.2021).
United Nations, Department of Economic and Social Affairs, Population Division (UN-DESA) (2019b): World Urbanization Prospects 2018: Highlights (ST/ESA/SER.A/421). Online: https://population.un.org/wup/Publications/Files/WUP2018-Highlights.pdf (accessed: 10.06.2021).
United Nations, Department of Economic and Social Affairs, Population Division (UN-DESA) (2019c): World Population Prospects 2019. Data Booklet. Online: http://www.europeanmigrationlaw.eu/documents/UN-WorldPopulationProspects2019-Databooklet.pdf (accessed: 20.07.2021).
United Nations Population Fund (UNFPA) (2012): Population Matters for Sustainable Development. New York: UNFPA.

Education for Sustainability as a Critical Theory of the Social Relationship to Nature

Christian Stache

1. Introduction

Since the 1990s, the concept of "Education for Sustainable Development (ESD)" (introducing Overwien 2014) has experienced a rapid rise. According to the "National Action Plan for Education for Sustainable Development", its focus is on the acquisition of skills that should enable the individual to behave in a way that is conducive to sustainable development. In concrete terms, for example, alternative forms of mobility and consumption and values such as "generational justice" are to be practised (National Platform Education for Sustainable Development 2017: 7-8).

Reflecting and changing one's own way of life is by no means in toto wrong. The transition to a sustainable form of society *also* requires a civil society cultural revolution of the way of life. But ESD misses the actual problems of the current social relationship with nature, such as climate change or the social relationship with animals. I will only mention two main points of criticism here (for a detailed critique of the ESD programme see e.g., Kehren 2016).

Firstly, the social relations of exploitation and domination, as they exist in particular in socio-economic production relations, as the cause of the destruction of nature and social antagonisms in our society (cf. e.g., Burkett 1999; Foster et al. 2010; Stache 2017) fall outside the ESD grid. The same applies to their reflection and criticism. This problem can be traced back to the birth of the concept of sustainable development (cf. Brand & Görg 2000).

Secondly, the ways out of a non-sustainable society are being shortened in accordance with the insufficient understanding of the problem to paths of ecological modernisation of the existing relations of exploitation and domination. On the Internet portal "Education for Sustainable"

Development of the German Commission for UNESCO it says, for example a social transformation towards sustainable development "requires strong institutions, participatory decision-making and conflict resolution, knowledge, technology and new patterns of behaviour" (German Commission for UNESCO n.a.). The revolution of political-economic relations and structures, through which nature in our present society is despotically appropriated and over-exploited in the production of goods, is not on this list, nor are the relations and structures of domination in state and society. But if these are excluded, the transition to a sustainable society becomes the transformation to an ecologically modernised, capitalist society.

If ESD education is for the ecological modernisation of capitalism and, therefore, inadequate to understand the causes of the destruction of nature and social contradictions and to outline how to overcome them, what would be the alternative? In the following it is argued that a critical theory of the social relation to nature would be one.

What this essentially consists of and why it requires a forward-looking return to the Marxist programme of political economy is outlined in the next section. Subsequently, using the model of Donna Haraway's postmodern philosophy and her concept of naturecultures, it will be developed that a certain negation of ideologism is necessary for a critical theory of the social relationship to nature in keeping with the times. Its purpose is to contain the overemphasis of cultural and ideological theory in current social criticism and to understand real socio-natural developments. In a second step, with reference to the socio-relational theory of capitalism, it will be shown that the relationship between bourgeois society and nature should be conceived as a dialectical contradiction if the current destruction of nature is to be understood and a practice developed to halt climate change or animal goods production and to solve the socio-ecological crisis as a whole. Finally, in the last chapter, some ideas are presented on how the bourgeois state and the dualism of nature and society could be understood within a critical theory of the social relationship to nature.

2. Outlines of a Critical Theory of Social-natural Conditions

A critical theory of social natural relations means at least three things. First, the mutual relationship between society and nature must be presented in its historically specific, socio-economic and political-cultural depth structure. Secondly, its representation should be used to criticise the deep structure. Thirdly and finally, the critical theory of the social relationship with nature should be able to indicate how and by whom the current bourgeois social relationship with nature can be changed in order to reconcile society and nature with each other. An education for sustainability was based on the findings of such a critical theory of the social relation to nature. Its programme, outlined here like a woodcut, is also the programme of Marxist *Kapital*. Today it is necessary to return to it for at least three reasons.

Although it is certainly part of the theory and critique of social relations to nature to demystify naturalizations of social and socio-natural relations – the main concern of critical cultural and ideological theory – it is firstly impossible to explain in this way why, how, by whom and in whose interest the various destructions of nature can be produced and overcome. Criticism of culture and ideology is not enough to fully understand problems such as the greenhouse effect or the so-called livestock farming and the class struggles to shape, continue or end them. For this we need the classical political economy.

Moreover, we find ourselves in a new historical constellation that requires a reflection on the previous significance of ideology and cultural criticism for critical social theory. Adorno (1973: 15) once argued that philosophy kept itself alive "because the moment of its realisation was missed". "After philosophy has broken the promise that it is one with reality or is about to be created, it is forced to criticise itself ruthlessly" (ibid.). In the middle of the last century, Adorno thus justified the necessity of ideology and cultural criticism as (auto)correction, expansion and perhaps as Marxism's measure of survival without alternative, by saying that the revolution had failed. Critical theory was, therefore, forced to reflect on why this was the case. But, and this is my second argument, it is time to reflect again on ideology and cultural criticism in the light of the current situation in which the ruling forces have integrated democratic elements of cultural and ideological theory in the sense of "progressive neoliberalism" (Fraser 2017: 46). If liberal cultural theory has been adapted by the ruling bloc to reform politics, culture and thinking in such a way that exploitation and domination are consolidated rather than relaxed, ideology and cultural criticism cannot continue as it has been until now.

The third argument in favour of a return to the Marx programme arises from the interaction between the first two. Today, capitalist development confronts us not only with the integrative recognition (Hawel 2007: 125) of groups of subalterns into the Western cultural and political establishment by means of cultural pluralization and individualization. It also forces us to confront what in the first instance is not discursive, symbolic, ideal, pictorial, theoretical, etc.: the socio-economic practice of society and the practice of nature. According to the Swedish human ecologist Andreas Malm (2018), with the greenhouse effect at the latest, these have brought about a new quality in social development and in our relationship with nature, which the majority of society on the planet cannot ignore on pain of their own demise. "History has sprung alive, through a nature that has done likewise," Malm writes (ibid.: 11). Climate change "represents history and nature falling down on society" (ibid.: 15). Malm calls this new historical-natural constellation "the warming condition" (ibid.: 1). The concepts of cultural and ideological theory do not suffice to change the terminology. What is needed here are the natural sciences as well as the Marxian critique of economics and especially those terms that describe the social as class structure and the sphere of production. The place where human society and nature in practice have always been in mutual exchange and where the modern greenhouse effect was created.

A return to the Marxian programme *does not*, it should be explicitly noted here, mean the replacement of cultural and ideological theories by political economy. Rather, it is about turning away from "ideologism" (Gramsci GH 3: 494) – the complement of "economism" – i.e., from the overemphasis on culture, politics, ideology, philosophy etc. and their extensive disconnection from economics in the analysis and critique of social and natural development. Furthermore, the aim is to define more precisely the relationship between political economy and ideology and cultural theory and vice versa. In other words, natural and socio-historical development gives rise to at least three requirements for a critical theory of the social relationship to nature. It requires the certain negation of ideologism, the reappropriation of political economy and the reconfiguration of political economy and theory of culture and ideology. In the following, I will present in a very condensed way how the first two tasks of a critical theory of social natural relations could be created. The third will be formulated here only rudimentary ideas.

Certain Negation of Ideologism: Donna Haraway's Naturecultures

The model of the so-called "naturecultures", the epistemological concept of the US biologist and cultural theorist Donna Haraway for the social relationship to nature, can be used as an example to show why a self-critique of cultural and ideological theory is needed. Haraway's basic idea about the social relationship with nature is that such a relationship does not (no longer) exist. For, according to her thesis, nature and society, which she describes by the term culture, are no longer separate entities. Rather, the poles of the classical dualism of the Western tradition of thought have imploded into each other. Nature has become society and society has become nature. Both are both at the same time and always. Nature and society exist only as diverse hybrids, as naturecultures or nature-cultures. "[N]atures and cultures have become one world" (Haraway & Goodeve 2000: 157), Haraway says: "situated naturecultures" (Haraway 2006: 110; cf. Haraway 2001: 120).

Haraway bases this position essentially on four arguments:

The "Great Divides" (Haraway 2006: 104; 2008: 9), i.e., the dualistic juxtapositions in Western thinking, are first of all the main problem of the network structure in which we live. For they formed the sedimentation of power relations that led to numerous exclusions of the so-called others. The modern contrast between nature and society is one of these dualisms. The nature-society dichotomy is a discursive strategy that makes the interactions between nature and society and their cultural productions invisible and naturalises them. Nature and society developed into discursive fetishes. In addition, power relations and exclusions with reference to an apparently given nature would be objectified and legitimised, and nature and its components would be turned into quantifiable resources. Hence, the mixing of nature and society is a way to avoid exclusions.

Haraway's second argument is based on her assessment of the development of productive forces after the Second World War. In particular, a "new historical configuration" (Haraway 1996: 366) had begun with the developments in the real life sciences, in computer and communication sciences. Humans are now capable of transforming or completely shaping everything that is usually perceived as nature. The development of technology and science thus permits the "final appropriation of nature by culture" (Haraway 1990: 142).

Thirdly, if nature can be appropriated and shaped in its entirety, it can no longer be the other thing in society. Rather, nature is "fully artifactual" (Haraway 1997: 108), "natural units" are accordingly "only crazy, mystical illusions" (Harway 1995b: 175). In other words: "Nature is constructed, historically constituted [...]" (Haraway 1995a: 156). It is, according to Haraway, "a cultural production" (Haraway 1983: 135), "genuinely social and actively relational" (Haraway 1991: 21). In Haraway's models, nature thus congeals into the epitome of reified cultural productions.

Fourthly, for Haraway, nature is not only a construct but also "society". A society as such does not exist. Rather, according to Haraway, it belongs to the "unlamented transcendental elements of the Enlightenment" which "disappeared into the funnel of gravity" (Haraway 1995b: 26). In Haraway's thinking, society is replaced by a network of material-semiotic actors and agents who formed natural cultures through cultural production.

This philosophy of culture is insufficient for a critical theory of social natural conditions for several reasons. The problems begin with the determination of the object of critical theory. Haraway's science-theoretical criticism of dualistic concepts of nature and culture or society is correct and urgently needed. But in her work she ultimately epistemologically idealistically reduces the problem of the social relationship to nature to a question of cultural-discursive production of nature and society. Instead of relating the critique of the modern dualism of nature and society and the critique of the mechanisms of their reproduction in the (natural) sciences to historical and natural development and their relation to each other, for Haraway these processes all coincide. She assumes the dualisms to be the product of modern knowledge production and power relations. Socio-natural development, for its part, withers away in Haraway's struggle for narratives of nature and society. The qualitative difference between nature and society in practice and their – right or wrong – conception in theory is ultimately levelled out. For Haraway, there is no longer any practice – either social or natural – outside of the epistemology, in the strict sense of her theory, which has been expanded in terms of cultural theory. Accordingly, the core problem of a critical theory of the social relationship to nature does not lie in how society's relationship to nature is shaped in practice. Rather, it is decisive what is understood as nature and culture and that they are thought and told differently.

Secondly, Haraway overestimates the scope of the bio-, communication sciences and computer science and the consequences this has for the conceptualisation of nature. It goes without saying that these have contributed to expanding the field of original accumulation and thus the appropriation of nature by capital. But this in itself is not a fundamental innovation of capitalist development. The history of the so-called livestock farming, for example, is a sequence of processes of separating direct producers from nature and of valorising nature through new technologies and political violence. It can also be seen relatively clearly in geoengineering, for example, that people, even those who continue the project of controlling nature in the traditional way, are reaching their limits in shaping nature despite all the development of productive forces. However, much capital tries to subjugate the earth, the qualitative autonomy and independence of nature from people and their society does not undermine this. However, this does not mean that there is still anything like untouched nature on our planet (cf. MEW 3: 44).

Even if Haraway's assessment were correct and we were in the age of technical reproducibility of nature, thirdly, nature would not be absorbed into culture. Contrary to what Haraway claims, nature does exist before and without us. It is not dependent on our relations with it. It also develops without our intervention. Human beings do not constitute nature. If this were so, we would not be able to explain the origin of man, for example. Nor could we really explain the (natural) greenhouse effect without a nature that is qualitatively different from human beings and their relations with each other.

This does not, however, deny that we can only relate to nature by mediation, nor that the concepts we make of nature are social constructions that are not identical with the object. This is the case (cf. MEW 20: 565). However, the mediation between nature and society cannot be limited to the culturally constructed concepts or the culturally constructed knowledge of nature. Rather, the terms and knowledge of nature are *a* part of the mediation that takes place throughout social practice, i.e., social work.

But nature is also not absorbed in the mediation through social work. One could rather say that through mediation it maintains itself, beyond it and against it, as an autonomous and independent entity. Reflecting its mediation, a positively determinable concept of nature is not only possible, but also necessary for critical theory today. Haraway, on the other hand, culturalises nature. She ultimately reduces it to an invention of discursive-cultural production.

Fourthly, Haraway rightly criticises the idea that "society" exists as a monolithic block, as ideological. But the same applies to the idea that society no longer exists. For one thing, it means abandoning the critique of social structures, relations and actors. If society does not exist, then – at least in theory – its structures, relations and agents no longer exist either. It therefore becomes impossible to differentiate between different constellations of social relations and socio-structural actors.

Furthermore, Haraway's alternative to the concept of society is by no means more viable. For them, coexistence consists of a multitude of spatially and temporally situated networks between actors and agents, which form a network of networks that is constantly changing. In these networks, human individuals, things and the relationships between them form the basic units. Haraway thus develops an intersubjective, more precisely an inter-agent cultural philosophy. The problem with this is that if the constellations between actors and agents are no longer situated in social structures, philosophy tips over into a democratised or agentially expanded subjectivism or methodological individualism. The starting point, reference point and vanishing point of theory are the actors, actants and their relationships. Beyond that, there are no other social contexts. What at first glance appears to be enrichment through microanalysis turns out to be a loss, a (self-)limitation of social theory, because the quality of society that goes beyond inter-agent relationships is abandoned.

Fifthly, Haraway mixes nature and society conceptually and speculatively by combining them into a hybrid (naturecultures), although they have been separated in real history. The historical course of class societies has led to an increasing separation of society and nature, to an increase in the subjugation and overexploitation of nature by and for the benefit of the ruling classes (MEW 42: 397). The blending of nature and society in the field of theory ultimately obscures the recognition of this relationship to one another, the relations of exploitation and domination and their development which are effective in it and which are non-discursive-cultural in the first instance. Strictly speaking, Haraway naturalises capitalist relations of exploitation and domination and thus implicitly accepts them as the inescapable basis of "natural cultural production". For Haraway, there are only manifold forms of its design with various inclusions and exclusions that can be shifted pragmatically. But overcoming them is no longer conceivable.

The blending of nature and society is, therefore, a postmodern actualisation, a shortening of the dialectic of nature and society. With dualistic approaches, the social relationship between nature and society is unthinkable, because the connection between nature and society cannot be thought of at all or only from one of the two poles. In hybridist readings, which are mostly culturalist-constructivist, as in Haraway's case (cf. Malm 2018: 44-79), nature and society are always one. One can no longer think of their difference.

In summary, Haraway thus narrows the focus of her critique of nature, society and their relationship in terms of cultural philosophy and refrains from feeding back into the entities of real history and their interaction. She exaggerates the development of the technological abilities of human beings and subsequently interprets nature in a culturally idealistic way as a social-relational construct. Nature is what is produced as such in bourgeois society. It replaces the concept of society with a democratised or agentially expanded methodological individualism. Finally, it mixes nature and society conceptually speculatively to the so-called natural cultures. Haraway's theory thus obscures the recognition of the reciprocal relationship between society and nature, of the relations of exploitation and domination that are effective within them, and of the possibility of their qualitative revolutionization.

The Dialectical Contradiction Between Nature and Civil Society

So far, the model of Haraway cultural philosophy has shown that it is not possible to tie in with this or related systems of thought in order to understand the current relationship between society and nature. In the following, we will focus on the second point of the programme for a critical theory of the social relationship between nature: the reappropriation of political economy.

In the sustainability discourse it is a commonplace that nature and society are in a reciprocal relationship. Marx (MEW 23: 57) generally refers to this in *Kapital* as "metabolism". This is a transhistorical condition of human existence and development. As Haraway's criticism should have made clear, however, it depends on how one imagines metabolism exactly.

In bourgeois society it is organised in a special dialectical way. In it, a double polar contradiction between nature and society constantly moves within their unity mediated by the historically specific, i.e., capitalist form of social work. Let us look at what this formulation says bit by bit.

In contrast to other species, human society has created a special form of social practice in which people relate to each other and to nature. In the course of the development of its relationships, human society has differentiated itself from societies of other animals and natural ecosystems. It has thus historically constituted itself as a human society.

Animated and inanimate nature has also developed and transformed over hundreds of millions of years. Certain animal societies have emerged, others have differentiated. Many have become extinct. The climate has changed and, as a result, the entire plant world and its global geography have changed. All this has happened without human society having been a significant factor. Nature has, therefore, developed largely autonomously. We can speak of an independent natural history.

To the extent that society is determined by the fact that it is the social product of human beings and that nature is the product of natural processes, they differ from one another. There is a difference between them.

However, neither nature nor human society are completely independent of each other. Human society depends on an exchange with nature in order to maintain and develop human individuals and human society. On the other hand, human beings are not necessary for nature to maintain and develop. But the way people behave changes not only themselves but also nature. Therefore, human society is not only historical-social, but also always natural, without being absorbed into nature. Nature, in turn, is not only natural, but also human-social, without being exhausted in it.

So there is not only a difference between nature and society. There is also an inner difference between nature and society on every pole. This does not mean, however, that nature is no longer nature or that society is no longer society, or that the two merge into each other. Nature is nature in the first instance, albeit socialised, society is society in the first instance, albeit natural.

However, this double polar difference between nature and society does not change the fact that nature and society also form a unity. For, as a socio-historical product of human beings, their society is first of all inevitably embedded in inanimate and animate nature. Secondly, people are never only social, human individuals, but also always animate natural beings. They are animals with special, socio-historically created abilities. The double polar difference between nature and human society thus exists, but only within their natural-social unity.

As already indicated, the double polar difference between nature and society is not ontologically given in the strict sense. It is rather the historical product of social work. Social work means that people, in their social practice of producing (and distributing) commodities, enter into relationships with each other and with nature in order to reproduce human individuals and human society. The human-social production and distribution of commodities is thus directly inherent in a relationship with nature. This is so because, in order to produce commodities, human beings must somehow appropriate nature and transform it in order to survive. At the same time, people change naturally and socially through social work.

Thus, through social work, a reciprocal process of socialisation of nature and naturalisation of society takes place in the course of human socio-economic practice, which at the same time encompasses the reproduction processes of nature and society. The result is that the double polar difference within its unity is reproduced in a historically and spatially specific form.

The present bourgeois social formation is characterised by a special organisation of social work. In societies with a capitalist mode of production there are specific relationships between people as well as a special relationship with nature. Their interplay leads to the fact that the double polar difference turns into a contradiction between nature and society.

According to Marx, we live in a society which, for all its innovations, developments and shifts in time and space, is socio-economically characterised by the capital relationship. By this he understands "a social relationship between persons mediated by things" (MEW 23: 793).

This sentence can be easily resolved using the "Architectonics of the three volumes" (Wolf 2013) of the *Kapital*. The first volume is mainly concerned with production conditions. The capitalist relations of production exist between the owners of the means of production and the wage labourers, who have nothing to sell but their labour. They face each other directly in the sphere of production. On the farm their relationship is, as Marx writes, "despotic" (MEW 23: 351). Capitalists allow wage labourers to work in their own interest and under their own command, appropriating the added value created in the production process. In other words: the profits that capitalists accumulate are ultimately produced by the workers. The relationship between capital and labour in production is therefore a relationship of exploitation and domination. Every production process reproduces this relationship and the underlying ownership relationship. The workers receive a wage, while the capitalists continue to have the means of production plus new capital.

The second volume of *Kapital* deals mainly with circulation, i.e., the relations between people in the market. Two things are crucial here. Firstly, by buying and selling goods, people enter into a relationship with each other in actu, which is reified in various interconnected forms. These forms are the (exchange) value of goods, money and capital. Together with property relations, they form the social structure which sets production for profit as the purpose of social action in bourgeois society. Secondly, the capital relationship between wage labourers and capitalists does not appear directly on the market as a relationship of domination and exploitation. For as sellers and buyers of goods on the market, people are politically free and equal.

But as Marx's analysis of production shows, this is not so. What is mediated through the buying or selling of labour in exchange for money – i.e., through things – is a relationship of exploitation and domination between the same capitalists and workers who face each other in the market as seemingly equals. Marx presents this unambiguously in the third volume of *Kapital*, which deals with the mutual interaction of circulation and production in the overall process of capitalist production. There it says that the capitalists as a class, "no matter how they prove themselves as false brothers in their competition with one another, form a true masonic alliance against the totality of the working class" (MEW 25: 208) in order to exploit it.

The capital relation is decisive here because the relation between society and nature, the social natural relation, is mediated in the capitalist formation of society through the capital relation, the relation of people to each other. In bourgeois society, the production process is not only the production process of commodities, but of capital. This means above all that it is in the interest and under the command of the capitalist class, its purpose is the accumulation of capital, while workers and nature, which are the sources of all wealth needed for production, are both merely means to that end. This does not mean that their exploitation is identical. But they both coincide in capitalist production.

The production of goods abstracts from the different qualities of nature as well as from its relative autonomy and laws of nature. The consequences of production and also of circulation, the individual and productive consumption of the produced goods for nature and finally the reproduction or the natural processes necessary for the reproduction of nature play at best a subordinate role for the class of capitalists. Lignite mining or meat production illustrate this.

Now the process of capital accumulation is potentially an infinitely growing process. This means that the appropriation and processing of nature, with all its consequences for the majority of people and nature, is increasing on a steadily growing scale. In the case of nature, however, ecological systems follow different, natural relations and processes than the society of capital. But when the class of capitalists subordinates natural relations and processes to the purpose of capital accumulation and abstracts from them in the above-mentioned way, the dialectical difference between social and natural relations and processes, between bourgeois society and nature becomes a contradiction. They are no longer compatible with each other. In the social metabolism with nature, capital causes successively increasing destruction, both quantitatively and qualitatively (cf. in detail Karathanassis 2015; Stache 2017: 431-534).

Civil State and the Dualism of Nature and Society

So far, it has been shown why, within the framework of a critical theory of the social relation to nature, cultural and ideological theory must be contained and political economy revived with regard to the dialectic between nature and society in order to take into account the development of capitalist society today. In the concluding section, some rudimentary ideas on the interaction of political economy, state and ideology are now presented, which are relevant for a critical theory of the social relationship to nature.

First to the political: In the capitalist social formation, the political form is relatively autonomous from the social form. This means that socio-economic exploitation and political domination do not coincide directly. Even though political power in capitalism comes from the factories (Gramsci GH 1: 132; GH 9: 2069), the bourgeois state constitutes itself as a political form of exercising power by separating economy and politics and society and state.

Nevertheless, the bourgeois state is a class state. First, it is based on the circulation relationship. The political power monopolised in the state guarantees the sale and purchase of goods and thus the undemocratic distribution of the total social product. Secondly, the state is also based on bourgeois property and production relations. The political violence monopolised in the state guarantees private ownership of the means of production and thus the undemocratic organisation of production and appropriation of the total social product. Finally, the state and its apparatuses as a political consolidation of social class relations and as a political field of class struggle are, due to unequal socio-economic conditions, unequally permeated by class relations and equally unequally occupied by classes and class factions.

Within this framework, the state acts in relative autonomy from the workers, from individual capitalists and capital fractions. It embodies the bourgeois "average rule" (MEW 3: 311). "The modern state authority is", according to Marx and Engels (MEW 4: 464), "a committee which administers the collective affairs of the whole bourgeois class". It is the "ideal total capitalist" (MEW 19: 222).

For the social relationship to nature, these provisions mean first of all that the despotic exploitation of nature in the economy is supplemented by the despotic rule over nature by the state. The socio-economic property relationship which the capitalists maintain with nature in production and which allows the free appropriation of nature and its productive forces is politically extended and supported by the bourgeois state. Although private ownership of nature is of course unequally distributed, it is also generalised in bourgeois society. Every citizen, not just a class, can in principle become the owner of a piece of nature. This is a central concession to build a consensus between the ruling and subaltern classes regarding private ownership and exploitation of nature.

At the same time, one of the functions of the state is to maintain and manage the natural production conditions for *all* capital and to create (new) access to them. How and to what extent this is done and who bears the costs is, however, the subject of political and economic class struggles. Mediated by taxes, the incomes of the subaltern class are generally used disproportionately to the profits. In the original accumulations for the exploitation of hitherto unexploited parts of nature, the state also actively and sometimes violently contributes to commodifying hitherto unexploited areas of nature, which in particular enables the capitals to monopolise nature.

Finally, at least two more things need to be added to the complex of social natural relations and the bourgeois state. Firstly, the growth of the overall profit and thus basically also the destruction of nature are in the self-preservation interest of the state to the extent that the state is dependent on a prospering economy. This is because it is financially dependent on the income generated by the economy. Secondly, in order to maintain itself, the state is also forced to promote the exploitation and domination of nature culturally, ideologically and financially in order to maintain the consent of the subalterns to bourgeois consensus. An important element in this context, which has been gaining influence for years, is the ideology that economy and ecology are compatible on a capitalist basis.

The scientist Dieter Wolf has done considerable preliminary work on the central nexus of capitalist production and circulation relations and the emergence of bourgeois-dualistic forms of thought. In it he ties in with Marx' logical-systematic derivation of a necessarily false consciousness from the social relations of capitalism. Marx shows how appearances must be created so that things like goods, money and capital acquire an independent character, a fetish character. In people's consciousness it looks as if these "things" face people as uninfluenceable structures ("factual constraints") because the social relations from which they emerge are no longer comprehensible to people.

Dieter Wolf, building on the Marxian argumentation, explains that people will have to explain the presumed independence of goods, money and capital differently if they do not see them as representations of social relations. As substitute intermediaries they were left with only two options: Either they ascribe to them their characteristics as natural or as ideal-cultural after the fact. "The inner connection between nature and society", as it exists in the socio-relational organisation of social work, is, as Wolf (2012: 3) writes, "understood in the form of the external and mutilating unity of the opposition of 'nature and spirit'". This means that the relative autonomy of commodity, money and capital is either assumed to be natural or interpreted as the result of an ideal, normative or cultural convention, but not as the result of the relations of socio-economic practice.

If, however, one does not penetrate the social relations in capitalist society, one cannot properly understand the social relation to nature either: "The wrong understanding of society has the wrong understanding of the relation between 'nature and society' on the other side" (Wolf 2012: 1). The unity of opposites can "only be explained by one of the extremes or a 'mishmash' of both" (ibid.: 3). Nature and society are either only conceived as poles of a dualism. The common scientific division of labour is based on this separation. Or nature and society are blended as hybrids. Both variants are makeshift constructions to explain the historically specific, dialectical interaction of nature and society. However, they lead to the culturalistic, naturalistic and hybridistic associations mentioned above.

3. Conclusion

As should have become clear from the above, the programme for a critical theory of social natural relations and its implementation not only exceeds the limits of this article, but also the strength, time and abilities of an individual by far. Nevertheless, education for sustainability cannot do without such a theory if the social nature relation of the bourgeois society is not only to be ecologically modernised, but a sustainable one is to be established.

A critical theory of social natural conditions includes the certain negation of ideologism, as it has been exemplarily developed here on the model of Donna Haraway's postmodern cultural philosophy, in order to be able to bring the core of exploitation and the destruction of nature in the current phase of capitalist development to the concept in a theoretically adequate way. Secondly, with Marx's economic theory, the relationship between bourgeois society and nature can be interpreted and criticised as a double polar contradiction. The origin of this contradiction is the capital relationship and the inherent over-exploitation relationship between capital and nature. Capital systematically abstracts from the qualities and processes of nature and thus produces the well-known destructions in the social relationship to nature, such as the radicalised greenhouse effect or the industrialised exploitation of animals.

In order to fully grasp the social natural relationship and its global crisis in social theory, however, it is not enough to determine the socio-relational and economic causes in the capitalist mode of production. This analysis must be supplemented by a theory of political domination over nature and the forms of thought in which nature and society are reflected upon. The suggestions made are to follow the materialist theory of the state and the Marxian fetish critique. With the former it can be shown that the bourgeois state, despite and through its ecosystem management in the sense of the average rule of the bourgeoisie, is the beneficiary and accomplice of capital in the exploitation and destruction of nature. It extends it to political domination of nature, enables nature exploitation in processes of original accumulation and protects it by making concessions to subaltern class factions and involving them in the regulation of the social relationship with nature. With the Marxian fetish critique it is finally possible to derive dualistic as well as hybridistic conceptions of nature and society from the inner workings of capitalism. They are substitute mediations for the misunderstood process of dialectical mediation between nature and society through social work.

At present, it cannot be assumed that the programme of a critical theory of social natural relations, which is only developed here in very rough outlines, will find its way into existing educational institutions. Nevertheless, in view of the socio-ecological crisis it is inevitable to leave the ecomodernist framework of "Education for Sustainable Development". Reconciliation with nature cannot be achieved through green consumption, global agreements or "sustainable" technologies alone. The "socialized man, the associated producers" must "bring the metabolism with nature [...] under their joint control" and "regulate it rationally" (MEW 25: 828). To find the way there, a critical theory of the social relationship with nature is needed.

Bibliography

Adorno, Theodor W. (1973): Negative Dialektik. In: Tiedemann, Rolf (ed.): Theodor W. Adorno. Gesammelte Schriften. Band 6. Frankfurt a. M.: Suhrkamp, pp. 7-412.

Brand, Ulrich/Görg, Christoph (2000): Die Regulation des Marktes und die Transformation der Naturverhältnisse. In: PROKLA 118, pp. 83-106.

Burkett, Paul (1999): Marx and Nature: A Red and Green Perspective. New York: St. Martin's Press.

Deutsche UNESCO-Kommission (n.a.): Was ist BNE? Online: https://www.bne-portal.de/de/einstieg/was-ist-bne (accessed: 29.07.2020).

Foster, John B./Clark, Brett/ York, Richard (2010): The Ecological Rift: Capitalism's War on the Earth. New York: Monthly Review Press.

Fraser, Nancy (2017): From Progressive Neoliberalism to Trump—and Beyond. In: American Affairs 1, 4, pp. 46-64.

Gramsci, Antonio (2012): Gefängnishefte. 10 Bände. Hamburg: Argument-Verlag.

Haraway, Donna (1983): Signs of Dominance: From a Physiology to a Cybernetics of Primate Society, C.R. Carpenter, 1930-1970. In: Coleman, William (ed.): Studies in History of Biology. Band 6. Baltimore/London: Johns Hopkins Univ. Press, pp. 129-219.

Haraway, Donna (1990): Investment Strategies for the Evolving Portfolio of Primate Females. In: Keller, Evelyn F./Jacobus, Mary (ed.): Body Politics. Women, Literature, and the Discourse of Science. New York/London: Routledge, pp. 139-161.

Haraway, Donna (1991): The Actors are Cyborg, Nature is Coyote, and the Geography is Elsewhere: Postscript to "Cyborgs at Large". In: Penley, Constance/Ross, Andrew (ed.): Technoculture. Minneapolis: Univ. of Minnesota Press, pp. 21-26.

Haraway, Donna (1995a): Die Neuerfindung der Natur. Primaten, Cyborgs und Frauen. Frankfurt a. M./New York: Campus.

Haraway, Donna (1995b): Monströse Versprechen. Coyote-Geschichten zu Feminismus und Technowissenschaft. Hamburg/Berlin: Argument-Verlag.

Haraway, Donna (1996): Anspruchsloser Zeuge@Zweites Jahrtausend. FrauMann©trifft OncoMouse™. Leviathan und die vier Jots: Die Tatsachen verdrehen. In: Scheich, Elvira (ed.): Vermittelte Weiblichkeit: feministische Wissenschafts- und Gesellschaftstheorie. Hamburg: Hamburger Edition, pp. 347-389.

Haraway, Donna (1997): Modest_Witness@Second_Millennium.FemaleMan© _Meets_ OncoMouse™. Feminism and Technoscience. New York/London: Routledge.
Haraway, Donna (2001): For the love of a Good Dog. Webs of Action in the World of Dog Genetics. In: Lammer, Christina (ed.): Digital Anatomy. Wien: Turia + Kant, pp. 115-139.
Haraway, Donna (2006): Encounters with Companion Species: Entangling Dogs, Baboons, Philosophers, and Biologists. In: Configurations 14, 1-2, pp. 97-114.
Haraway, Donna (2008): When Species Meet. Minnesota/London: Univ. of Minnesota Press.
Haraway, Donna/Goodeve, Thyrza N. (2000): How like a Leaf? New York: Routledge.
Hawel, Marcus (2007): Emanzipative Praxis und kritische Theorie – Zur Dialektik von integrativer Anerkennung und aufhebender Negation. In: Witt-Stahl, Susann (ed.): Das steinerne Herz der Unendlichkeit erweichen. Beiträge zu einer kritischen Theorie für die Befreiung der Tiere. Aschaffenburg: Alibri, pp. 125-141.
Karathanassis, Athanasios (2015): Kapitalistische Naturverhältnisse. Ursachen von Naturzerstörungen – Begründungen einer Postwachstumsökonomie. Hamburg: VSA.
Kehren, Yvonne (2016): Bildung für nachhaltige Entwicklung. Zur Kritik eines pädagogischen Programms. Baltmannsweiler: Schneider Verlag Hohengehren.
Malm, Andreas (2018): The Progress of This Storm. Nature and Society in Warming World. London: Verso.
Marx, Karl/Engels, Friedrich (1956-1990): Marx Engels Werke (MEW). Bände 1-43. Berlin: Dietz.
Nationale Plattform Bildung für nachhaltige Entwicklung (2017): Nationaler Aktionsplan Bildung für nachhaltige Entwicklung. Berlin.
Overwien, Bernd (2014): Umweltbildung und Bildung für nachhaltige Entwicklung. In: Sander, Wolfgang (ed.): Handbuch politische Bildung. 4th, revised edition. Schwalbach a. T.: Wochenschau, pp. 375-382.
Stache, Christian (2017): Kapitalismus und Naturzerstörung. Zur kritischen Theorie des gesellschaftlichen Naturverhältnisses. Opladen: Budrich UniPress Ltd.
Wolf, Dieter (2012): Gesellschaft und Natur, Strategien der Naturalisierung. Zur Verwandlung der Einheit von Natur- und Menschengeschichte in die Einheit des Gegensatzes von "Natur und Geist". Online: http://www.dieterwolf.net/pdf/Naturgeschiche_und_Menschengeschichte _Gegensatz_von_Natur_und_Geist.pdf (accessed: 29.07.2020).
Wolf, Dieter (2013): Zur Architektonik der drei Bände des Marxschen Kapitals. Online:°http://www.dieterwolf.net/pdf/Zur_Architektonik_der_drei_ Baende_des_Marxschen_Kapitals.pdf (accessed: 29.07.2020).

A Contribution from the Philosophy of Science for Education for Sustainable Development

Helge Kminek

1. Introduction[1]

In the scientific discourse on Education for Sustainable Development (ESD)[2] there is a trend of summarising the state of research in detailed questions and of determining research *desiderata*. For example, O'Flaherty and Liddy (2018) offered a synthesis of research findings on development education and ESD. A year later, Marcinkowski and Reid (2019) presented a summative paper on the more specific problem of the attitude-behaviour-relationship. And Verhelst et al. (2020) elaborated on a conceptual framework for an ESD-effective school organization based on a synthesis of the research findings.

In the wake of these developments, this article takes shape. The aim of the paper is to contribute to a formal theoretical framework for the field of ESD. For this, questions will be raised on a meta level. These questions are interwoven with questions of ESD discourse in the narrower sense, as will be shown. However, an attempt is made to locate the debates and research findings within the proposed framework.

The added value of such a theoretical framework is to systematically interrogate scholarly differences on how to work scientifically on advancing ESD theory, thus resolving those differences. Furthermore, this framework could be useful to identify research needs. In line with an early critique by Bob Jickling, who spoke of an impediment to the development of ESD due to a lack of philosophical reflection (1994: 5), this paper

---

1   I would like to thank Simone Blandford, Jürgen Braun, Anna Geyer and Markus Siewert for helpful comments on this article and the thorough editing.
2   ESD is understood broadly here, i.e., approaches to Environmental Education or Environmental Education for Sustainable Development are also included under the term, as the different concepts seem to me to merge into one another.

reflects on basic issues of the *theory of science* – as a branch of theoretical philosophy – of ESD.

The guiding questions of this paper are (a) which problems of the philosophy of science are to be taken up and reflected upon in the ESD field and (b) how can we work on an ESD theory that combines results of individual studies and research projects into an ESD grand theory and/or elaborates ESD paradigms and puts them up for discussion? The framework of this paper does not allow for a fundamentally systematic discussion of these questions, therefore, it does not claim to be a comprehensive contribution. Instead, it proceeds inductively and reflexively in search of relevant problems. In doing so, the article takes the first steps towards a ESD meta-theory, which is also necessary for the development of ESD paradigms. With the emergence of these paradigms, the further development of ESD theory is a justifiable prospect.

A model for a formal, content-free ESD theory is presented in section two. The added value of the model lies in the fact that controversies within ESD discourse can be systematically located. In addition, the model is kept so abstract and formal that it marks central cornerstones that would have to be considered and filled with content in the formation of paradigms of ESD theories. In the following sections, aspects of the model are examined. The first aspect reflected in the third section is the question of a descriptive and normative understanding of science, the two basic (thought-experimental) poles of science in general and ESD in particular. The considerations of the problem of normativity lead to the question of the significance of the (so far) underdetermined definition of sustainability for ESD theory. This question is explored in section four. In the fifth section a model is introduced and developed that captures ESD's pedagogical practice (formal, non-formal, informal) and at the same time the contentious nature of sustainability for ESD theory building. The paper ends with further reflections as a résumé in section six.

2. A Contribution to a Formal ESD-Model

Figure 1 displays the proposed model which interconnects central fields and positions of research in the field of ESD. It should not be claimed here that the proposed model and the systematisation envisaged by the model cannot be improved or presented more appropriately. The model is an initial proposal. But the advantage of the abstractness of the model is that the entire ESD research on (almost all) the cornerstones and areas identified as central can be located within it.

A Contribution from the Philosophy of Science for ESD

In addition, the model is characterised by the fact that it causes little or (in the best case) no opposition from representatives of different positions. This makes it possible to not only locate differences in different ESD-relevant issues, but also to determine convergences or even agreements. In my view, the possibility of concretely fixing differences and agreements seems a necessary condition for the prospect of ESD theory development. Moreover, such a model is also useful for the purpose of developing and constituting different paradigms of ESD theories. This model or one that will be further developed in the future can be used for this purpose.

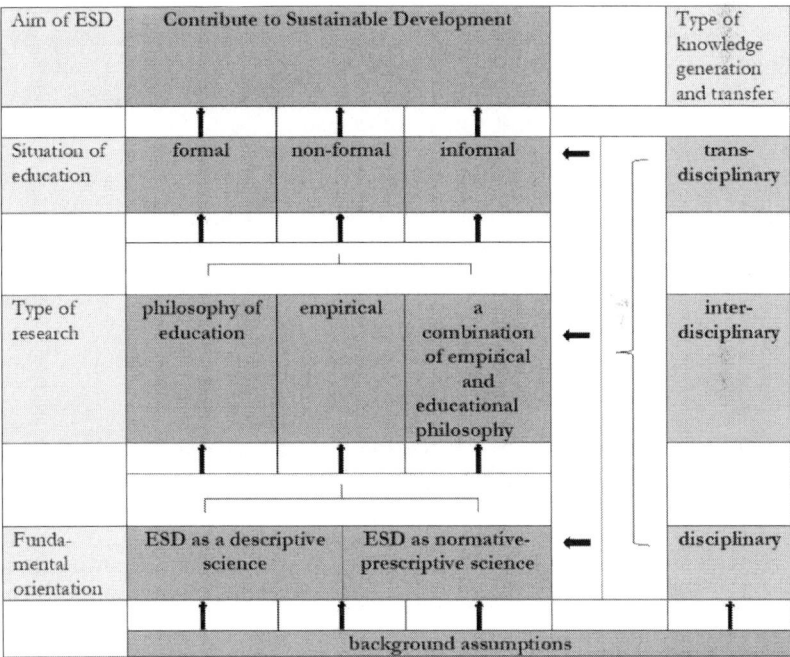

Figure 1: Proposal of an ESD theory framework[3] (Source: own illustration.)

Every theory has *background assumptions* that are rarely reflected. Due to this, it is suggested to designate them as the base of the model. However, the background assumptions cannot be reflected permanently. If one were to try to permanently reflect one's background assumptions, theory

---

3   The figure tries to be a concrete fixed point in which the following explanations are brought together in a concentrated way. The figure is not essential, but the textual explanations are. The size and thickness of the arrows or the boxes, for example, are also of no significance.

development would be practically impossible; at the very least, there is a threat of infinite loops of reflection and exaggerated doubts about principles. Instead of work regarding ESD, one would be practising philosophy, i.e., today's scientific discipline which is permanently working on basic questions. ESD theories cannot constantly reflect their background assumptions either. And yet it is not only scientifically honest, but also necessary for theory building and the further development of pedagogical practice to raise awareness of the background assumptions and to be able to sound out possible alternatives of theory and practice that there is no awareness of due to unreflected background assumptions.

A second fundamental question plays into the questions of ESD and all theoretical and research approaches. It is the question of whether the theory and research are disciplinary, interdisciplinary or transdisciplinary. This distinction was introduced on the right side of the Figure 1. The braces in connection with the three black arrows going from right to left are to be read as an expression of the fact that these three types of knowledge generation and transfer are possible at all levels (fundamental orientation, type of research and situation of education).[4] To avoid overloading the display, arrows from all three positions to each of the three levels have been omitted.

Based on considerations of the philosophy of science, it is now proposed to first distinguish between a descriptive and a normative-prescriptive variant of ESD. In the following section, this distinction is further elaborated, justified and reflected.

These two basic types of theory (descriptive and normative-prescriptive) can lead into three different concrete types of research (philosophy of education, empirical and a combination of philosophy of education and empirical research). These possibilities of different transfers into concrete research types are again shown with a brace and with three black arrows. Here, the three arrows must be read so that a connection is possible from the two positions of fundamental orientation to all three types.

At the last level, the distinction between formal, non-formal and informal situations of education is introduced. Education is to be

---

4   One can ask why a link was not also made to the goal of contributing to sustainable development. The reason for this is that (1) the model is designed for the theorisation of Education *for* Sustainable Development. Accordingly, the definition of the goal must be set from the outside. According to this understanding, ESD and its' theory–building has no influence on the goal–setting and stays out of the question of which way (disciplinary, interdisciplinary or transdisciplinary) the goal is determined. It would be a different case if a thesis were put forward, or if it were regarded as established knowledge, that educational theories and the way they are theorised must be consulted on the question of goal setting. This is an extremely demanding and at the same time very interesting question for the philosophy of education, which can only be called up as a question here.

understood broadly here, so that education – in the sense of learning – and *Bildung*[5] fall among the term.

All pedagogical practices are now characterised by the fact that they contribute to sustainability at least according to their aim and motive, although empirically this can of course be questioned. For this reason, the model concludes with the umbrella term "Contribute to Sustainable Development".

In the following three sections the reflections will be deepened in three areas of the model. The discussion will thus be richer in content and the corresponding areas will also be enriched in terms of content.

3. A Contribution about ESD as Descriptive or Normative Science

Interwoven with the question of sustainability and ESD is the diagnosis of crisis and urgency. It is extremely rare to find scientists who approach the field in an exclusively descriptive manner. The vast majority of scientists, including the author (cf. Kminek et al. 2021), claim to work scientifically and at the same time want to use their scientific work to promote ESD and thereby the transformation towards sustainable social relationships with nature.

However, this does not exclude the possibility of approaching the field of ESD in a fundamentally different way, namely a scientifically distanced and descriptive approach, even if a scientist takes a negative stance towards ESD. The descriptive variant is characterised by the abstinence from normative requirements, expectations and value judgements. This variant, at least according to the awareness of possible representatives,

---

5 "Bildung has no obvious English–language substitute. It has been translated variously as education, edification, formation, learning, culture, cultivation, and literacy. Bildung was given canonical definition by Wilhelm von Humboldt as "the linking of the self to the world to achieve the most general, most animated, and most unrestrained interplay" (Humboldt, W. 1792; in: Flitner & Giel (ed.) 1980: 58). In keeping with the breadth of this phrasing, Benner and Brüggen (2004) define Bildung as "the process of the forming (die Formung) of humans, as well as the determination (Bestimmung) of the goal and purpose of human existence"—further underscoring the vast, ill–defined semantic space that this term occupies in the German language. In addition, Bildung signifies the ideal of the autonomous, self–determined, and self–reflected personality in its full realization. But Bildung goes beyond this as well. Bildung cannot be completely contained by terms such as "education," "socialization," "instruction," or "schooling". Bildung identifies a kind of "becoming human" that spans biographical, the collective, institutional and historical dimensions. As such it opens up the possibilities of a generative process through which we are formed by the world, form ourselves, and form the world (immediately) around us" (Kminek 2022, page still unknown).

should not mean that another variant could not contribute to substantially developing – indeed improving – ESD. The idea here is that an alienated, scientifically distanced view and abstinence from being interwoven with the normative questions, problems and expectations in connection with the topic of sustainability can see and raise awareness of, but not limited to, aspects, structures and argumentative fallacies, that would otherwise remain hidden.

In principle, this argument is not new. It originates from Max Weber's philosophy of science, adapted here to ESD. Weber's argument can be identified in the context of his discussion on whether a chair of law should be held by an anarchist. Weber writes:

> Now, of course, one has wanted to open up certain barriers purely "logically". One of our very first jurists, in speaking out against the exclusion of socialists from the lecterns, occasionally declared: he would not be able to accept at least one "anarchist" as a teacher of law, since he would negate the validity of law as such altogether, – and he obviously considered this argument to be decisive. I am of the exact opposite opinion. The anarchist can certainly be a good legal scholar. And if he is, then that very Archimedean point, so to speak, outside the conventions and presuppositions which we take so much for granted, on which his objective conviction – if it is genuine – places him, can enable him to recognise in the fundamental views of the usual doctrine of law a problematic which escapes all those to whom it is all too self-evident. For the most radical doubt is the father of knowledge (Weber 2002: 366 – translation H. K.).[6]

If Weber's argument is accepted for ESD, this means that ESD approaches, or scholars who approach ESD in an exclusively descriptive manner, are not to be classified as inappropriate from the outset. Hence the first distinction in the theory of science is made, namely between a (A1) descriptive and a (A2) normative-prescriptive understanding of the science of ESD (compare table 1).

---

6 Max Weber does not call for a value–free approach to the objects of science. According to him, this would not be possible. This means that a value–free approach is not a prerequisite for certain statements, models and theories to be classified as scientific. What Weber demands, however, is an "is–ought" dichotomy with regard to scientific systems of propositions. I will come back to the question of the is–ought dichotomy.

A Contribution from the Philosophy of Science for ESD

A - Fundamental orientation on the how and why of ESD			
A1-ESD ESD as a descriptive science	A2- ESD ESD as normative-prescriptive science		
A1-ESD$_{1...n}$	A2-ESD-1	A2-ESD-2	A2-ESD-3$_{1...n}$

Table 1: Fundamental orientation on the how and why of ESD
(Source: own illustration.)

To the author's knowledge, ESD approaches that could be considered exclusively descriptive are not currently available. In principle, different approaches are conceivable; what unites these approaches is that they would fall into the category of (A1) descriptive ESD theories. What would distinguish the approaches, however, is that they would be based on different background theories and assumptions. The potential plurality of theories that fall under this type have been taken into account in table 2 with A1-ESD$_{1...n}$.

For the normative-prescriptive variety of ESD theories, an assortment of different approaches are available. A generally accepted systematisation has already been presented by Vare and Scott (2007). As is well known, they distinguish between ESD 1 and ESD 2. ESD 1 comprises of approaches that are intended to promote behaviour and ways of thinking in a short time. Approaches subsumed under ESD 2 have in common that the promotion of critical thinking and testing of ideas should be/are at the core of ESD.

Vare and Scott argue for a "yes-and" approach, that is, if you will, an ESD 3 concept that combines the two approaches of ESD 1 and 2. In principle, it is conceivable that there could be other types of ESD. This has been taken into account in the table with A2-ESD-3$_{1...n}$.

3.1 Reasons as Challenges for Further Development

Is it simply a question of whether one locates oneself as a scientist in the field of (A1) descriptive theories or in the field of (A2) normative-prescriptive theories? Of course, positioning towards one of the two must be supported with reasons. In the following, possible arguments that can be used to justify a position are contrasted. The core of the two arguments for each type is outlined in table 2 in order to identify the problems to which the respective arguments refer.

Arguments for the type A1-ESD	Arguments for the type A2-ESD
I	
The first argument is one commonly advanced in positivist social sciences. The social sciences have to investigate how the social world is, not how it could or should be. Social sciences that would make value judgements are worldview but not scientific.	This line of argument contends that (a) there are no social theories that are free of value judgements, especially since (b) social sciences are so interwoven with their own object of research that a supposed freedom from value judgements is a confirmation of current conditions.
And this fundamental argument also applies to the question of the transformation towards a sustainable society of social natural relations. It is precisely a value-free science that presents people with (factual) knowledge about the world with its value-free statements. How they use this (factual) knowledge is up to them.	And especially with regard to the question of the transformation towards a sustainable society of social natural relations, it must be added that the necessity of such a transformation is normatively of such relevance that an (artificial) distancing from this necessity can be seen as ethically irresponsible.
II	
Another argument to justify descriptive theorising of ESD is to say that the task of transformation towards a sustainable society within the planetary boundaries is one to be dealt with politically and not pedagogically. In and through ESD, the responsibility of the adult generation would be shifted to those who are predominantly underage.	The fact that the younger generations are not only at the mercy of the structures and processes of unsustainable development and, moreover, are not prepared for the task of transformation that will occupy many generations, legitimises ESD.
Furthermore, it can be asked today whether, with regard to the need for rapid steps towards change in order to minimise at least the worst consequences of climate change, these can factually only be dealt with politically and not pedagogically. For example,	Furthermore, since the Enlightenment, it has been the task of pedagogy to "create and preserve a world worth living in" (Blankertz 1982: 306 – translation H. K.). Whether pedagogy (in practice and theory) is aware of this task or not, and whether pedagogy accepts the task or not,

Greta Thunberg argues accordingly (cf. Thunberg 2019: 34).	is irrelevant according to Blankertz. The task exists objectively and, one may add, the task also exists when political changes are urgently needed.

Table 2: Two arguments for ESD-1 and ESD-2 respectively
(Source: own illustration.)

The arguments given here as examples, juxtapose and challenge one another. The challenge of the other type of theory offers the potential to further develop one's own position as it requires an argumentative response. This is to be evaluated positively as a further development.

Moreover, such controversies – at least from the author's point of view – allow for the possibility of developing theory building, in this case the theory building of ESD as a whole. If one of the two types of theory was to be abandoned due to the unforced momentum of the better argument (compare Habermas 1987), then this would also be an enrichment of ESD theory as a whole. The gain would consist in the arguments developed for the argumentative conviction of the other type of theory.[7]

3.1.1 The Is-Ought Dichotomy as a Common Basis and an Occasion to Reflect

The shared scientific-theoretical basis of the different, previously outlined types of theory can be seen as the "is-ought" dichotomy. What is meant by this is that nowadays it is likely that no scientist disputes that no ought-statements may be drawn from as-is-statements, or that such a conclusion is invalid. An example of such an *invalid* conclusion is the following syllogism:

Premise 1: All human beings are mortal.
Premise 2: Socrates is a human being.
Conclusion: Socrates should die.

However, while all scientists would likely consider this conclusion invalid, arguments in the field of sustainability and ESD are not only much more complex, but also raise the question of whether as-is-statements do not also contain ought-statements. This problem will be illustrated by another example syllogism. The question is whether the syllogism is valid or not.

Premise 1: The pupils of a rural primary school x eat a very meat-heavy diet.

---

7   This would not be a rejection or refutation of Weber's position. For new arguments can of course be put forward by a critic against the position that is (provisionally) assumed to be correct.

Premise 2: The consumption of meat is more harmful to the climate and biodiversity than a vegan diet.
Conclusion: The pupils should be educated to eat a vegan diet.

Leaving aside, for the sake of the problem discussed here, whether this second syllogism formally corresponds to the first syllogism and that it is questionable whether an exclusively vegan diet has negative consequences for biodiversity and other side effects that can be considered negative, the two syllogisms seem to be formally identical. However, while in the first case the conclusion, i.e., the implication, was undoubtedly evaluated as invalid, this is not clearly the case in the second syllogism.

The ambiguity of the conclusion of the second syllogism is a consequence of how its second premise is read. Is the premise to be read merely as an is-statement? Or does the second premise not factually contain an ought requirement that does not need to be specifically investigated? To put it another way: Does the as-is-statement that a vegan diet does not harm the climate as much as a meat diet imply the ought-to-be demand to eat a vegan diet?

With this concrete outline of the problem, the abstract scientific-theoretical topic of the so-called positivism dispute, conducted between Karl Popper and Hans Albert on the one hand and Theodor W. Adorno and Jürgen Habermas on the other, is raised (cf. for example: Adorno & Maus 1969; Kminek 2006).

It is not the purpose of this paper to contribute a new argument on the controversy of the positivism dispute (within the ESD field). It is merely a matter of raising awareness of the problem of the philosophy of science and its relevance for ESD theory building. For this reason, the discussion of the problem will end here. Specifically, the issue of nourishing the arguments that have just been presented has called up the question of the concept of sustainability and its possibly implicit normative demands. Following on from this, the concept of sustainability and its significance for ESD theory formation will be questioned.

4. On the Concept of Sustainability and its Problematisation

The term sustainability is omnipresent today. But what does the term mean and/or entail? Answering this question is crucial if ESD is to be stringently linked and/or operationalised to the goal of sustainability and not merely postulated to contribute to sustainability.

A Contribution from the Philosophy of Science for ESD

Three references are often used to define what is meant by sustainability. Historically, reference is made to the definition from the so-called Brundtland Report of the World Commission on Environment and Development (*Our Common Future*). It states that, "Sustainable development is development that meets the needs of the present without compromising the ability of future generations to meet their own needs" (WECD 1987: 41).

To define the term sustainability, the triple-bottom-line concept of sustainability is often invoked as a concept as well (compare the overview article by Purvis et al. 2019). The three bottom lines, which are also conceptualised as pillars, are ecology, economy and social issues.

Finally, reference is often made to the seventeen United Nations Sustainable Development Goals (SDGs) and the elaboration on them (compare UN 2016).

The relevant question for the present context is (i) whether these definitions are universally accepted and if not, (iia) whether it has an impact on ESD and if so, (iib) what is the impact?

4.1 On the Critique of Sustainability Definitions

There are numerous criticisms of the (i) definitions which can be divided into at least three classes (A-C) of criticisms.

(A) The first class of criticism is particularly well illustrated by the definition of the Brundtland Report previously quoted. The critique now presented is exemplary for the mode of critique. This class of criticism can be titled "lack of determined".

The criticism is that the definition is underdetermined. An underdetermined term means that it is determined, i.e., defined, on the one hand. On the other hand, however, the definition of the term is insufficient to distinguish it from other terms or – and this is decisive here – it cannot be clearly determined whether something falls under the term or not. What is meant by this can be explained by the following example. In the Rhine-Main region, Frankfurt Airport is one of the largest employers. There is no doubt that air traffic contributes significantly to man-made climate change, i.e., the increase in the average global temperature. This has the well-known negative consequences that affect the needs of future generations. This could lead to the conclusion that the growth of air traffic should be prevented, or at the least, a process of shrinkage should be initiated. However, this is offset by the need for people's jobs today.

The example illustrates the criticism of the Brundtland Report's definition of sustainability. Based on the definition, it is not possible to decide whether priority should be given to jobs today or to the reduction of aircraft movements for the living conditions of people tomorrow (and in many regions of the world, today). And thus, it is not clearly determinable what exactly the contribution of ESD will be if the goal is not precisely defined, regarding the ESD-concept of UNESCO (2018) (cf. Kminek 2020).

(B) John Elkington coined the triple-bottom-line model in 1994. The three components (social, ecological and economic) are partly differentiated, which is not relevant here. For the problem to be unfolded, only the critique of this model is of interest. What is disputed with regard to this concept is above all the definition of the relationship between the social, the ecological and the economic. Different proposals have been made. For example, that it is or should be a matter of three independent pillars standing side by side and supporting the roof of "sustainability". This conceptualisation is being criticized by arguing that even if the three components are conceived as independent areas, they have common intersections. Or it is argued for a nested and priority model that sees the foundation as being the ecology component, followed by the social component and finally the economy. The respective models are always a critique of the models from which they distance themselves. This means that in this form of critique there is agreement on the central characteristics with which sustainability is to be determined, but there is disagreement on the theoretical modelling.

(C) Finally, there is a form of criticism that will be outlined here using the SDGs as an example. The 17 sustainability goals (UN 2016) are intended to promote sustainability, and the pursuit and achievement of these goals should lead to sustainable development worldwide. Even though the concept as a whole and the seventeen individual goals were coordinated worldwide and adopted within the framework of the United Nations, there are many criticisms of the concept and goals. Here, once again, the aim is only to encourage a kind of critique of concepts of sustainability rather that attempt to define the concept of sustainability. Therefore, the entire discussion around the SDGs is not yet unpacked.

What is being questioned here is the criticism that accuses the SDGs of not pursuing the right goals or, to put it mildly, not pursuing the right goals consistently enough. Two examples may be mentioned that originate from ESD discourse. But according to the structure of the critique, it can also be found outside of ESD discourse in other disciplines (e.g., sociology and philosophy), and from these discourses outside of ESD they took up the criticism.

For Helen Kopnina (2020), the concept of sustainable development, and consequently ESD, places too much emphasis on the economic and social aspects of sustainability. As a result, for the co-concept of sustainability (and also ESD), ecological justice and the related recognition that non-humans also have a right to exist and flourish are not taken into account. Kopnina wants to address the critique with a reformed undergraduate curriculum in which students have to deal with a fourth concept, that of ecological justice.

According to Stein et al.'s (2020) critique of the SDGs and ESD, both wrongly assume the possibility of perpetual growth and consumption on a finite planet. They combine their presuppositions of neoliberal economics underlying the SDGs with a plea for an ESD that works to undo the denial of the negative consequences of modernity and coloniality.

Three forms of criticism were developed with regard to different attempts to define the term sustainability: (A) insufficient definition of the term, (B) contentiousness of the modelling and the accompanying setting of priorities and finally (C) criticism from the outside which, for example, bring other theories of reference to the fore and consider the theories of reference chosen by a sustainability concept as at least secondary, if not obstructive.

4.2 On the Consequence for ESD Due to the Questionability of Sustainability

Due to the controversial nature of what is meant by sustainability, the question for ESD is whether the theorisation of ESD is affected by the controversy. This brings us to the questions that have already been addressed. They are (iia) whether the fact that definition(s) of sustainability are not universally accepted has an impact on ESD and if so, (iib) what is that impact?

The first answer is that it is irrelevant for ESD whether it is already clear what sustainability is defined as. According to this position, it can be argued that the determination of what is to be understood by sustainability and how and by whom action is to be taken to achieve a then defined goal of sustainability is to be decided jointly and democratically by different actors. It is this idea of finding solutions that underlies UNESCO's ESD concept (UNESCO 2018).

Undoubtedly, this idea is once again not universally shared. This is unsurprising as this idea is itself a normative position of Political Philosophy among others. Underlying the concept is the idea that everyone should be equally involved in processes of finding solutions. This can be argued with further good reasons.

But the idea of equally finding joint solutions can also be criticized and rejected as insufficient because, for example, the people of the future cannot participate in the processes even if they are significantly affected by the decisions. And if an awareness is not created for this, then the initial position is not properly understood, precisely because of the notion of joint, supposedly democratic solution finding underlying the ESD concept.

Yet, one does not necessarily have to call on future generations and their possible rights to problematise. For example, it is not only Andreas Malm (2016: 267) who points out that people are impacted extremely differently depending on where on earth they live. Unlike almost anyone else, he challenges the thesis that all people are in the same way responsible for climate change:

> Capitalists in a small corner of the Western world invested in steam, laying the foundation of the fossil economy; at no moment did the species vote for it either with feet or ballots, or march in mechanical unison, or exercise any sort of shared authority over its own destiny and that of the earth system. *It* [humankind – H. K.] *did not figure as an actor on the historical stage* (Malm 2016: 267).

My point here is not to accept Malm's thesis as incontrovertibly correct, but to show that ESD is built on background assumptions of Political Philosophy and other assumptions, for example, about history, society and economy. And because the background assumptions can be questioned, different theories of ESD are conceivable, based precisely on different background assumptions.

The fact that background assumptions influence research is not a new or surprising insight. With regard to the already highly complex field of ESD research, the significance of the different background assumptions further increases the complexity and consequently complicates the joint work on an ESD theory.

For the time being, an ESD theory *cannot* be assumed at all. Even though the goal of an ESD theory will most likely never be achieved, this goal must be strived towards, otherwise any theory building would appear arbitrary. The condition of the possibility of achieving this goal is to expand ESD approaches into comprehensive theories and thus establish ESD paradigms. These ESD paradigms would either prove themselves or they would have to be discarded on the way to a comprehensive ESD theory.

The reflections on the concept of sustainability have not only highlighted the controversy over what is to be understood by the term, but also what is to be considered sustainable. Furthermore, the importance of background assumptions for theory building have been reiterated. But what does this mean for ESD theory building? In the following section, a first proposal is made, and in the section that concludes the article, this proposal is brought together with other reflections developed throughout.

A Contribution from the Philosophy of Science for ESD

5. A Theoretically Open Modelling Proposal for ESD

The question to be negotiated here has already been asked. The question was (see iib above) about the impact of the plurality of sustainability ideas on ESD theory. It is proposed here – for the moment – to include the plurality of conceptions of sustainability in a theoretically open modelling proposal for ESD respectively, to explicitly emphasise the plurality, which is often at least implicitly contained in every individual contribution on ESD. For without an implicit conception of sustainability and how education would possibly contribute to sustainability, no approach and contribution that locates itself in the ESD field can get by. In order to systematically locate the plurality of sustainability, a theoretical modelling of didactic theory is used.

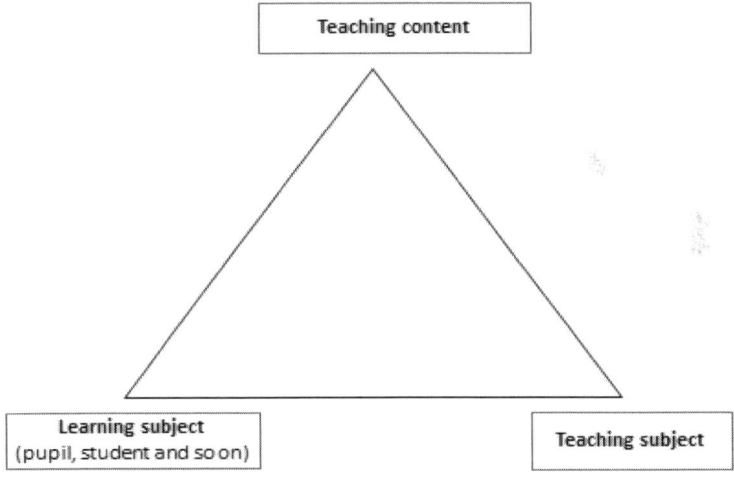

Figure 2: Didactic triangle (Source: own illustration.)

The plurality is presented in a further development of the so-called didactic triangle. The didactic triangle is well known in education science and used to model the situation of teaching in an abstract way. It models the three teaching components: learning subject, teaching subject and the content of teaching and the mutual relationship structure. It is claimed that the teaching process is visualised in this triangle.

A further development, which was named didactic pyramid by Andreas Gruschka (2002), is proposed here in a manner applied to ESD.[8] It is so strongly formalised that the modelling can be used for a wide variety of theoretical designs for formal, non-formal, as well as informal education practise.

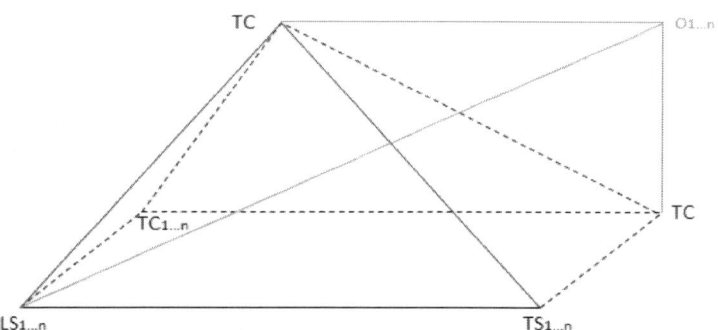

Figure 3: Didactic pyramid as a formal model of ESD teaching practice (Source: own illustration.)

The didactic pyramid also includes the teaching content (TC), the learning subject (LS) and the teaching subject (TS) as the didactic triangle. So far, it is the didactic triangle. From now on, the description of the model not only becomes more complex, but the complexity described is at certain points only implied in the model. If the whole complexity was to be implemented in the model, then the aim of illustration would be counteracted and the model would become confusing.

O is the object of learning/the educational process, which is (to contribute to) sustainability. 1…n stands for the different ideas of sustainability or the questionability of what sustainability is. Therefore, $O_{1…n}$ as a whole stands for the diversity of ideas of sustainability. In order to keep the model as clear as possible, a more complex representation in which several O (O_1, O_2, O_3) are represented, at least by way of example, was dispensed with. If one considers the different possibilities ($O_{1…n}$), one immediately becomes aware of the complexity of the practice as well as the theory of ESD.

$LS_{1…n}$ (LS = learning subject) always means the person who learns something and/or who undergoes a fundamental process of learning, i.e.,

---

[8] On the development and predecessors of this modelling, see Gruschka 2002 and Kminek 2018: 252ff.

a process of *Bildung*.⁹ Depending on the context, especially for formal and non-formal education, this can also be several persons ($S_{1...n}$) at the same time.

Depending on the context, $TS_{1...n}$ (TS = teaching subject) means one or more teachers (formal context), one or more pedagogues (non-formal context) or one or more very different persons (informal context, e.g., members of the peer group or characters in literature or films). In the case of informal education, it is not a structurally distinct person from $LS_{1...n}$.

TC stands abstractly for the didactic object in cases of practices of formal and non-formal education. The didactic object, i.e., the teaching content, can be anything from a worksheet to a film. Also, a project through which a change in the sense of sustainability is to be contributed can represent a didactic object for itself. This is because in and through the project, learning is to take place beyond the project with regard to sustainability. In the case of informal education, there is no didactic object in the strict sense. And yet there is an object on which something can be learned, can be educated in of itself. This object can be, for example, the topic of a play (e.g., the working conditions in factories in Bertolt Brecht's *Saint Joan of the Stockyards*) or a topic of a conversation of a peer group (e.g., is the climate balance to be taken into account when planning a holiday together or not). In the case of informal education, it is of course also possible that one learns/educates oneself in the direct confrontation with the world. In such a case, there is no didactic object. In these cases, DO coincides with O. The coincidence of DO with O is an exception in the areas of formal and non-formal education.

$TC_{1...n}$ (TC = teaching content) expresses the fact that each pupil or student views the didactic object TC differently and has a different view of this object. This means that, for example, in the case of a school class with 25 pupils, there are 25 different views of TC. Especially in the field of formal and non-formal education, this perspective is not likely to be identical with the perspective of TS – the teacher – on LC. This circumstance is symbolised and located in the modelling by means of the position TC.

TC here stands for the way the teacher sees the didactic object. By marking this position, it is made clear that the teacher sees and perceives the didactic object differently than the pupil or pupils.

Actual learning and educational processes of $S_{1...n}$ are not visible to P. They take place behind a façade, on the back of the pyramid, at the place $DO_{1...n}$. This means that actual learning and educational processes are not identical with the learning processes that P can plan and observe.

---

9   Compare footnote 3.

A large part of educational theory is concerned with the empirical enlightenment of this state of affairs or proposals to increase the probability of success of the planned process, i.e., that a pupil or student will reach or be brought to the "actual" goal of O more securely, better and often more quickly by dealing with the didactic object DO.

As desirable as it is that pupils, for example, reach O safely, better and/or faster by dealing with DO, this process cannot be technically planned and simply "produced" by the processing of meaning (compare Luhmann & Schorr 1982). Pedagogical theories that overlook the technological deficit of pedagogy make a logical-pedagogical conclusion error. They confuse ought with being. The error is that the conclusion is drawn from the ought (e.g., all pupils should learn this in a safe, better, faster way) to the being that all pupils *would* learn O, which is often not the case.[10]

If one adds, as already developed, that it is unclear what O, i.e., the goal, is in the first place, the vagueness of (i) what ESD should lead to and (ii) how ESD practice is empirical becomes apparent. It is precisely this circumstance that makes a model, like the one presented here, and its further development or the development of another potentially better model necessary for further research in order to determine the research needs and differences between different theorisations for the purpose of improving the theory (or theories).

6. Another Reflection as a Résumé

The article has attempted to put ESD into perspective in terms of the philosophy of science by means of theoretical references selected by the author, and to present initial ideas for reflections on the philosophy of science in the field of ESD.

The proposal(s) put forward here could quickly be criticised as working against the goal of sustainable development by abstract modelling and by keeping open the questions of what sustainability is in general and in terms of ESD. By leaving the questions open, the goal of sustainability and ESD for contributing to sustainability would become arbitrary.

In my view, the criticism is justified and unjustified at the same time. It is justified because the possibility of sustainability appearing as supposedly arbitrary is given. However, it is not only the possibility of arbitrariness that is argued against, but also the fact that this arbitrariness

---

10 At the very least, the performance (e.g., in action, in linguistic utterances) of the pupils is not as desired.

has already been argued against frequently and will probably continue to be argued against. At the very least, the scientists in the ESD field have it in their own hands to decide whether or not to leave the supposed arbitrariness on the table. Furthermore, and this motive underlies the entire essay, this first proposal for a more abstract ESD theorising is linked to the idea that concrete reference points for ESD theorising are needed so that work can be done (even) more systematically on further developing ESD theory. For this goal, this model is only meant to provide a component on a meta-level.

For me, one question keeps popping up now and then. Namely, the question of whether, in view of the challenges facing humanity, a fundamental socio-ecological transformation, a completely new kind of thinking, philosophy of science and theory and practice of pedagogy is needed. If one answers the question affirmatively, then the thoughts developed here are worthless. My answer, at least for the time being, is yes and no.

Yes, a fundamentally new theory and practice is needed – for example, comparable to the transformation of thought associated with the philosophy of René Descartes.[11] The idea of a steady progress of human history (Hegel 2001) was already identified as unsustainable in the middle of the 20th century at the latest (Adorno & Horkheimer 1999). *But* – read: *no* – a fundamentally new, further or better development of theory and practice will not be able to start again from scratch. For this reason, previous theory and practice must also be reflected with regard to the question of what can be discarded and what can be retained. For this form of reflection, a maximum distancing from theory and practice is necessary. A scientific-theoretical questioning of one's own theory and practice is suitable precisely for this purpose. The purpose of this paper is to contribute to such a scientific-theoretical questioning of one's own theory and practice as a first step on the way to a framework of an ESD-meta-theory.

Bibliography

Adorno, Theodor W./Horkheimer, Max (1999 [1944]): Dialectic of Enlightenment. London: Verso.
Adorno, Theodor W./Maus, Heinz (1969): Der Positivismusstreit in der deutschen Soziologie. Neuwied [a.o.]: Luchterhand.

---

[11] The question of whether primacy lies in theory or in practice is probably comparable to the question of the chicken and the egg.

Blankertz, Herwig (1982): Die Geschichte der Pädagogik. Von der Aufklärung bis zur Gegenwart. Wetzlar: Büchse der Pandora.

Brecht, Bertolt/Willett, John (1991): Plays, poetry and prose / Bertolt Brecht. Ed. by John Willett. Vol. 3. Pt. 1. Saint Joan of the Stockyards. London: Methuen.

Brunner, Karl-Michael (2019): Sustainable Consumption and the Dynamics of Demand. From individualistic to systemic concepts of transformation. In: Luks, Fred (ed.): Opportunities and Limits of Sustainability Transformation Economic and Sociological Perspectives. Wiesbaden: Springer Gabler, pp. 167-184.

Jickling, Bob (1994): Why I Don't Want My Children To Be Educated for Sustainable Development. In: Journal of Environmental Education 23, 4, pp. 5-8.

Flitner, Andreas/Giel, Klaus (1980): Wilhelm von Humboldt – Werke in fünf Bänden. Band I: Schriften zur Anthropologie und Geschichte. Darmstadt: Wissenschaftliche Buchgesellschaft.

Ford, Daniel/Blenkinsop, Sean (2021): Letters From a Dying College: How the Climate Crisis Demands a Wilder Pedagogy and Wilder Policies. In: Policy Futures in Education, Special Issue: Wilding educational policy - Hope for the future, pp. 1-13.

Friesen, Norm (2021): The necessity of translation in education: Theory and practice. In: Willmers, Annika/Jornitz, Sieglinde (ed.): International perspectives on school settings, education policy and digital strategies. Opladen/Berlin/Toronto: Barbara Budrich, pp. 337-351.

Gruschka, Andreas (2002): Didaktik: das Kreuz mit der Vermittlung; elf Einsprüche gegen den didaktischen Betrieb. Wetzlar: Büchse der Pandora.

Habermas, Jürgen (1987/1981): Theory of Communicative Action, Volume Two: Lifeworld and System: A Critique of Functionalist Reason (Book). Translated by Thomas A. McCarthy. Boston, Mass.: Beacon Press.

Hegel, Georg W. F. (2001): The Philosophy of History; with prefaces by Charles Hegel and the translator, J. Sibree. Kitchener, Ont.: Batoche.

Kraft, Volker (2007): Zwischen Reflexion, Funktion und Leistung: Facetten der Erziehungswissenschaft. Bad Heilbrunn: Klinkhardt.

Kminek, Helge (2006): Werturteilsstreit und erziehungswissenschaftliche Forschung. Master's thesis (unpubl.).

Kminek, Helge (2018): Philosophie und Philosophieren im Unterricht: empirische Erschließung einer widersprüchlichen Praxis. Opladen/Berlin/Toronto: Barbara Budrich.

Kminek, Helge (2020): Concept of Education in Education for Sustainable Development – the Necessity of Exposing the Uncertainty. In: Kminek, Helge/Bank, Franziska/Fuchs, Leon (ed.): Kontroverses Miteinander. Interdisziplinäre und kontroverse Positionen zur Bildung für eine nachhaltige Entwicklung. Frankfurt a. M.: Goethe-Universität, FB04-Dekanat, pp. 153-168.

Kminek, Helge/Wallmeier, Philip (2020): Nicht abschließbare Problemorientierung als Leitprinzip – Zur Bildung für die sozial-ökologische Transformation in polarisierten Zeiten. In: Eicker, Jannis/Eis, Andreas/Holfelder, Anne-Katrin/Jacobs, Sebastian/Yume,

Sophie/Konzeptwerk Neue Ökonomie (ed.): Bildung Macht Zukunft. Lernen für die sozial-ökologische Transformation? Schwalbach a. T.: Wochenschau.
Kminek, Helge/Holfelder, Anne-Katrin/Singer-Brodowski, Mandy (2021): Zukunft war gestern – Zur Legitimität der Pädagogik in Zeiten der sozialökologischen Krise. In: Zukunft – Stand jetzt. Jahrbuch für Pädagogik 2021. Redaktion: Bünger, Carsten/Czeijkowska, Agnieszka/Lohmann, Ingrid/Steffens, Gerd. Weinheim: Beltz (forthcoming).
Kminek, Helge (2022): Survival through Bildung: On the Topicality of Heinz-Joachim Heydorn's Philosophy of Education. Opladen: Budrich (forthcoming).
Kopnina, Helen (2020): Education for Sustainable Development Goals (ESDG): What Is Wrong with ESDGs, and What Can We Do Better? In: Education Science 10, 10, pp. 1-14.
Kuhn, Thomas S. (1962): The Structure of Scientific Revolutions. Chicago: Univ. of Chicago Press.
Lassman, Peter (1989): Max Weber's "Science as a vocation". London [a.o.]: Unwin Hyman.
Luhmann, Niklas/Schorr, Karl E. (1982): Das Technologiedefiziz der Erziehung und die Pädagogik. In: Luhmann, Niklas/Schorr, Karl E. (ed.): Zwischen Technologie und Selbstreferenz. Frankfurt a. M.: Suhrkamp, pp. 11-40.
Malm, Andreas (2016): Fossil Capital. The Rise of Steam Power and the Roots of Global Warming. London: Verso.
Marcinkowski, Tom/Reid, Alan (2019): Reviews of research on the attitude-behavior relationship and their implications for future environmental education research. In: Environmental Education Research 25, 4, pp. 459-471.
O'Flaherty, Joanne/Liddy, Mags (2018): The impact of development education and education for sustainable development interventions: a synthesis of the research. In: Environmental Education Research 24, 7, pp. 1031-1049.
Purvis, Ben/Mao, Yong/Robinson, Darren (2019): Three pillars of sustainability: in search of conceptual origins. In: Sustainability Science 14, pp. 681-695.
Ritsert, Jürgen (2003): Einführung in die Logik der Sozialwissenschaften. Münster: Westfälisches Dampfboot.
Rucker, Thomas (2017): Erkenntnisfortschritt (in) der Erziehungswissenschaft. Lernt die Disziplin? Bad Heilbrunn: Verlag Julius Klinkhardt.
Stein, Sharon/Andreotti, Vanessa de Oliveira/Suša, Rene/Ahenakew, Cash/Čajková, Tereza (2020): From "education for sustainable development" to "education for the end of the world as we know it". In: Educational Philosophy and Theory 54, 3, pp. 274-287.
UN (2016): Transforming Our World: The 2030 Agenda for Sustainable Development. A/RES/70/1. Online: https://sustainabledevelopment.un.org/content/documents/21252030%20Agenda%20for%20Sustainable%20Development%20web.pdf (accessed: 09.09.2021).
UNESCO (2018): Education for Sustainable Development Goals. Learning Objectives. Paris.
UNESCO (2020): Education for Sustainable Development. A Roadmap. Paris.

Umweltbundesamt (2017): Szenario Luftverkehr Deutschland unter Einbezug von Umweltaspekten. Von: Maibach, Markus/Peter, Martin/Killer, Maura/Bieler, Cuno/Zandonella, Remo/Notter, Benedikt/Bertschmann, Damaris; INFRAS Forschung und Beratung, Zürich. Im Auftrag des Umweltbundesamtes. Dessau-Roßlau: Umweltbundesamt.

Vare, Paul/Scott, William (2007): Learning for a Change. In: Journal of Education for Sustainable Development 1, 2, pp. 191-198.

Verhelst, Dies/Vanhoof, Jan/Boeve-de Pauw, Jelle/Van Petegem, Peter (2020): Building a conceptual framework for an ESD-effective school organization. In: The Journal of Environmental Education 51, 6, pp. 400-415.

WCED (1987): Our Common Future. Oxford: Oxford Univ. Press.

Weber, Max (1989 [1917]): Max Weber's "Science as a vocation". Ed. by Peter Lassman. London [a.o.]: Unwin Hyman.

Weber, Max (2002 [1917]): Der Sinn der »Wertfreiheit« der soziologischen und ökonomischen Wissenschaften. In: idem (ed.): Schriften: 1894 - 1922 / Max Weber. Ausgew. und hrsg. von Dirk Kaesler. Stuttgart: Kröner, pp. 358-394.

Autonomy and Second Nature: A Hegelian Account of Education for Sustainable Development

Beer Albers

1. Introduction

In ongoing academic and political debates about Education for Sustainable Development (ESD), a recurring pattern can be identified that presents itself as a (supposed) conflict between two claims simultaneously associated with ESD. Insofar as ESD is a form of education, the "normative claim of pedagogy since the Enlightenment" (Kminek 2020: 153) is addressed to it. It is the claim to enable students to be autonomous individuals. At the same time, however, ESD is linked to a clear goal: In the face of worsening ecological crises and under increasing time pressure, it aims to bring about a transformation of people's lives for the sake of sustainability. The two claims addressed to ESD are thus autonomisation and transformation. A conflict between these claims would arise if the realization of one of them were possible only at the expense of the other. This would be the case if autonomisation did not lead to transformation, or, in other words, if transformation could only be accomplished by non-autonomous means – for example, by manipulatively conditioning students to act sustainably. In this case, ESD would be permeated by a constitutive contradiction that could only be resolved if one of the two claims constituting it were given up. However, this would mean that the idea of ESD would have to be given up as a whole since ESD is only constituted as a unity of both claims.

Based on Georg Wilhelm Friedrich Hegel's theory of education (*Bildung*[1]), this paper argues that it is a mistake to abstractly pit the claim to

---

1   It is well-known that the German word *Bildung* cannot easily be translated into other languages. Not even in its ordinary German meaning is *Bildung* a semantic equivalent to 'education', 'culture', 'cultivation' or 'civilization' (cf. Kosellek 2006: 109-110). This problem is exacerbated when speaking of Hegel's technical use of the word. Aware of this problem, *Bildung* is translated as 'education' throughout this paper for the sake of terminological consistency. However, it is

autonomisation of educational subjects against the necessity of social transformation (also) brought about by conditioning elements. Drawing on Hegel, I argue that it is instead necessary to perceive autonomisation and conditioning as two sides of a tension-filled unity of the concept of education itself, or more precisely, of education as the formation of a *second nature*.² One must, in other words, move beyond an abstract opposition of the two concepts.

To this end, I will first analyse argumentative patterns which operate with an abstract – i.e., exclusionary – opposition of autonomisation and conditioning (chap. 2). Subsequently, Jürgen Menthe's proposals for a subject-critical ESD are reconstructed (chap. 3). In view of an (assumed) far-reaching ineffectiveness of ESD, Menthe argues for the formation of a sustainable habitus of students, which is to be brought about by conditioning elements. It will be argued that his proposal, which relies on a conception of second nature, requires further clarification. To achieve such clarification, an account of Hegel's theory of education will be given (chap. 4). This will include a treatment of what Christoph Menke calls Hegel's *critical* theory of second nature (cf. Menke 2018: 145). It will be demonstrated that Hegel does not conceive of autonomisation and conditioning as exclusive opposites, but rather understands the process of education as a tension-filled unity of autonomisation and conditioning that takes place in the acquisition of a second nature. The aim of reconstructing Hegel's theory of education is to show that education can at the same time contain conditioning elements *and* be a process of liberation. If this is the case, then there is not necessarily a fundamental conflict between autonomisation and social transformation for the sake of sustainability. In a final return to subject-critical ESD, I will draw on Hegel to argue that ESD only undermines the normative claim of modern educational institutions if it renders the students' own self-reflection impossible (chap. 5).

---

important to keep in mind that 'Bildung' in Hegel's terminology is not identical to what is commonly associated with 'education'. Regarding the German semantic of Bildung and the related problems of translation, see also Kminek 2022 (in this volume), footnote 5, p. 74. As for the translations of the quoted texts in general, I have used English translations if they were available and adequate. If one of these factors was not given, I have used my own translations. Alterations to existing translations have been indicated by footnotes.

2 I generally follow Menke (cf. Menke 2018: 120) in interpreting Hegel's theory of education from the perspective of his theory of second nature.

2. ESD between Autonomisation and Conditioning

Normative academic and political debates about ESD have long been troubled by the concern that the concept of ESD might contain a fundamental contradiction (cf. for example, Jickling 1992: 6). The (supposed) contradiction arises from the assumption of an incompatibility of two claims simultaneously attached to ESD. The first claim is that, as education, it ought to enable autonomy (cf. ibid.: 8). The second claim is that ESD should lead to an ecological transformation of everyday routines for the purpose of sustainability (cf. van Poeck & Östman 2020: 1004). The concern around an incompatibility of these two claims is not only raised by fundamental critics of ESD (cf. for example Jickling 1992) but also appears to trouble its advocates (cf. for example van Poeck & Östman 2020).

Taken on their own, both claims are convincing for different reasons. The claim to autonomy is grounded in a generally shared normative understanding of education: That autonomy is to be attained through education is a semantic core of modern concepts of education, i.e., an invariant of otherwise diverse modern understandings of education, as Reinhart Koselleck has shown (cf. Koselleck 2006: 137). In turn, over the past few years, the "urgent need for a transition towards a more sustainable world" (van Poeck & Östman 2020: 1003) has ever more strongly been brought to our attention by (among other things) political protests, findings in the fields of environmental science, and natural catastrophes.

In accordance with their fundamental persuasiveness, both claims are frequently brought forward in current debates. On the one hand, the demand not to instrumentalize students and educational processes for the sake of achieving extra-educational political ends is insistently articulated in the name of the claim to autonomy (for an overview, cf. ibid.: 1005-1006). On the other hand, in view of the urgency of current ecological problems, discussions about ways to effectively bring about ecological transformation through ESD are increasing. Here, the issue of conditioning tends to make an appearance (cf. Kminek 2020: 153).

However, the issue of conditioning is not a new one in the context of normative debates surrounding ESD. As early as 1992, Bob Jickling formulated an understanding of the interrelation between the concepts of education, autonomy and conditioning, which, in its basic features, is shared by proponents and opponents of ESD to this day. According to this understanding, education is supposed to bring about autonomy, as already noted above (cf. Jickling 1992: 8). Prescribing certain ways of thinking or acting is said to be incompatible with this goal. In line with this, it is considered "wrong to persuade, influence or even educate people towards pre- and expert-determined ways of thinking and acting" (Wals 2010: 150), as this is thought to be "repugnant to the development of autonomous thinking" (Jickling 1992: 8). Jickling explicitly emphasizes the opposition of education and conditioning presupposed by this: "I would rather have my children *educated* than *conditioned* to believe that sustainable development constitutes a constellation of correct environmental views" (ibid., emphasis added).

In this generally shared understanding, autonomisation and conditioning are seen as abstract opposites. Processes of conditioning, the idea goes, cannot be processes of autonomisation. The process of autonomisation, as which education is conceived, is therefore understood as a process that does not (and *may not*) contain conditioning elements. This paper aims at rethinking the relationship between the concepts of autonomisation and conditioning with reference to Hegel's theory of education. My aim is thus to reinterpret what Arjen Wals calls the "tension between the call for self-determination on the one hand, and the call for sustainable social norms [...] on the other" (Wals 2010: 150). To do so, I will first look at a conception of ESD which affirms conditioning elements and then interpret this conception against the background of a Hegelian account of education.

3. ESD and the Critique of Autonomous Selfhood

Jürgen Menthe has proposed what can be called a *subject-critical* (*subjektkritische*) conception of ESD.[3] Subject-critical ESD is characterized by a critique of conceptions of subjectivity underlying theories and educational policies oriented towards what Menthe perceives as a naïve, rationalist image of autonomy. In contrast to these, the subject-critical conception advocates that ESD should not be designed primarily as a rational appeal to (supposedly) rational subjects but should instead shift its focus towards other factors influencing the students' actions apart from autonomous insight.

In order to establish his stance, Menthe follows Markus Rieger-Ladich (2002) in assuming an alternative between "two interpretations of the concept of Enlightenment" (Menthe 2017: 130) corresponding "to the different receptions of the tradition of Enlightenment in France and Germany" (ibid.: 131). Both receptions depart from Immanuel Kant's canonical treatment of the concept of Enlightenment (Kant 1996) but

---

3 The German word 'Subjektkritik' is difficult to translate into English. It generally denotes the critique of certain abstract philosophical conceptions of subjectivity.

emphasize different aspects of it. The first understanding of Enlightenment, which is attributed to the German tradition, is said to presuppose a robust subject which – through education – can be enabled "to make use of its intellect in order [...] to decide and act autonomously, freely and rationally" (Menthe 2017: 131). According to Menthe, this understanding of subjectivity is accompanied by a conception of action that essentially regards "rational, conscious deliberative processes" (ibid.: 130) as decisive for a subject's actions. This in turn corresponds to a conception of ESD that assumes that rationally addressing students in the context of educational processes will result in changes of their behaviour in terms of greater sustainability (cf. ibid.: 131).

Since, according to Menthe, such behavioural changes fail to be achieved despite rationally addressing students, he suggests turning to a second, "subject-critical concept of Enlightenment" (ibid.). According to Menthe, this conception originated "primarily from French, more sociologically oriented authors" (ibid.) and recognizes that individuals are subjected to "multiple economic constraints, biographical factors, and social relations of power and domination" (ibid.: 133). Menthe stresses that the subject-critical concept of Enlightenment is based on the insight that subjectivity is not immediately given, but rather "the result of complex interactions (power relations) between the individual and society" (ibid.). In view of what Menthe calls the "heteronomous constitution of the subject" (ibid.: 130), he advocates that ESD should not limit itself to an "intellectual approach" (ibid.: 135). Instead, it should shift its focus to the social practices involved in the formation of acting subjects in the first place (cf. ibid.: 137). According to Menthe, this is necessary to effectively bring about more sustainable behaviour and to thereby establish "a living culture of sustainability" (ibid.).

The departing point of Menthe's reconstruction of the French reception of the Enlightenment tradition is Kant's claim that immaturity (*Unmündigkeit*) "has become almost nature" (Kant 1996: 17) to man. By conceiving the subject as essentially rational and self-transparent, the German reception of (Kantian) Enlightenment seems unable to appropriate the subject's *almost natural* immaturity (cf. Menthe 2017: 132-133). Accordingly, it is unsurprising that Menthe refers to authors operating with a concept of *second nature* in order to object to the conception of subjectivity attributed to the German tradition. Menthe draws particularly on Pierre Bourdieu's concept of *habitus* (cf. ibid.). According to Bourdieu, the habitus of an individual comprises dispositions that are individually embodied and at the same time socially mediated (cf. Rieger Ladich: 317). Habitus is thus "history turned into nature" (Bourdieu 2000a: 263). Historically emergent social relations (namely class relations, cf. Rieger-Ladich 2002: 305-308) shape the dispositions of individuals and are realized as their "second nature" (Bourdieu 2000a: 263). This means that individuals embody habitual dispositions as if they belong to them as a set of *natural* dispositions, although in fact they are effects of social practices (cf. Rieger-Ladich 2002: 305-308). Since habitually conducted practices are carried out prereflexively ("below the level of consciousness and discursive thinking, therefore beyond the reach of deliberate scrutiny or control", Bourdieu 1979: 543), they are structurally akin to natural processes. For this reason, Bourdieu refers to the structures of habitus as "quasi-natures" (Bourdieu 2000a: 263).

Drawing on this pre-reflexive action-guiding character of habitus, Menthe argues for its potential to effectuate lasting change in students' behaviour. If enabling students to reflect on their decisions and calling on them to do so does not bring about the desired outcomes in terms of sustainable action, a pre-reflexive habitus of sustainability is supposed to provide a remedy (cf. Menthe 2017: 136). According to Bourdieu, habitus is not primarily induced by rational instruction, but rather by pre-reflexive practice (Bourdieu speaks of a *conditioning* (cf. Bourdieu 1980: 88) or even of a *dressage*[4]). In line with this, Menthe advocates bringing about habitual changes on the part of students at a pre-reflexive level.[5] His proposals are thus not fundamentally incompatible with educational interventions shaping "the students' routines without the students being aware of it" (Kminek 2020: 154). This has been understood as an endorsement of conditioning elements in ESD (cf. ibid.: 153). And indeed, Menthe clearly proposes that the implementation of sustainable practices and the accompanying changes in students' behaviour should not be made dependent on their insight but should instead be brought about at a level preceding reflection (cf. Menthe 2017: 137). In short, he argues for the formation of a second nature aligned with the goal of sustainability – a formation which includes conditioning elements.

This proposal has been criticized as being at odds with the claim to autonomy linked to modern pedagogy, or even being at risk of becoming essentially indistinguishable from educational programmes of totalitarian states (cf. Kminek 2020: 158). This would be the case if Menthe argued for *mere* conditioning of students. Menthe's treatment of Bourdieu would then ignore fundamental aspects of Bourdieu's treatment of habitus. It would be in line with Bourdieu only insofar as Menthe acknowledges that habitual formations can be an obstacle to social transformation and can

---

4 "Although making things explicit can contribute, only a true work of counter-dressage, involving repeated exercises similar to athletic training, can achieve a lasting transformation of habitus" (Bourdieu 2001: 220).

5 This follows from Menthe's claim that reflection "can only ever take place post hoc" (Menthe 2017: 137).

thus prevent the emergence of sustainable routines of action. After all, the core of his critique of the 'rationalist' conception of ESD consisted precisely in claiming that it is rendered ineffective by the prevailing unsustainable habitus of students. But Menthe's solution to the problem of the "extraordinary inertia" (Bourdieu 2000b: 172) of habitus would already depart from Bourdieu in that it would not rely on the (faint) hope that habitually acting subjects can be enabled to reflexively become aware of and transform their own practice. Menthe's solution would then merely amount to proposing the replacement of a worse (less sustainable) habitus with a better (more sustainable) one. Pre-reflexive habitus, originally introduced as a problem for ecological transformation, would uncritically be redeclared as a solution to this problem. A sustainable habitus would no longer be considered problematic, but instead be presented as a solution to the problem of ESD's lack of effectiveness. The normative evaluation of second-natural formations would thus be made dependent (in a utilitarian manner, as it were) on their *consequences*, completely leaving aside the normative evaluation of their *structure*.

This would overlook the fact that habitual formations are not only critically examined by Bourdieu because of their consequences (e.g., unsustainable actions), but also because structurally they are mechanisms "that operate the continued subjugation of human beings and prevent their self-determination" (Rieger-Ladich 2002: 286). Bourdieu's treatment of habitus is critical insofar as it considers habitual formations in terms of their role in the blind, i.e., irreflexive and thus heteronomous reproduction of social orders (cf. ibid.: 285). According to Rieger-Ladich, Bourdieu's thought is therefore "guided by a normative concept of free and self-determined life" (ibid.) and aims at "making the meaning of their behavior available to subjects again" (Bourdieu 1974: 39, as cited in Rieger-Ladich 2000: 285). Thus, by merely demanding that a worse habitus be replaced by a better one, one falls short of this normative claim of Bourdieu's thought. Judged by Bourdieu's standard, it is not enough to rely on ESD to bring about a second nature that results in better (i.e., more sustainable) ways of acting. If one wants to do justice to Bourdieu's reflections, one must critically examine second-nature formations not only in terms of their *consequences* but also in terms of their *structure*. Advocating educational programmes aimed at the transformation of students' habitus without critically examining the structure of second nature regresses behind Bourdieu's critical project. This regression would likewise be a regression behind the "normative claim of pedagogy since the Enlightenment" (Kminek 2020: 153). Against such proposals, the criticism of being close to totalitarian educational programmes is justified.

Whether this criticism is also valid regarding Menthe's subject-critical conception of ESD depends on which status Menthe assigns to the concept of autonomy within it. The treatment of this question can proceed on two levels. *Firstly*, it can be asked whether Menthe's proposal contains an explicit affirmation of a clearly defined concept of autonomy. *Secondly*, it can be asked whether Menthe's proposal necessarily amounts to an affirmation of heteronomy or whether it is in principle conceptually compatible with a reformulated concept of autonomy.

As for the first question: In relation to Menthe's staunch critique of the 'rationalist' understanding of subjectivity and the strong notion of autonomy associated with it, his remarks on an alternative notion of autonomy are remarkably scarce. The fact that Menthe speaks of the "illusion of the responsible, autonomous individual that acts consciously and on the basis of values and preferences" (Menthe 2017: 130) at times suggests that he intends to depart from the normative claim to autonomy altogether. In contrast to this, it becomes clear elsewhere that he is rather concerned with overcoming a "dichotomous understanding of maturity [*Mündigkeit*, B.A.] vs. immaturity [*Unmündigkeit*, B.A.]" (ibid.: 131). It nonetheless remains obscure how exactly such an overcoming should be imagined. Moreover, Kminek has pointed to the unclear status of subjective reflection in Menthe's considerations (cf. Kminek 2020: 158). In fact, Menthe remains vague on this point. Admittedly, he speaks of "reflection of one's own actions" as playing a "special role" (Menthe 2017: 137) within subject-critical ESD. But apart from claiming that this reflection "can only ever take place post hoc" (ibid.) – a claim which is not explained further –, Menthe is silent about what this 'special role' is supposed to consist of and how it is to be incorporated into educational practice. From this we can conclude that Menthe's reflections do not offer or affirm a well-defined concept of autonomy. It remains unanswered how exactly the connection between social practice and autonomy, between conditioning and reflection, is to be conceived.

Regarding the second question, I do not think that one must necessarily ascribe the abovementioned affirmation of a manipulative educational approach to Menthe, for he leaves room (albeit abstractly) for reflection on one's own sustainable habitus (cf. ibid.). He does not offer an elaborated alternative to the 'rationalist' conception of autonomy, but he also does not propose anything that is fundamentally incompatible with a revised concept of autonomy.[6] Understood in this way, Menthe is in line with his central point of reference Rieger-Ladich who dedicated his

---

6   This reading presupposes that Menthe's remark that reflection is only possible *post hoc* is taken to mean that although reflection takes place *post hoc* insofar as it has non-reflexive preconditions, it can still be directed at future actions. This understanding is plausible because Menthe attributes to subjects a limited capacity to change their own habitus through "self-reflexive practice" (cf. Menthe 2017: 135). Such changes would have to occur with regard to future actions. The reflection bringing these changes about would thus in a sense also be a reflection *ex ante*.

theoretical project to the aim of "sketching the contours of a new concept of autonomy" (Rieger-Ladich 2002: 20).

As I will argue below, essential elements of this project can be grasped in Hegelian terms. In doing so, my aim is to show that in a Hegelian framework the relation of social norms and subjective freedom can be understood in a way that does not abstractly pit autonomisation and conditioning against each other. The tension between them is instead to be understood as an internal tension constitutive of the concept of education. If it is true that subject-critical approaches can be reformulated in terms of Hegelian theory, then it follows that the alternative construed by Rieger-Ladich and Menthe between a German and a French reception of the Enlightenment is a *false alternative*. As Kminek has already shown with regard to Theodor W. Adorno (cf. Kminek 2020: 155-156), it is not the case that there has been no reflection on heteronomous moments of the constitution of subjectivity and on the embeddedness of subjects in social practices within the German Enlightenment tradition.[7] In what follows, it will be shown that what Menthe understands by subject critique (*Subjektkritik*) is not an innovation of twentieth-century French theory. On the contrary, it is argued that essential elements of subject-critical thought can already be found in Hegel's philosophical reflections on education (*Bildung*) in early 19th century Germany.[8] Indicating that the suggested alternative between a German Enlightenment tradition that uncritically presupposes a fully rational, self-transparent subject and a French Enlightenment tradition that recognizes the subject's embeddedness in social practices is a false alternative is not only done for the sake of historical accuracy. The reference to Hegelian theory is primarily made for argumentative reasons. I argue that Hegel's theory of education, reconstructed from the perspective of his "critical concept of second nature" (Menke 2018: 48), equips us with an understanding of education in which both the social mediation of the subject and its individual freedom are reflected. Thus, Hegel's theory of education can simultaneously present itself as an affirmation of the idea of autonomy *and* avoid the mistake of overlooking the prereflexive, socially mediated involvements of acting subjects. In this way, it succeeds in not pitting autonomisation and conditioning abstractly against each other and instead

---

7 Such a portrayal of the German Enlightenment tradition is inaccurate even if one limits oneself (as Rieger-Ladich does) to the pedagogical discourse about *Mündigkeit* in postwar Germany, for Adorno can clearly be attributed to this discourse. It is remarkable that Adorno's well-known remarks on 'education for maturity' (*Erziehung zur Mündigkeit*) are not mentioned in Rieger-Ladich's analysis of the discourse about maturity/autonomy (*Mündigkeit*) in postwar Germany even though he situates his reflections in the tradition of Critical Theory (cf. Rieger-Ladich 2002: 11-12).

8 Bourdieu was aware of this, as can be seen from the fact that he regarded Hegel's theory of habit as a precursor to his own concept of habitus (cf. Bourdieu 1990: 12).

conceptualizes them as a structural nexus of a "dialectic of second nature" (ibid.: 46) internal to the process of *Bildung* itself.

4. Mechanism of Autonomy? – Hegel on *Bildung* and Second Nature

> Education [*Pädagogik*] is the art of making human beings ethical [*sittlich*, B.A.]: it considers them as natural beings and shows them how they can be reborn, and how their original nature [*erste Natur*, B.A.] can be transformed into a second, spiritual nature so that this spirituality becomes habitual to them. (Hegel 2003: 195)

Hegel develops his theory of education along the distinction between the concepts of *nature* and *spirit*. "As spirit", Hegel claims, "man is a free being [*Wesen*] who is in a position not to let himself be determined by natural drives [*Naturimpulse*, B.A.]" (Hegel 2003: 51). Two central assertions are contained in this sentence: *Firstly*, man is characterized as a *spiritual* being – a being that, as we shall see, is spiritually determinable and (more importantly) able to spiritually determine itself. *Secondly*, the relation of man's spirituality towards his naturalness is characterized as a relation of *negativity*: Man is spiritual insofar as he can distinguish himself from his naturalness and place himself in a relation of negativity to it – in this respect, he is spiritual insofar as he is *not natural*. Hegel's basic assumption is that man is both a natural and a spiritual being. In order to reconstruct Hegel's theory of education which proceeds from this assumption, it is first necessary to explain both sides of this "*twofold* nature of man" (Beuthan 2021: 106).

That a human being can relate negatively to its natural impulses presupposes that such impulses are inherent within it. Hegel refers to the totality of these impulses as the "lower faculty of desire [*niederes Begehrungsvermögen*, B.A.] by which man behaves as a natural being" (Hegel 1993b: 205). This faculty inheres animals and human beings alike (cf. ibid.: 217) and therefore belongs to the *animal* side of human life (cf. Hegel 2007: 56). As a natural being, a human individual is dependent on things external to it (e.g., food or another individual of his species) in order to reproduce its own life as well as the life of its species (cf. Hegel 2004: 409-411). This integration into a natural environment corresponds to the human drives (*Triebe*), which express themselves in desires (*Begierden*) directed at individual objects (cf. Hegel 1993a: 58). Translated into the terminology of contemporary philosophy, it can be said that as biological individuals, humans have specific natural dispositions (cf. Testa 2019: 293). Hegel refers to these dispositions as man's first nature: "man's *first nature* is his immediate animal existence" (Hegel 1975: 97).

In the opening quote it has already become apparent that human beings can relate negatively to their natural impulses; they can renounce their desires (cf. Hegel 2007: 132). This does not imply that man can completely rid himself of his natural impulses, nor that he can only attain freedom through their complete renunciation.[9] Hegel's reference to the fact that man can posit himself in a negative relation to himself as a naturally determined being is rather to be understood as a recognition of a structural possibility constituting man's spirituality: As a spiritual being, he is able to transcend his immediate natural determination through "reflection" (Hegel 2003: 37) and is, therefore, not identical to it. A human being is thus more than just a biological individual. Unlike the animal, which is identical with its naturalness, man is able to abstract from his natural determinacy (cf. ibid.: 38). However, man's mental capacities are not limited to the mere negative capacity of abstraction but, moreover, enable him to replace negated natural determinations with the positivity of self-imposed spiritual determinations (cf. ibid.: 39-40). This capacity is a necessary condition of autonomy in the sense of self-determination: As a spiritual being, a human being has the capacity of "positing [...] itself as something determinate" (ibid.: 39).

As a being capable of spiritual self-determination, man can go beyond immediately given desires and pursue higher-level purposes. Hegel refers to the faculty to do so as the "higher faculty of desire [*höheres Begehrungsvermögen*, B.A.]" (Hegel 1993b: 206) which he equates with the *will* of man (cf. ibid.).[10] In contrast to determinations of the lower faculty of desire, determinations of the will do not immediately result from natural impulses but are outcomes of the intellectual involvement with "reasons

---

9 Indeed, Hegel explicitly contradicts both of these claims. Since drives belong to man's nature, they cannot be eliminated by a decision of will: "man does not posit his drives himself, but has them immediately, that is, they belong to his *nature*" (Hegel 1993b: 218). For a human being it is nonetheless possible to relate to its natural impulses in a way that reduces them to a subordinate moment of its life. Note, however, that Hegel thinks of this subordination not in terms of renunciation but in terms of satisfaction: "desires, urges are dulled by the habit of their satisfaction. This is the rational liberation from them; monkish renunciation and forcible repression do not free us from them, nor are they rational in content" (Hegel 2007: 132). Regarding the general structure of this model of subordination and its role in Hegel's concept of *ethical life (Sittlichkeit)*, see Henrich 2010: 172-181.

10 In English, the semantic difference between the German expressions 'Begehren' and 'Begierde' cannot be reproduced at the lexical level. It is, therefore, important to keep in mind that the 'higher faculty of desire' (*höheres Begehrungsvermögen*) is precisely not concerned with desires in the sense of particular object-oriented expressions of natural drives (*Begierden*), but with rational determinations of the will. In Hegel's terminology, natural desires belong to the 'lower faculty of desire' (*niederes Begehrungsvermögen*).

[*Beweggründen*, B.A.]" (ibid.). Unlike animals, humans have a "responsiveness to reasons" (McDowell 2009: 166). If a human individual acts in a certain way, it "renders them [reasons, B.A.] its own" (Hegel 1993b: 206).

At this point, a basic terminological clarification of the Hegelian concept of action is necessary. Whoever acts realizes an *end* (cf. Hegel 2003: 42-43). This is the case regardless of whether the acting person consciously reflects on his action or acts unconsciously. Hegel's point is that the realization of a purpose is structurally inscribed into the successful execution of an action. For example, I realize an end with my daily walk to the train station even if I do not consciously reflect on this end every single day but act out of habit instead. One could find out about my end by asking me about my reasons for walking to the train station. As Brandom puts it, whoever acts has (explicit or implicit) reasons for acting the way he does: "the acts we perform count as *actions* just insofar as it is proper to offer and inquire after reasons for them" (Brandom 1994: 5). Thus, being able to act presupposes responsiveness to reasons: Only those biological individuals who are responsive to reasons can be considered agents. Because man inhabits the "the realm, common to all, of reasons" (Hegel 2007: 71),[11] he can be considered an acting subject. Or, to put it in the terminology of contemporary philosophy, man is an "inhabitant of the space of reasons" (McDowell 2009: 181).

However, man's spiritual faculties are not inherent in him at birth – they must first be acquired. Since a human biological individual is a subject of action only if it has acquired spiritual faculties, the acting subject is not uncritically presupposed in Hegel's thought. Quite the opposite: For Hegel, an autonomous humane agent is the result of the process of acquiring spiritual faculties. Hegel's treatment of education aims to describe the structure of this process.

Hegel's theory of education – or at least the 'ontogenetic' or 'subjective' aspect of it[12] – proceeds from the description of the unborn child's mode of life inside the womb of its mother. In this state, the child lives "in undivided soul-unity with its mother" (Hegel 2007: 89) and "is not yet *Itself*, not a subject reflected into itself" (ibid.). It does not yet have drives and desires, as these presuppose an already constituted self which relates to entities external to it. As the unborn child "has as yet no proper

---

11   For the sake of terminological consistency, I have altered Wallace's/Miller's translation of the German word 'Gründe' to 'reasons' (Wallace/Miller translate it as 'grounds').
12   In treating Hegel's concept of education, I mainly focus on the aspects of the concept concerning the education of the individual. Even though I do not explain these aspects as isolated from historically emergent social forms, I nevertheless largely bracket the strand of Hegel's theory of *Bildung* that conceives the historical development of humanity as a process of *Bildung*. On this aspect, see Forster 2012: 81-82, 88, Beuthan 2012: 111-113, and Brandom 1979: 194-195.

individuality, no individuality to enter into relationship with particular objects in a particular manner" (ibid.: 55), it lacks the drives and desires characteristic of animal life. Its mode of life is therefore not yet animalistic; for Hegel, it rather "resembles the life of a plant" (ibid.: 56).

Through the "tremendous leap" (ibid.) of birth, however, the child traverses from "completely oppositionless life into the state of separation" (ibid.) and thereby "passes into the animal mode of life" (ibid.). It now "establishes its independence" (ibid.) as a being separated from its mother. Unlike a plant, it now has a self-feeling (*sense of self, Selbstgefühl*, cf. Hegel 2004: 336) and is a needy being equipped with drives and desires. In this respect, it resembles an animal organism (cf. Hegel 2007: 56). According to the above discussion, the newborn, whose utterances of life are essentially identical with its utterances of natural impulses, does not yet have any spiritual abilities. It is not yet responsive to reasons and thus not an acting subject. In other words, it is still in the "state of nature" (Hegel 1993b: 223), i.e., in an "uncivilized [*ungebildeten*] condition" (Hegel 2003: 51).

The newborn faces a world which is not merely a natural world. Although it only relates to material objects in its surroundings, these objects do not constitute the totality of the world surrounding it. Even if it is not yet receptive to it at first, it is, nevertheless, surrounded by a "world of spirit" (ibid.: 35) which in Hegel's thought also goes by the name of *objective spirit*.[13] It is a spiritual world insofar as it is the result of human interactions that are not identical with the mere acting out of natural impulses of biologically human individuals. In the idiom of contemporary philosophy, it can be said that this spiritual world consists of *social practices* (cf. Menke 2018: 20).

As inhabitants of the world of objective spirit, the adults surrounding the child usually do not act in accordance with their immediate, merely factual natural impulses, but are "also aligned with a normative being exemplified in concrete social and political structures" (Beuthan 2012: 111). This can be rephrased in terms of roles: Adults act in different roles, each of which is associated with certain normative standards, i.e., certain rules constitutive of the practice in question (cf. Menke 2018: 28-29). Those surrounding the child act, for example, as moral, political, legal and economic subjects and thus take part in social practices constituting the

---

13   In other words, Hegel distinguishes two worlds: "There are two worlds, the natural and the ethical [*sittliche*, B.A.]" (Hegel 2005: 232). The ethical world (i.e., the world of objective spirit) is also characterized as a "second nature" (Hegel 2003: 35). To draw a more comprehensive picture of Hegel's theory of second nature, one would have to distinguish between subjective and objective second nature and deal with the latter in more detail. Here, more emphasis is placed on subjective second nature. On the distinction between subjective and objective second nature in Hegel, see Testa 2019: 291, and Menke 2018: 43.

objective world of spirit. Unlike nature, objective spirit is dependent on human action insofar as it is itself but an "ensemble of practices" (Menke 2018: 29) that is only "maintained and [...] groomed by the continuing practice of a community" (McDowell 2009: 167). These practices are, at least in principle, alterable by reflexive intervention on the part of the subjects involved in them.

Such normatively oriented action presupposes, however, that the acting individuals are responsive to the spiritual mode of being of the world of spirit. This is not yet the case with the child. It does not yet think in (e.g.,) moral, political, or legal categories and does not yet pursue purposes of these kinds. How does the newborn get out of the state of identity with its natural impulses? In other words: How does it become a subject capable of acting in the world of spirit?

Hegel answers this question within the framework of his theory of second nature: The human individual not yet responsive to reasons transforms into an acting subject by being initiated into the world of spirit through practice (i.e., exercise). The first (natural) birth is thus followed by a "second birth of the children, their spiritual birth" (Hegel 2007: 230). Hegel claims: "the individual activities of man acquire by repeated practice [*Übung*, B.A.] the character of *habit*" (ibid.: 136). According to Hegel, this applies not only to the bodily mediated practical handling of objects at hand (like in writing, cf. ibid. or in playing the piano, cf. Hegel 1986b: 189) but to any subjective spiritual activity: "Habit is a form that embraces all kinds and stages of spirit's activity" (Hegel 2007: 132).[14]

Hegel's mention of 'repeated practice' implies that the 'second birth', which takes place as a "production of habit" (ibid.: 131), is not a single event but rather a lengthy process. From a Hegelian perspective, it would be incoherent to describe this process as a series of autonomous acts of the subject acquiring a second nature. This is because spiritual abilities, and thus the possibility of autonomy, are acquired only through the acquisition of a second nature. Therefore, the acquisition itself cannot be a series of fully autonomous acts. As Menke puts it, "the break with the existence as a natural being [...] cannot be a free act of self-liberation" (Menke 2018: 74). Accordingly, Hegel describes education as a process involving external conditioning elements: Education necessarily contains an element of "being *habituated* [*gewöhnt werden*, B.A.]" (Hegel 2017: 249).[15]

---

14 For the sake of terminological consistency, I have altered Wallace's/Miller's translation of the German word 'Geist' to 'spirit' (Wallace/Miller translate it as 'mind').

15 Note that Hegel uses a passive form (*gewöhnt werden*). This implies an external conditioning aspect in the process of the individual being habitualised. From this perspective, education can be described as the individual's *"process of adapting itself to* [...] limitations" (Hegel 2003: 224) imposed on it by the world of spirit. The fact that education involves an element of adjustment to given social practices is, according to Hegel, the reason for "the disfavor which it incurs" (ibid.: 225).

However, because of this, one does not have to ascribe to Hegel the claim that education is a wholly heteronomous, externally controlled process. On the contrary, Hegel also emphasizes what he calls "the immanent moment of all education [*Erziehung*, B.A.]" (Hegel 2007: 57). From a certain point, children actively want to be part of the adults' world and develop a "striving after education on the part of children" (ibid.).[16] What can be attributed to Hegel on the basis of this argument, however, is the claim that education and external conditioning are not abstract opposites.

The spiritual contexts of concrete social practice – within which a self becomes a subject capable of action – structurally and temporally precede its subjectivity. Therefore, only *after* an individual has been initiated into these practices can the status of a subject of action be ascribed to it (cf. Menke 2018: 122). This shows that Hegel's theory of subjectivity does not uncritically presuppose an immediately given subject independent of social practices, but on the contrary understands subjectivity as socially and practically mediated. Rephrased in the words of Robert Brandom, one becomes capable of agency only by "subjecting oneself to the [...] discipline of a set of social practices" (Brandom 1979: 195).

This can be exemplified by the acquisition of a language which contemporary Hegelians regard as a paradigmatic example for the entanglement of conditioning and autonomisation typical of educational processes (cf. Menke 2018: 106-111; Brandom 1979: 193, McDowell 2009: 168). Their shared assumption is that autonomy presupposes the ability to determine oneself based on reasons (cf. exemplarily Brandom 1994: 5). But only after an individual has acquired a language, John McDowell argues, can it be responsive to reasons: "It is not that prelinguistic human beings are already responsive to reasons" (McDowell 2009: 168). Since it is a prerequisite of an action that the subject performing it is an inhabitant of a *space of reasons*, a human being, according to a Hegelian understanding, cannot be a subject of action prior to its acquisition of a language. For it to acquire a certain language, it must submit to a set of norms (in terms of implicit rules) constituting it (cf. Brandom 1979: 188). If a language is constituted by a set of norms, then being a competent speaker of that language presupposes a submission to those norms. And since language is a social phenomenon (i.e., it exists only within social communities of speakers, cf. McDowell 2009: 167) commanding a language means having to subordinate oneself to the norms of a social practice (cf. Brandom 1979: 193). In fact, commanding a language means turning it into one's second nature, so that it is "unresistingly and fluently" (Hegel 2007: 132) available as a medium of thought, speech and action. Since agency can only be

---

16 In other words: The more autonomous an individual becomes in the process of its education, the more it can autonomously govern the further course of this process.

ascribed to beings who command a language, it is true that only those who have submitted to the inherent normativity of an existing practice can be subjects capable of agency. Through this submission does the individual gain "the ability [...] of critical reflection on an existing normative reality" (Beuthan 2012: 112) – e.g., on language itself – and can transformatively engage with it (cf. the examples in Brandom 1979: 195).

As already noted, the form of habit is not limited to language but "embraces all kinds and stages of spirit's activity" (Hegel 2007: 132).[17] It there-fore encompasses all human activity that is not traceable to immediate natural dispositions. This includes fundamental human patterns of behaviour (Hegel even considers the upright stance of humans to be a habit, cf. ibid.) as well as habits of thinking (cf. ibid.).[18] As spirituality's form, habits are indifferent to their content, which does not necessarily have to be rational: "Entirely contingent content can of course, like every other content, take the form of habit" (ibid.: 133). In this paper, I will focus largely on Hegel's normative evaluation of habit as a *form* of spirit's realization and thus for the most part set aside Hegel's theory of the rationality of spiritual *contents*.

Hegel's normative evaluation of habit as a form of spirit's realization starts with emphasizing the enabling aspect of habit. It is a liberating force insofar as it enables spiritual content "to *belong*" to a subject as its own, not as "cut off from action and actuality, but in its [the subject's, B.A.] very being" (ibid.). Through the acquisition of a second nature man develops dispositions which – unlike first-natural dispositions – are not alien to spiritual contents but instead conform to them: In habit, the human soul "has made itself so at home in the [spiritual, B.A.] content, that it moves about in it with freedom" (ibid.: 134). For Hegel, this makes habit "the most essential feature of the *existence* of all spiritual life in the individual subject" (ibid.: 133).

However, Hegel's theory of second nature offers not only a description of the liberating character of habit but can also be understood as a critical treatment of habit's structure. The core of Hegel's critique of second nature is that, although it is "most essential" (ibid.) for spiritual subjectivity, it nevertheless conflicts with freedom due to its form: "although, on the one hand, by habit a man becomes free, yet, on the other

---

17 For the sake of terminological consistency, I have altered Wallace's/Miller's translation of the German word 'Geist' to 'spirit' (Wallace/Miller translate it as 'mind').
18 On the relation of thought and habit, see Hegel 2007: 132: "*Thinking*, too, though wholly free, and active in the pure element of itself, likewise requires habit and familiarity, this form of *immediacy*, by which it is the unimpeded, pervaded possession of my *individual self*. Only through this habit do I exist for myself as thinking. Even this immediacy of thinking togetherness-with-one-self involves bodiliness (deficient habituation and long continuation of thinking cause headaches)" Furthermore, see Hegel 2003: 195.

hand, habit makes him its *slave*" (ibid.: 134). This is due to the fact that "habit is the determinacy of feeling (as well as of intelligence, will, etc. [...]) made into something that is natural, mechanical" (ibid.: 131). In habit, spirit as distinct from nature is realized in a *natural form*. The educated individual which has acquired a spiritual second nature is no longer identical with its natural impulses, but its spirituality is threatened to be given in a merely natural manner (cf. Menke 2018: 42). Putting it succinctly, Hegel writes: "In habit man's mode of existence is natural, and for that reason he is unfree in it" (Hegel 2007: 131). As habit operates pre-reflexively (cf. Testa 2019: 291), i.e., in the "form of *immediacy*" (Hegel 2007: 132), it enables humans to interact in the world of spirit in an unimpeded manner (cf. ibid.). But, although it is "not an immediate, first nature, dominated by the individuality of sensations", it is, nevertheless, "still a *nature*, something *posited* that assumes the shape of *immediacy*" (ibid.: 134). Habitually realized spirit is thus "not mere nature, but merely like nature" (Menke 2018: 42). This "enslavement to nature [*Naturverfallenheit*, B.A.] of man's spirit" (ibid.: 43) concerns its form of realization as second nature. Habit is therefore a deficient form of realization of spirit even if it is "the habit of right in general [*des Rechten überhaupt*, B.A.], of the ethical [*des Sittlichen*, B.A.]" and thus "has the content of freedom" (Hegel 2007: 131).

According to Hegel, processes of education are essentially processes of liberation of the individual from its immediate naturalness:

> Education, in its absolute determination, is [...] *liberation* and *work* towards a higher liberation; it is the absolute transition to the infinitely subjective substantiality of ethical life, which is no longer immediate and natural, but spiritual and at the same time raised to the shape of universality. (Hegel 2003: 225)

However, through the process of education, the individual acquires a second nature which has itself the form of naturalness, i.e., immediacy. Because education is precisely about overcoming naturalness, it cannot end with bringing oneself (or being brought) into mechanical conformity with the respective prevailing forms of objective spirit through "reflectionless habit" (Hegel 1986a: 134). To the contrary, Hegel stresses that "the cultivated [*gebildete*] [...] human being wills that he should himself be present in everything he does" (Hegel 2003: 136-137). Though in habit "our consciousness is [...] *present*" (Hegel 2007: 136) in a given spiritual practice, insofar as we are acquainted to it, we are "yet conversely *absent* from it, *indifferent* towards it" (ibid.) since habits operate prereflexively (cf. ibid.), i.e., below the level of conscious deliberation or even attention. Therefore, to be an educated human being can not be the same as merely being governed by one's habits, i.e., by internalizations of objective spirit acquired in education. Education would not be a process of liberation if it did not enable the capability of reflexive distancing from and critical appropriation of these internalizations.

In line with this, Hegel stresses it to be "[t]he principle of the modern world [...] that whatever is to be recognized by everyone must be seen by everyone as entitled to such recognition" (Hegel 2003: 355). Accordingly, a Hegelian account of education does not point towards a reflectionless and mechanical conformity of an individual with the social norms that have become its second nature. It emphasizes quite the opposite: Education enables the individual to a "refraction and critical reflection" (Beuthan 2012: 112) of the process of its own formation – a capacity rendered possible only *through* this formation, i.e., through the acquisition of the ability to speak, think and judge. The individual can turn its second-nature abilities against themselves, i.e., it can turn them against their merely natural form.[19] In this way, it either appropriates the particular determinacy in which it finds itself out of habit "as its own" (Hegel 2003: 41) or dispenses with it (cf. ibid.: 37-39). Not by the mere acquisition of a spiritual second nature but only through its critical reflection does the subject attain its *"self-determination"* (ibid.: 41), i.e., autonomy, which constitutes the *telos* of the educational process.[20]

5. Subject-critical ESD in View of Hegel's Theory of *Bildung*

The reconstruction of the Hegelian theory of education yielded the following results: (1) Autonomisation and conditioning cannot be understood as abstract opposites but must instead be conceived as a tension internal to the process of *Bildung*. In other words, if one wants to understand the process of autonomisation, as which education is usually conceived, one must understand that it involves conditioning elements. Only through the acquisition of a second nature, which contains a conditioning moment of habituation, can the individual gain the capacity

---

19 In this way, previously irreflexive determinations can become reflexive. This does not mean, however, that spirit's form of realization as second nature can as such be sublated (cf. Menke 2018: 45). One reason for this is that each act of reflection of second-natural determinations is itself a spiritual activity and as such makes use of second-natural capacities, which is why a "reflexively uncapturable [*uneinholbares*, B.A.] moment" (ibid.: 44) necessarily arises.

20 As Menke has shown, it follows from this consideration that autonomy, in the Hegelian understanding, must be thought of not as a *state* but as a never-ending *process* of liberation identical with "the determinate negation of any given concrete expression of unfreedom" (Adorno 2006: 243, as cited from the German edition in Menke 2018: 51).

to be a self-determined acting subject. As Menke puts it: "Disciplining dialectically turns into liberation [*schlägt dialektisch in Befreiung um*, B.A.]" (Menke 2018: 76). (2) The second-nature capacities enable the subject to act within the world of spirit. These capacities are mediated by social practices. The individual does not acquire its autonomy beyond these practices but in them: It becomes capable of acting within a concrete social practice temporally and structurally preceding it. (3) Autonomy is simultaneously enabled and hindered by second-nature habits. It is enabled because man can act in the world of spirit because of his second nature. At the same time, it is hindered because the form of habit leads to prereflexive processes (in everyday language one could say: to unconscious routines) which become an alien force conflicting with the subject's freedom. To realize its freedom, the subject must therefore use its second-nature habits to turn them against their own natural form by reflexively appropriating their contents (cf. Menke 2018: 33, 36, 48-49).

What conclusions can be drawn from the insights of Hegel's theory of education for the evaluation of the subject-critical conception of ESD? Based on the Hegelian theory outlined, one can agree with Menthe's criticism of a naively-rationalist conception of subjectivity and action. Although this criticism does not apply to the German Enlightenment tradition as broadly as Menthe suggests, it is, nevertheless, essentially justified (also in this regard, see Kminek 2020: 155). From the perspective of Hegel's theory of education, it is oversimplified to assume that "rational, conscious deliberative processes of autonomously acting subjects" (Menthe 2017: 130) are typically causal for choices and/or changes of action. As shown, according to Hegel, subjects are enabled to act against the background of their second nature habits which most of the time operate "pre-reflexively behind their shoulders" (Testa 2019: 302) and are mediated by concrete social practice.[21]

If one sees in Menthe's proposals a tendency of falling into the vicinity of a totalitarian manipulation that fundamentally breaks with the claim to autonomy in modern pedagogy, one can object to them with reference to Hegel. But even if Menthe is not committed to such a position, Hegel can help us to better understand this modern claim to autonomy in its relation to social practices. We can learn from Hegel that educational processes certainly include moments of habitualisation. Therefore, if educational processes are processes of liberation, then an abstract objection to habituating elements of education cannot be formulated in the name of freedom. At the same time, however, we can learn from Hegel that ESD may not be limited to mere 'training' in sustainable ways of acting. Against

---

21 This Hegelian insight is in line with Menthe's argument in section 3.2 of his text ('*ESD and the Role of Social Practices*', Menthe 2017: 136-137).

such ideas, it is important to keep in mind that Hegel's concept of second nature is a *critical* concept. Hegel's critique of second nature reveals that, despite its liberating character, second nature conflicts with freedom as it develops a momentum of its own that opposes the self-determination of the subject. This is the case even if a given habit has a rational content (as Hegel puts it: "the content of freedom", Hegel 2007: 131). Habitualisation (even if it includes elements of conditioning) can therefore not be thought of in abstract opposition to freedom. But *mere* conditioning that leads to mechanic, reflectionless behaviour contradicts the above-mentioned "principle of modern times" (Hegel 1986c: 404). The *"right of the subjective will"* that accompanies this principle is the "right to recognize nothing that I do not perceive as rational" (Hegel 2003: 159). Any educational programme neglecting the subject's "highest right" (ibid.) to rationally reflect on the normative orders it is embedded in would regress behind the normative self-understanding of modern societies. Without empowering subjective reflection and enabling subjective insight into the reasonableness of ESD-related educational contents, ESD would (in Hegel's words) aim at bringing about conditions of pre-modern *ethical life* [*Sittlichkeit*] in which (as Hegel pictures it) a given citizen "did virtually by instinct what was expected of him" (Hegel 1975: 97) without further reflection. Attempts to bring about such conditions in the modern world would undermine the modern consciousness of freedom (*Freiheitsbewusstsein*) and thus the legitimizing basis of modern educational institutions.

With Hegel's theory in mind, one can say that whether the normative self-understanding of modern educational institutions is undermined by ESD does not depend solely on the question of whether or not a habitualisation of sustainable routines of action takes place in educational institutions. The mere fact that the individual becomes habitually familiar with existing social practices in the course of its education does not automatically render the institutions bringing this about illiberal or even totalitarian. What matters more is that educational institutions enable subjects to critically reflect and thus reflexively appropriate (or reject) their own habitual determinations. The central question is not whether habitualisation is brought about by schools (this question is wrongly posed from Hegel's point of view, because "all kinds and stages" (Hegel 2007: 132) of spiritual activity are realized habitually), but whether education makes it possible for subjects to adopt a conscious attitude towards their habits acquired through education. If it is true that educational institutions inevitably contribute to the habitualisation of ways of acting and thinking by shaping the students' second nature, then a political and pedagogical reflection on what the content of these habits should be seems not only appropriate but necessary.

Bibliography

Adorno, Theodor W. (2006): History and Freedom. Lectures 1964-1965. Edited by Rolf Tiedemann. Translated by Rodney Livingstone. Cambridge: Polity Press.
Beuthan, Ralf (2012): Bildung und Freiheit? Wie man mit Hegel einen Weg aus einem gegenwärtigen Dilemma findet. In: Vieweg, Klaus/Winkler, Michael (ed.): Bildung und Freiheit. Ein vergessener Zusammenhang. Paderborn: Schöningh, pp. 101-113.
Bourdieu, Pierre (1974): Zur Soziologie der symbolischen Formen. Translated by Wolfgang Fietkau. Frankfurt a. M.: Suhrkamp.
Bourdieu, Pierre (1979): La distinction: critique sociale du jugement. Paris: Les Éditions de Minuit.
Bourdieu, Pierre (1980): Le sens pratique. Paris: Les Éditions de Minuit.
Bourdieu, Pierre (1990): 'Fieldwork in Philosophy'. In: idem (ed.): In Other Words. Essays Towards a Reflexive Sociology. Translated by Matthew Adamson. Stanford: Stanford Univ. Press, pp. 3-33.
Bourdieu, Pierre (2000a): Esquisse d'une théorie de la pratique, précedé de Trois études d'ethnologie kabyle. Paris: Éditions du Seuil.
Bourdieu, Pierre (2000b): Pascalian Meditations. Translated by Richard Nice. Stanford: Stanford Univ. Press.
Bourdieu, Pierre (2001): Meditationen. Zur Kritik der scholastischen Vernunft. Translated by Achim Russer, Hélène Albagnac & Bernd Schwibs. Frankfurt a. M.: Suhrkamp.
Brandom, Robert (1979): Freedom and Constraint by Norms. In: American Philosophical Quarterly 16, 3, pp. 187-196.
Brandom, Robert (1994): Making it Explicit. Reasoning, Representing, and Discursive Commitment. Cambridge/Mass.: Harvard Univ. Press.
Forster, Michael N. (2012): Bildung bei Herder und seinen Nachfolgern. Drei Begriffe. In: Vieweg, Klaus/Winkler, Michael (ed.): Bildung und Freiheit. Ein vergessener Zusammenhang. Paderborn: Schöningh, pp. 75-89.
Hegel, Georg W. F. (1975): Lectures on the Philosophy of World History. Introduction: Reason in History. Translated by Hugh Barr Nisbet. Cambridge: Cambridge Univ. Press.
Hegel, Georg W. F. (1986a): Vorlesungen über die Philosophie der Geschichte. Vol. 12 of 'Werke'. Edited by Eva Moldenhauer & Karl Markus Michel. Frankfurt a. M.: Suhrkamp.
Hegel, Georg W. F. (1986b): Vorlesungen über die Philosophie der Religion I. Vol. 16 of 'Werke'. Edited by Eva Moldenhauer & Karl Markus Michel. Frankfurt a. M.: Suhrkamp.
Hegel, Georg W. F. (1986c): Vorlesungen über die Geschichte der Philosophie I. Vol. 18 of 'Werke'. Edited by Eva Moldenhauer & Karl Markus Michel. Frankfurt a. M.: Suhrkamp.
Hegel, Georg W. F. (1993a): Philosophische Enzyklopädie für die Oberklasse (1808ff.). In: idem (ed.): Nürnberger und Heidelberger Schriften 1808-1817.

Vol. 4 of 'Werke'. Edited by Eva Moldenhauer & Karl Markus Michel. 2nd edition. Frankfurt a. M.: Suhrkamp, pp. 9-69.

Hegel, Georg W. F. (1993b): Rechts-, Pflichten- und Religionslehre für die Unterklasse (1810ff.). In: idem (ed.): Nürnberger und Heidelberger Schriften 1808-1817. Vol. 4 of 'Werke'. Edited by Eva Moldenhauer & Karl Markus Michel. 2nd edition. Frankfurt a. M.: Suhrkamp, pp. 204-274.

Hegel, Georg W. F. (2003): Elements of the Philosophy of Right. Edited by Allen W. Wood. Translated by Hugh Barr Nisbet. 8th edition. Cambridge: Cambridge Univ. Press.

Hegel, Georg W. F. (2004): Hegel's philosophy of nature: being part two of the Encyclopedia of the philosophical sciences (1830) translated from Nicolin and Pöggeler's edition (1959) and from the Zusätze in Michelet's text (1847). Translated by Arnold Vincent Miller. 2nd edition. Oxford: Oxford Univ. Press.

Hegel, Georg W. F. (2005): Die Philosophie des Rechts. Vorlesung von 1821/22. Edited by Hansgeorg Hoppe. Frankfurt a. M.: Suhrkamp.

Hegel, Georg W. F. (2007): Philosophy of Mind. Translated by William Wallace & Arnold Vincent Miller. Oxford: Oxford Univ. Press.

Hegel, Georg W. F. (2017): Grundlinien der Philosophie des Rechts oder Naturrecht und Staatswissenschaft im Grundrisse. Mit Hegels eigenhändigen Notizen und den mündlichen Zusätzen. Vol. 7 of 'Werke'. Edited by Eva Moldenhauer & Karl Markus Michel. 15th edition. Frankfurt a. M.: Suhrkamp.

Henrich, Dieter (2010): Hegels Theorie über den Zufall. In: idem (ed.): Hegel im Kontext. Mit einem Nachwort zur Neuauflage. Frankfurt a. M.: Suhrkamp, pp. 158-187.

Jickling, Bob (1992): Viewpoint: Why I Don't Want My Children to Be Educated for Sustainable Development. In: The Journal of Environmental Education 23, 4, pp. 5-8.

Kant, Immanuel (1996): An answer to the question: What is enlightenment? In: idem (ed.): Practical philosophy. Edited and translated by Mary J. Gregor. Cambridge: Cambridge Univ. Press, pp. 11-22.

Kminek, Helge (2020): Concept of Education in Education for Sustainable Development – the Necessity of Exposing the Uncertainty. In: Kminek, Helge/Bank, Franziska/Fuchs, Leon (ed.): Kontroverses Miteinander. Interdisziplinäre und kontroverse Positionen zur Bildung für eine nachhaltige Entwicklung. Frankfurt a. M.: Universitätsverlag, pp. 153-168.

Koselleck, Reinhart (2006): Zur anthropologischen und semantischen Struktur der Bildung. In: idem (ed.): Begriffsgeschichten. Studien zur Semantik und Pragmatik der politischen und sozialen Sprache. Frankfurt a. M.: Suhrkamp, pp. 105-154.

McDowell, John (2009): Towards a Reading of Hegel on Action in the "Reason" Chapter of the *Phenomenology*. In: idem (ed.): Having the World in View. Essays on Kant, Hegel, and Sellars. Cambridge/Mass.: Harvard Univ. Press, pp. 166-184.

Menke, Christoph (2018): Autonomie und Befreiung. Studien zu Hegel. Frankfurt a. M: Suhrkamp.

Menthe, Jürgen (2017): Verklärte Aufklärung. Der Subjektbegriff im Konzept der Bildung für nachhaltige Entwicklung. In: Greco, Sara A./Lange, Dirk (ed.): Emanzipation. Zum Konzept der Mündigkeit in der Politischen Bildung. Schwalbach a. T.: Wochenschau, pp. 129-138.
Rieger-Ladich, Markus (2002): Mündigkeit als Pathosformel. Beobachtungen zur pädagogischen Semantik. Konstanz: UVK Verlagsgesellschaft.
Testa, Italo (2019): Selbstbewußtsein und zweite Natur. In: Vieweg, Klaus/Welsch, Wolfgang (ed.): Hegels Phänomenologie des Geistes. Ein kooperativer Kommentar zu einem Schlüsselwerk der Moderne. 4th edition. Frankfurt a. M.: Suhrkamp, pp. 286-307.
van Poeck, Katrien/Östman, Leif (2020): The Risk and Potentiality of Engaging with Sustainability Problems in Education—A Pragmatist Teaching Approach. In: Journal of Philosophy of Education 54, 4, pp. 1003-1018.
Wals, Arjen (2010): Between knowing what is right and knowing that is it wrong to tell others what is right. On relativism, uncertainty and democracy in environmental and sustainability education. In: Environmental Education Research 16, 1, pp. 143-151.

Networking for Sustainability in Education

Franz Rauch, Günther Pfaffenwimmer and Renate Hübner

1. Introduction

In this contribution, we offer perspectives on communication practices and strategies within a network related to sustainability in education, based on the description of a network at school level. We describe the potential, challenges and instruments/methods of networking with the goal of enhancing learning about and for sustainability. In doing so, we want to point out the "intervening" character of networks specifying communication about and for sustainability. In order to illustrate communication and learning processes we will present the Austrian ECOLOG-Schools-Network, its national impact and its international embedding. We describe theoretical concepts and the organization of the ECOLOG-network. Based on evaluation and research studies, lessons learned from networking for sustainability on individual and institutional level will be presented and reflected upon. To sum up, spaces for exchange and reflection offered by the network, constructively support the ability to deal with tensions and dilemmas. The overall challenge of the network might be described as keeping momentum between structures and processes or, in other words, between flow and stability in order to enable sustainable communication and learning. Educational systems are places of organised learning processes and thus of high rationality, but as a social institution, it is also committed to future generations. Therefore, it can be argued that schools should act as "models for sustainability", in the sense that sustainability should not only be taught, but also realized in practice. We describe a national school network across disciplinary and structural borders. The major challenge is how to support teachers willing to engage in SD and institutionalize communication processes between teachers, pupils, schools, scientists and administration. The chapter will close with lessons learned and some reflections on networking as a context for communication on sustainability.

2. Education and Sustainable Development

Current discussions around Education for Sustainable Development (ESD) in Austria focus on the notions of sustainable development, on environmental education, on development education (or global learning or global citizenship education) and international peace as well as civic education. These have all sparked debates on the nature of education in general (Rauch & Steiner, 2013). Current international United Nations programmes such as Sustainable Development Goals – especially goal 4 "for Quality Education" (UNESCO 2017) or the 2015 UNESCO Global Action Programme on Education for Sustainable Development are in line with the conceptualisation of ECOLOG.

As with human rights, sustainable development may be regarded as a regulative idea (Kant 1956). Such ideas do not determine an objective but serve as heuristic structures for reflection. They give direction to research and learning processes. In terms of sustainability, this implies that the contradictions, dilemmas and conflicting goals inherent in this vision need to be constantly re-negotiated in a process of discourse between participants in each and every concrete situation (Minsch 2004). This implies a major challenge, but also has considerable potential to enhance learning and innovative developments in education (Rauch 2015).

Responsible political decisions are undoubtedly necessary for social change. However, it is also essential that not only individuals develop skills of (self) critical reflection and process competence, but also groups, organizations or social subsystems. Such a common (social) learning process requires skills that have to be developed, such as the ability for collective decisions and actions based on long-term-oriented reflection. The ability to empathize is also essential. Experiencing and enduring contradictions emotionally, enables people to deal with the moral demands that result from the normativity of the sustainability concept (Rauschmayer & Oman 2012).

Communication is a central dimension within processes of Education for Sustainable Development. The development of the term sustainability communication is accompanied by the call for responsible human interaction with the natural and social environment. This entails a process of social understanding that deals with the causes and with possible solutions. The task of sustainability communication is to critically evaluate and introduce an understanding of the human-environment relationship into social discourse (Godemann & Michelsen 2011), which includes reflection upon dilemmas and contradiction (Hübner 2012; Hübner et al. 2014).

Furthermore, the development of a learning community as the core element of a new learning culture can also be seen as an innovation: students and r/teachers work out relations and options for joint actions, and reflect on these actions as well as on the learning process, thus following Bateson's concept of first and second order learning (Bateson 1972; Vare & Scott 2007).

A central goal is to develop and enhance the abilities necessary for the transformation of individual, organizational and societal patterns towards sustainability. Learning is transformative "when the learners, integrate and reinterpret knowledge into their own frames and put it into practice in their own lives. Learning is also one mechanism for changing the society and for transforming the society" (Reardon, 2010, 9). Transformative education involves experiencing a deep structural shift in the basic premises of thought, feelings and actions. It involves people's relationship with nature and with other humans and is basically a collective learning process. Transformative learning also demands change to those cultures and structures which are hindering the process. This concept neglects indoctrination with the ideals of ESD as well as the reinforcement of fears without any perspective towards possible solutions (O'Sullivan et al. 2002: xvii; Singer-Bodrowski 2016).

3. Theoretical Background of Networks in Education

In the early 1980s, the notion of "networks" became very popular within society as a whole, and within the scientific community in particular. Naisbitt (1984) talked about a "megatrend" of transformation of and within hierarchies, arguing that informal networks of small groups become necessary in order to optimize organisational problem-solving processes which can no longer be performed by hierarchical structures.

According to Castells' (2000) notion, networks constitute a new social morphology in society, where dominant functions and processes are increasingly organised around networks. New information technologies provide the material basis for its pervasive expansion throughout the entire social structure. Castells (2000) conceptualises his notion of 'network' as a highly dynamic, open system consisting of nodes and flows.

In the wake of these general social trends and this structural transformation, networks in educational contexts have also become increasingly attractive in educational systems. In the 1990s systemic school modernization processes were launched by policymakers, prompted by the need for reformatory change in the light of the results of international assessments (like the TIMSS and PISA studies). Having proclaimed "school autonomy" as the goal, the central administration here has focused increasingly on contextual steering activities, whilst delegating responsibilities to decentralised units (Posch & Altrichter 1993; Fullan 2007; Rauch & Scherz, 2009). Less bureaucratic steering generates a need for alternative coordination. Intermediate structures (Czerwanski et al. 2002) such as networks are conceived and expected to fill a structural gap and take over functions traditionally assigned to the hierarchy. Ideally, networks are conceived as an interface and an effective means of pooling competencies and resources (Posch 1995; OECD 2003). As intermediate structures, they manage autonomy and interdependent structures and processes, and try to explore new paths in learning and cooperation between individuals and institutions (Rauch 2013).

- In this process, authors consider the following aspects paramount:
- Mutual Intention and Goals (Lieberman & Wood 2003)
- Trust Orientation (McLaughlin et al. 2008)
- Voluntary Participation (Boos et al. 2000; McLaughlin et al. 2008)
- Principle of Exchange (Win-Win Relationship) (OECD 2003; McCormick et al. 2011)
- Steering Platform (Dobischat et al. 2006)
- Synergy (Schäffter 2006)
- Learning (Czerwanski et al. 2002; O'Hair & Veugelers 2005)

Per Dalin's (1999) description of how networks function in education, there is an important theoretical basis which underlies the formation of regional networks in ECOLOG (case one). Networks in education have an informative function, which becomes visible in a direct exchange of practice and knowledge for teaching and schools, and act as a bridge between practice and knowledge. Beyond their informative function, networks also have a function for agenda setting and identity building of groups across borders of different kinds, such as disciplines or generations (case two).

Through networking, further opportunities for learning and competence development (professionalization) are encouraged by the members who are establishing the learning function. Trust is a prerequisite for cooperation within a network. It is the basis for the psychological functioning of a network, which encourages and strengthens individuals. In the political function of networks, enforceability of educational concerns increases, following the motto "together we achieve more".

In order to enhance trust it is not enough only to be expert in teaching and learning sustainability and transformation, but also to be ready for experiences made together in designing and/or implementing measures to bring sustainability to reality.

4. The Austrian ECOLOG-Schools Programme – History, Structure, Lessons Learned and Impact of a Network[1]

This case describes ECOLOG, a key action programme and network for the greening of schools and education for sustainability in Austria.

4.1 ECOLOG as an International Project

It was developed in 1996 by an Austrian team of teachers working on the international ENSI project (Posch 1999).

In December, 1985, the CERI Governing board[2] accepted the proposal for the ENSI project from Austria. This basic concept, in which the OECD highly esteemed demand for "dynamic qualities" was linked with the promotion of "environmental awareness", stated that dynamic qualities could best be developed if students are enabled to take constructive initiatives in their close environment (Posch 1990). Action research (AR) was chosen and has proved to be the method to make dynamic qualities observable, to facilitate reflection and observe their enhancement, through, for example, environmental-oriented project teaching. ENSI was the first project to focus on dynamic qualities and to link them to environmental awareness and environmental education, which is still an ongoing task in the different member states (Rauch & Pfaffenwimmer 2018).

In 1986 in Austria, a team of experienced teachers from different regions and types of schools was chosen, and formed the ENSI teacher team which was coordinated by staff at the Ministry of Education and scientifically facilitated by academics from Universities. The teacher team received training in action research to be able to document and publish their innovative work as case studies. The ENSI team built bridges between practice, policy and research for many years until 2017. In the summer of 1995, the Minister of Education commissioned the ENSI teacher team to design the ECOLOG school network, which after a two-year pilot phase developed into a wider school network. The ECOLOG-school network contributed to the development of pedagogical criteria for "The Austrian Eco-label for Schools and Teacher Training Colleges"[3] which has been awarded by the government since 2002.

---

1   ECOLOG is the abbreviation for the Ecologisation of Schools.
2   CERI is a research department of the OECD Directorate for Education and Skills – see online: http://www.oecd.org/education/ceri/
3   https://www.umweltzeichen.at

In 1999, Austria joined the Australian-led ENSI project "Learnscape" (1999 – 2001) with the involvement of eight Austrian schools. Learnscapes has become a focal topic for the ECOLOG school network and was also the starting point for the still on-going collaboration with the Austrian Institute for School and Sport Facilities (ÖISS). One important result of this collaboration was its recommendations for the design of school grounds (Mellauner & Clees 2005).

In 2002, Austria submitted the first proposal for an ENSI-EU-project "School Development through Environmental Education SEED" (2002-05). The proposal was successful, and Austria coordinated the SEED Project from 2002 through to 2005.[4] The most influential publication is "Quality Criteria for ESD-Schools" (Breiting et al. 2005) which is translated into many languages. In order to facilitate understanding and implementation of the Quality Criteria for ESD-Schools, the ENSI teacher team designed and piloted an in-service seminar for heads and coordinators of ECOLOG-schools (Lechner & Rauch 2014).

Collaborations between schools and their surrounding communities are crucial for real development and change in society. Therefore, the last project of ENSI, CoDeS (School and Community Cooperation for Sustainable Development) focused on this collaboration by gathering 29 experts and 17 countries. The project ran from 2011 to 2014 and was funded by EU Comenius funds.[5]

4.2   Structure of ECOLOG

ECOLOG is based upon an action research approach, as was described earlier. Schools analyse the ecological, technical and social conditions of their environment and, consequently, define the objectives, targets, concrete activities and quality criteria to be implemented and evaluated. Students as well as all the other stakeholders of a school should be involved in a participatory fashion, and collaboration with authorities, businesses and other interested parties is encouraged. The measures concern, among others, areas like saving resources (energy, water etc.), reduction of emissions (i.e., waste, traffic), spatial arrangement (from the classroom to the campus), the culture of learning (communication, organisational structure), health promotion as well as the opening of the school to the community. All in all, over 550 schools with about 15,000 teachers and approximately 110,000 students are currently part of the

---

4   https://www.ensi.org/projects
5   https://www.ensi.org/Projects/Our_Projects/CoDeS/

network. Many others are reached through the website, teacher in-service-training seminars and newsletters (Rauch & Pfaffenwimmer 2019).

Given the uncertainty of what constitutes adequate action in complex situations, such as networking and the differences of understanding conceptions like education and sustainable development, there is a need to reflect on one's actions. This helps to nurture an ability and readiness for the further development of one's actions in response to the outcome of the reflection process. Competent, professional action in complex situations, hence, requires concomitant learning processes as a *sine qua non*. Inversely: professional learning requires the experience of acting in complex practical situations. From these perspectives, professional action and professional learning coincide in one stream of action. As professional learning happens in practical situations, which, in turn, are seen to require reflection and further development, knowledge and skill development go hand in hand with practical situational development (Altrichter & Posch 2009). Stern et al. (2014) have recently offered reflections on good action research. They argue that good action research pursues worthwhile practical purposes, connects theory with praxis, and is responsive and collaborative.

ECOLOG is a national support system with the aim of promoting and integrating an ecological approach into the development of individual schools, with attempts being made, through regional networks, to embed the programme in Austria's nine federal states (Rauch & Steiner 2006). In order to provide support, a network structure involving ECOLOG regional teams in the nine states has been developed; furthermore, a scientific advisory board has been established. Central support is provided by the Ministry of Education and by the Institute of Instructional and School Development at the Alpen-Adria-University, Klagenfurt. Additional support measures are provided by the FORUM Environmental Education (an NGO) as well as via seminars for heads and coordinators of ECOLOG network schools, the Education Support Fund for Health Education and Education for Sustainable Development, as well as via the National Environmental Performance Award for Schools and University Colleges of Teacher Education (Rauch & Pfaffenwimmer 2020).

4.3 Impact of ECOLOG

The following Table 1 gives an overview of the EE/ESD-developments in Austria since the 1990s. The overview shows the context of the ECOLOG-schools-programme in Austria. In this subchapter we focus on the contribution and connectedness of ECOLOG to some of these initiatives.

An early impact of ECOLOG was the implementation of the *National Environmental Performance Award* for Schools and University Colleges of Teacher Education. This is a national government-based award to acknowledge top level performance since 2002 (Rauch & Pfaffenwimmer 2014). The Ecologisation Programme serves as an important source for the formulation of the pedagogical criteria (Pfaffenwimmer 2004).

Since the 1990s ECOLOG has established itself as a reference point for other thematic networks in Austria focusing on ESD, such as "climate alliance schools"[6], "climate schools"[7], "nature park schools"[8], UNESCO schools[9] and "healthy schools"[10].

From 1997 to 2004 the ENITE-project (Environmental Education and ESD in Teacher Education) was carried out by the University of Klagenfurt as a research and development network which supported the development and study of initiatives in teacher education and was inspired by ECOLOG, especially at Universities of Teacher Education (Posch et al. 2000; Kyburz-Graber et al. 2003). The main outcome of the ENITE-network so far is the National Teacher Training Course "Innovation in Teacher Education – Education for Sustainable Development" (BINE) offered by the Institute of Instructional and School Development at the University of Klagenfurt in cooperation with Universities of Teacher Education (Rauch & Steiner 2015). Since 2006-07 teacher education is involved in a dynamic reform process based on new legislation for teacher training. One positive result of the ENITE-network and the BINE courses is that communication and collaboration and also participation between the University of Teacher Education and the ECO-school network has been stabilised and enhanced (Rauch & Pfaffenwimmer 2014).

---

6   https://www.klimabuendnis.at/english
7   https://klimaschulen.at
8   https://www.naturparke.at/schulen-kindergaerten/schulen/
9   https://www.unesco.at/bildung/unesco-schulen/
10 https://www.gesundeschule.at/

	ESD-Implementation and relevant legal developments	ECO School Network (ECOLOG)	Teacher Education	Higher Education	International initiatives
1995		Start of ECO-school concept			ENSI decision on focus topics: ECO-schools, teacher education, (IT)-networking and quality assurance.
1996		Start of ECO-school pilot phase (1996–1998)			
1997			ENITE-research project (Environmental Education in Teacher Education)		
1998					

1999		Concept for ECO-school network	
2000			
2001		Start of ECO-school network	ENITE-network
2002	ESD platform in Ministry of Education (2002–2008)	"National Environmental Performance Award" for Schools and Teacher Training Universities		EU-ENSI-SEED-network project (2002–2005)
2003			
2004			First national teacher training university course "Innovation in Teacher Education – Education for Sustainable	EU-ENSI-CSCT-project (2004–2007)

		Development" (BINE).	
2005	Vilnius declaration ESD Strategy process (2005–2007)	International conference "Committing Universities to Sustainable Development"	UNECE Vilnius declaration
2006	ESD Strategy Process EU-ESD-Conference	Research project "Competences for Education of Sustainable Development" (KOM-BiNE) (2006–2008).	UNECE evaluation
2007	UNESCO Award		"Sustainability Award" established	EU-ENSI-SUPPORT network project (2007–2011)
2008	ESD Strategy decision	Second National Teacher Training		

	Austrian Agency for Education for Sustainable Development ("Dekadenbuero")		University Course BINE		
2009					UNECE evaluation
2010		300 ECO-schools	ECO-school-network with teacher training universities		
2011	Legislation on quality management in schools				EU-ENSI-CoDeS-network project (2011–2014)
2012		400 ECO-schools	Third national teacher training university course BINE	Alliance of Sustainable Universities	
2013					
2014					
2015	Global Action Programme				

Sustainable Development Goals (International initiatives)			
2016		Fourth national teacher training university course BINE	
2017	500 ECO-Schools (ECO-School-Network ECOLOG)		
2018			Project UniNEtZ (Higher Education)
2019	600 ECO-Schools		

Table 1: Overview of the ESD-developments in Austria. (Source: own illustration.)

In her recent evaluation study, Ziener (2017) writes that the annual reports by the participating schools, which are published on the ECOLOG-Website (https://www.oekolog.at/welcome.html), serve as outreach and impact of the programme. Her analysis indicates the wide variety of external partners with whom schools regularly cooperate, such as parents' associations, municipalities/mayors, farmers, nature conservation associations, environmental education associations, national parks/nature parks, local universities and colleges, the health and social sector, industries, tourism, local media and so on.

Throughout the history of Environmental Education and ESD in Austria and especially since the Ministry´s basic decrees for Environmental Education for Sustainable Development in 1985 and 2014 (Austrian Federal Ministry for Education and Women´s Affairs, 2014), the engagement in locally relevant educational activities has been a central focus. Partnerships with external agencies and actors have proved a valuable approach (Lukesch et al. 2009). In the years 2012 – 2014 "School-Community-Collaboration" was a focal topic for the ECOLOG-programme, also contributing to the ENSI-EU-Project CODES (2011-2014). (https://ensi.org/Projects/Our_Projects/CoDeS/) (Rauch & Pfaffenwimmer 2019).

In 2006, the Austrian UNESCO-Commission decided to give awards to projects within the UN Decade Education for Sustainable Development (DESD) that met the international criteria of ESD. From 2007 to 2014, 201 projects from168 organisations were awarded and documented in four publications of the UNESCO commission as well as in the "Bildungslandkarte" (Education Landscape)" of the FORUM Umweltbildung (Environmental Education FORUM) (https://www.bildungslandkarte.at/). The "Education Landscape" is an electronic search tool to find Austrian organisations which are active in the field of ESD and offer learning opportunities. Currently 525 organisations (actors) are registered. Since 2016 these institutions also have had the opportunity to apply for the Award "Education for sustainable development - BEST OF AUSTRIA" within the framework of the UN Global Action Programme.

5. Lessons Learned During the ECOLOG-schools-programme in Austria

Throughout the past twenty years of the ECOLOG-schools network's existence, a series of evaluations, inquiries and studies have been produced

(Thonhauser et al. 1998; Ehgartner 1999; Payer et al. 2000; Schober-Schlatter 2002; Rauch & Schrittesser 2003; Heinrich & Mayr 2005; Knoll & Szalai 2009; Rauch & Dulle 2012; Ziener 2017). Based on these studies the following lessons learned may be extracted.

ECOLOG is a highly demanding programme: As a comprehensive concept of school development promoting Education for Sustainable Development, which connects teaching and learning processes, school organisation and the school's collaboration with external partners, ECOLOG is a highly demanding programme.

The ECOLOG network supports further development: Building upon already existing experiences at schools, the ECOLOG network supports further development, for example, through regional exchange of experiences and information, the generating of new ideas, the provision of educational materials and through financial resources.

ECOLOG has effects in numerous areas: The effects of ECOLOG are seen in numerous areas. Among them are changes in teaching methods (increased project-based learning and social learning, for example), the increased integration of health-related topics as well as ecological and social topics in the teaching, the design and organisation of the school building (e.g., the schoolyard, measures of energy optimisation) and changes in school life (e.g., healthy foods for pupils and teachers).

ECOLOG depends on dedicated individuals: On the one hand, ECOLOG exists through the particular dedication of individual members of the teaching staff. On the other hand, a culture of mutual collaboration must be established in order for a sustainable school culture to thrive.

Ecologisation needs to be integrated into school processes and identity: Processes of ecologisation at schools are successful in the long-term if they are viewed both as dependent on the build-up of experiences and routines as well as on the development of new ideas.

The ECOLOG network schools face a number of challenges: Supporting the development of a sustainable school culture depends on taking the different interests of stakeholders seriously and on working collaboratively on common aims. Successful ECOLOG network schools have learned to deal with both internal as well as external change, and to embrace diversity.

6. Reflections on Networking ESD

The ECOLOG programme has been growing for many years and is the oldest network supported by the Ministry of Education. One reason for this is that ESD is always connected with current developments in the

Austrian education system, such as quality evaluation and quality assurance. Other factors for its success are the support system of the network, which keeps the projects going, as well as an active evaluation culture, which includes action research as well as external, formative evaluations, which provide feedback and confirmation (Rauch & Pfaffenwimmer 2019). The ECOLOG programme has influenced other developments in Austria, like the National Environmental Performance Award as well as other thematic school networks like Climate Alliance Schools, UNESCO Schools or Nature Park Schools. All in all, nearly 20% of the Austrian schools participate in one of these networks dealing with ESD issues. Beyond this impact the experiences and evaluation outcomes gained in the ECOLOG programme build the foundations and provide orientation for awards like the UNESCO Award on ESD (in the context of UN DESD) and the current award Best of Austria (in the context of the UN SDGs).

One challenge still posed is the sustainable anchoring of ECOLOG at schools at the interface of innovation, and as part of the dynamic everyday culture of these schools. In relation to regional support systems in the federal states, the respective professional and political contexts play a decisive role. The provision of stable and continuous support, which, at the same time, is flexible enough to dynamically respond to change, both make high demands on all parties involved and, at the same time, also require adequate resources.

The aim followed by ECOLOG is the implementation of ESD at individual schools in their respective local environment. ESD is conceptualised as the negotiation of conflicting interests. Without this, ESD cannot come to full fruition in the context of current social arrangements. Instead, ECOLOG challenges those conditions and formulates demands towards co-determination.

Hence, the ECOLOG programme is caught between the danger of being instrumentalised by a particular interest (e.g., one-sided economisation) and being overburdened (by its claim to formative influence). The creation of spaces for exchange, networking and reflection are central elements of the ECOLOG programme, through which it hopes to support ECOLOG network schools in their constructive handling of this area of tension (Rauch 2016).

7. Conclusions

With reference to the four functions of networking according to Dalin (1999), such initiatives as the university courses might be understood as networks in education which offer goal-oriented exchange processes among teachers (information function) in support of the professional development of teachers, i.e., fresh ideas for classroom teaching, or interdisciplinary cooperation of schools (learning function). Therefore, networks have the potential to create a culture of trust, with the effect of raising teachers' self-esteem and willingness to take risks (psychological function), while upgrading science at school (political function).

In the long run, a balance of Krainer's (1998) dimensions action/reflection (goal-directed planning and evaluation) and autonomy/networking (analysis of one's own situation, but also support by "critical friends") is paramount in order to set up a sustainable support system for teachers and schools. Evaluation and research need to be driven by an interactive link between an interest to gain new knowledge and a developmental interest. Therein, an action research culture of self-critical and collective reflection may flourish (Rauch 2013).

In the following, five dimensions are sketched out, all taking into account that networking for ESD necessitates dealing with conflicting issues and views, and with keeping them in a certain balance.

Networking for ESD needs both visible challenges and visible success

In order to stimulate the necessity for change, the key stakeholders of change need a clear rationale. The examples described here show that teachers need to get support and opportunities to share their experiences in order to make both their success and remaining challenges visible. These new challenges are again a starting point for new innovations. This kind of "innovation culture" needs challenges that lead to success. On the other hand it needs success that leads to new questions. Each of the examples reported above can be understood as examples of interplay between challenge and success.

Networking for ESD needs both individual and organizational efforts

Projects for change need to foster both teachers' autonomy and networking, supported by knowledgeable others (internal or external experts). However, in order to raise the likelihood and sustainability of success, their organizations (e.g., schools) need to support these individuals in their efforts to learn and bring about change.

Networking for ESD needs both flexible plans and the use of windows of opportunity

Although ECOLOG has a good reputation in Austria as well as internationally, it was never really easy to increase their numbers, or to establish them at all in the Austrian education system. However, with the growing issue of climate change, for instance, and the societal movement Fridays for Future (plus accompanying developments), it was again possible to dynamise the network.

Networking for ESDs needs active insistence and resilience as well as patience

Networking needs a lot of time, and tolerance of frustration by all people concerned. Of course, conflicts of interest arise and need to be solved constructively. Thus, they need a long-term perspective; something that is not possible at the moment might be dealt with later on. They also need qualified and dedicated stakeholders who have plenty of creativity, endurance and patience. Larger initiatives open the view for the general and the holistic (e.g., the educational system); but also for the particular and the small (e.g., good ideas by a student in a classroom).

Networking for ESD means both accepting responsibility and allocating it

Long-term initiatives need to transfer from a short-term status into a stable sustainable project anchored in the educational system. Ideally, a reform project is successful in the long run when it has become unnecessary. The process of accepting responsibility is increasingly accompanied by a process of allocating responsibility to the new institutions that may have been established in the meantime. Collaborations (with Colleges for Teacher Education, Universities, Local School Authorities etc.) are a central issue of all of the cases described above. These co-operations are based on negotiated contracts and allow the emergence and development of mutual responsibility and trust.

The overall challenge might be described as maintaining the momentum between structures and processes or, in other words, between stability and dynamics, to enable sustainability in education that is supported by communication and networking.

Bibliography

Altrichter, Herbert/Posch, Peter (2009): Action Research, Professional Development and Systemic Reform. In: Noffke, Susan E./Somekh, Bridget (ed.): The SAGE handbook of Educational Action Research. London [a.o.]: SAGE Publications Ltd., pp. 213-225.
Austrian Federal Ministry for Education and Women's Affairs (2014): Basic decree on environmental education for sustainable development. Wien.
Bateson, Gregory (1972): Ökologie des Geistes – anthropologische, psychologische, biologische und epistemologische Perspektiven. Frankfurt a. M.: Suhrkamp.
Boos, Frank/Exner, Alexander/Heitger, Barbara (2000): Soziale Netzwerke sind anders. In: Journal für Schulentwicklung 3, 4, pp. 14-19.
Castells, Manuel (2000): The Rise of the Network Society (The Information Age: Economy, Society and Culture, Vol.1.). 2nd edition. Oxford: Blackwell Publishers Ltd.
Czerwanski, Annette/Hameyer, Uwe/Rolff, Hans-Günter (2002): Schulentwicklung im Netzwerk—Ergebnisse einer empirischen Nutzenanalyse von zwei Schulnetzwerken. In: Rolff, Hans-Günter/Bauer, Karl-Oswald/Klemm, Klaus/Pfeiffer, Hermann/Schulz-Zander, Renate (ed.): Jahrbuch der Schulentwicklung. München: Juventa, pp. 99-130.
Dalin, Per (1999): Theorie und Praxis der Schulenwicklung. Neuwied: Luchterhand.
Dobischat, Rolf/Düsseldorf, Christina/Nuissl, Ekkehard/Stuhldreier, Jens (2006): Lernende Regionen—begriffliche Grundlagen. In: Nuissl, Ekkehard/Dobischat, Rolf/Hagen, Kornelia/Tippelt, Rudolf (ed.): Regionale Bildungsnetze. Bielefeld: Bertelsmann, pp. 23-33.
Ehgartner, Michaela (1999): Ökologisierung von Schulen. Ein Projekt des BMUK. (Diploma thesis – equivalent to a Master's thesis). Vienna: Univ. of Vienna.
Fullan, Michael (2007): The New Meaning of Educational Change. London: Routledge.
Godemann, Jasmin/Michelsen, Gerd (2011): Sustainability Communication. Interdisciplinary perspectives and Theoretical Foundations. Dordrecht/Heidelberg/London/New York: Springer.
Heinrich, Martin/Mayr, Petra (2005): ÖKOLOG-Oekologisierung von Schulen—Bildung für Nachhaltigkeit. Analyse und Ausblick. Zusammenfassender Bericht über die systematischen Reflexionen von Erfahrungen in den ÖKOLOG-Schulen. Linz: Univ. of Linz.
Hübner, Renate (2012): Nachhaltigkeitskommunikation reloaded. Aporien als Chance für gesellschaftliche Lern- und Entwicklungsprozesse. In: GAIA 21, 4, pp. 262-265.
Hübner, Renate/Rauch, Franz/Dulle, Mira (2014): Implementing an Interfaculty Elective "Sustainable Development" – an Intervention into a University's Culture between Organised Scientific Rationality and Normative Claim. In: Muga, Helen/Thomas, Ken (ed.): Cases on Pedagogical Innovations for

Sustainable Development. Hershey (PA): IGI Global / IGI Publishing (IGIP), pp. 510-522.

Knoll, Bente/Szalai, Elke (2009): ÖKOLOG und Gender – ÖKOLOG-Schulen aus dem Blickpunkt Gender betrachtet. Wien: BMUKK.

Krainer, Konrad (1998): Some considerations on problems and perspectives of inservice mathematics teacher education. In: Alsina, Claudi/Alvarez, José M./Hodgson, Bernard/Laborde, Colette/Perez, Antonio (ed.): 8th International Congress on Mathematics Education: Selected lectures. Sevilla, Spain: S.A.E.M. Thales, pp. 303-321.

Kyburz-Graber, Regula/Posch, Peter/Peter, Ursula (2003): Challenges in Teacher Education – Interdisciplinarity and Environmental Education. Innsbruck/Vienna/Munich/Bozen: StudienVerlag.

Lechner, Christine/Rauch, Frank (2014): Quality Criteria for Schools Focusing on Education for Sustainable Development (ESD). In: Rauch, Frank/Schuster, Angela/Stern, Thomas/Pribila, Maria/Townsend, Andrew (ed.): Promoting Change through Action Research. Rotterdam: Sense Verlag, pp. 65-76.

Lieberman, Ann/Wood Diane R. (2003): Inside the National Writing Project. Connecting Network Learning and Classroom Teaching. New York: Teacher College Press.

Lukesch, Robert/Payer, Harald/Pfaffenwimmer, Günther/Posch, Peter (2009): Emerging partnerships between school and community – Results from a pilot study in Austria. In: Czippan, Katalin/Varga, Attila/Benedict, Faye (ed.): Collaboration and Education for Sustainable Development. Case studies collected by SUPPORT members 2008-2010. Oslo: Norwegian Directorate of Education and Training.

McCormick, Robert/Fox, Alison/Carmichael, Patrick/Procter Richard (2011): Researching and Understanding Educational Networks. London: Routledge.

McLaughlin, Colleen/Black-Hawkins, Kristine/McIntyre, Donald/Townsend, Andrew (2008). Networking Practitioner Research. London: Routledge.

Minsch, Jürg (2004): Gedanken zu einer politischen Kultur der Nachhaltigkeit. Aufbruch in vielen Dimensionen. In: Radits, Franz/Braunsteiner, Maria-Luise/Klement, Karl (ed.): Bildung für eine Nachhaltige Entwicklung in der LehrerInnenbildung. Baden: Teacher Education College Baden, pp. 10-18.

Naisbitt, John (1984): Megatrends. 10 Perspektiven, die unser Leben verändern werden. Bayreuth: Heyne Verlag.

OECD (2003). Schooling for Tomorrow. Networks of Innovation. Paris: OECD.

O'Hair, Mary J./Veugelers, Wiel (2005): The case for network learning. In: Veugelers, Wiel/O'Hair, Mary J. (ed.): Network Learning for Educational Change. Maidenhead: Open Univ. Press, pp. 1-16.

O'Sullivan, Edmund/Morrell, Amish/O'Connor, Mary A. (2002): Expanding the boundaries of transformative learning: Essays on theory and praxis. New York: Palgrave.

Payer, Harald/Winkler-Rieder, Waltraud/Landsteiner, Günther (2000): Ökologisierung von Schulen. Umwelteffekte und Wirtschaftsimpulse. Wien: ÖAR-Regionalberatung.

Pfaffenwimmer, Günther (2004): ENSI Study: Quality criteria for ECO school development. Austrian Report. Austrian Federal Ministry for Education, Science and Culture. In: Mayer, Michela/Mogensen, Finn (ed.): Environmental Education ECO-schools: trends and divergences. A comparative Study on ECO-School development processes in 13 countries. Wien: BMUKK.

Posch, Peter (1995): Professional Development in Environmental Education: Networking and Infrastructure. In: OECD (ed.): Environmental Learning for the 21st Century. Paris: OECD, pp. 47-64.

Posch, Peter (1999): The Ecologisation of Schools and its Implications for Educational Policy. In: Cambridge Journal of Education 29, 3, pp. 341-348.

Posch, Peter/Altrichter, Herbert (1993): Schulautonomie in Österreich. Innsbruck: StudienVerlag.

Posch, Peter/Rauch, Franz/Kreis, Isolde (2000): Bildung für Nachhaltigkeit. Studien zur Vernetzung von Lehrerbildung, Schule und Umwelt. Innsbruck/Vienna/Munich/Bozen: StudienVerlag.

Rauch, Franz (2013): Regional networks in education: a case study of an Austrian project. In: Cambridge Journal of Education 43, 3, pp. 313-324.

Rauch, Franz (2015): Education for Sustainable Development and Chemistry Education. In: Zuin, Vânia/Mammino, Liliana (ed.): Worldwide Trends in Green Chemistry Education. Cambridge: Royal Society of Chemistry, pp. 16-26.

Rauch, Franz (2016): Bildung für eine nachhaltige Gesellschaft – Konzept und Befunde aus österreichischer Perspektive. In: Diendorfer, Gertraud/Welan, Manfried (ed.): Demokratie und Nachhaltigkeit. Verbindungen, Potenziale und Reformansätze. Innsbruck: StudienVerlag, pp. 121-148.

Rauch, Franz/Dulle, Mira (2012): Auf dem Weg zu einer nachhaltigen Schulkultur—15. Jahre ÖKOLOG-Programm, 10 Jahre Netzwerk ÖKOLOG. Wien: BMUKK.

Rauch, Franz/Pfaffenwimmer, Günther (2014): Education for Sustainable Development in Austria. Networking for Education. In: Jucker, Rolf/Mathar, Reiner (ed.): Schooling for Sustainable Development in Europe. Dortrecht: Springer, pp. 157-176.

Rauch, Franz/Pfaffenwimmer, Günther (2020): The Austrian ECOLOG-Schools Programme – Networking for Environmental and Sustainability Education. In: Gough, Annette/Lee, John C. K./Tsang, Eric P. K. (ed.): The Green Schools Movement Around the World: Stories of impact on Education for Sustainable Development. Dortrecht: Springer.

Rauch, Franz/Pfaffenwimmer, Günther (2019): The Austrian ECOLOG-Schools Programme – History, Structure, Lessons Learned and Impact of a Network. In: Hungarian Educational Research Journal 9, 4, pp. 589-606.

Rauch, Franz/Pfaffenwimmer, Günther (2018): ENSI pillars – Action Research and Dynamic Qualities: In: idem (ed.): Environment and School Initiatives. Lessons from the ENSI Network – Past, Present and Future. BMBWF: Wien, pp. 40-45.

Rauch, Franz/Scherz, Hermann (2009): Regionale Netzwerke im Projekt IMST: Theoretisches Konzept und bisherige Erfahrungen am Beispiel des

Netzwerks in der Steiermark. In: Krainer, Konrad/Hanfstingl, Barbara/Zehetmeier, Stefan (ed.): Fragen des Bildungswesens – Antworten aus Theorie und Praxis. Innsbruck: StudienVerlag, pp. 273-286.

Rauch, Franz/Schrittesser, Ilse (2003): Networks as Support Structure for Quality Development in Education. In: Center for School Development of the Austrian Federal Ministry for Education, Science and Culture/Center for Interdisciplinary Studies of Austrian Universities (ed.). Klagenfurt: Univ. of Klagenfurt.

Rauch, Franz/Steiner, Regina (2006): School Development through Education for Sustainable Development in Austria. In: Environmental Education Research 12, 1, pp. 115-127.

Rauch, Franz/Steiner, Regina (2013). Competences for Education for Sustainable Development in Teacher Education. In: Centre for Educational Policy Studies Journal 3, 1, pp. 9-24.

Rauch, Franz/Steiner, Regina (2015): BINE: Professional development ESD course for higher education teachers, Austria. In: Kapitulčinová, Dana/Dlouhá, Jana/Ryan, Alexandra/Dlouhý, Jiří/Barton, Andrew/Mader, Marlene/Tilbury, Daniella/Mulà, Ingrid/Benayas, Javier/Alba Hidalgo, David/Mader, Clemens/Michelsen, Gerd/Vintar Mally, Katja (ed.): Leading Practice Publication: Professional development of university educators on Education for Sustainable Development in European countries. Prague: Charles Univ., pp. 114-119.

Rauschmayer, Felix/Omann, Ines (2012): Transition to Sustainability: Not Only Big, But Deep. Reaction to M. Bilharz, K. Schmitt. 2011. Going Big with Big Matters. The Key Points Approach to Sustainable Consumption. In: GAIA 20, 4, pp. 232-235.

Reardon, Betty A. (2010): Human Rights and Human Rights Learning as a Vehicle for the Renewal of the University. MS. Klagenfurt.

Schäffter, Ortfried (2006): Auf dem Weg zum Lernen in Netzwerken – Institutionelle Voraussetzungen für lebensbegleitendes Lernen. In: Brödel, Rainer (ed.): Weiterbildung als Netzwerk des Lernens. Bielefeld: Bertelsmann, pp. 29-48.

Schober-Schlatter, Petra (2002): Schule auf dem Weg zur Nachhaltigkeit. Bedingungen und Hemmnisse eines ökologie-orientierten Wandels von Schulen. (Dissertation). Linz: Univ. of Linz.

Senge, Peter (1996): Die fünfte Disziplin. Stuttgart: Clett-Cotta.

Singer-Brodowski, Mandy (2016): Transformative Bildung durch transformatives Lernen. Zur Notwendigkeit der erziehungswissenschaftlichen Fundierung einer neuen Idee. In: ZEP 1, pp. 13-17.

Stern, Thomas/Townsend, Andrew/Rauch, Franz/Schuster, Angela (2014): Action Research, Innovation and Change: International and Interdisciplinary Perspectives. London/New York: Routledge.

Thonhauser, Josef/Ehgartner, Michaela/Sams, Jörg (1998): Ökologisierung von Schulen. Evaluation eines OECD-Projekts. Salzburg: Univ. of Salzburg.

UNESCO (2017): Education for sustainable development goals: Learning objectives. Paris: UNESCO.

Vare, Paul/Scott, William (2007): Learning for a change. Exploring the relationship between education and sustainable development. In: Journal of Education for Sustainable Development 1, 2, pp. 191-198.

Ziener, Karen (2017): Das ÖKOLOG-Netzwerk: Begleitforschungsstudie in der Phase 2015 bis 2016. Klagenfurt: Alpen Adria Universität.

ESD in the Museum: The Project BioKompass
A Practical View from the Senckenberg Natural History Museum Frankfurt

Leon Fuchs, Christina Höfling and Lena Theiler

1. Introduction

How do we want to live in 2040? Will housing be regulated; will we eat meat from the laboratory and will we mainly get from A to B in the cities by bicycle? How do we create a sustainable and liveable future? The German Advisory Council on Global Change (WGBU 2011) speaks of a "Great Transformation" that is necessary for a society shaped according to sustainability principles. Such a transformation will profoundly change the way we think and act, as well as existing structures in a wide range of societal areas.

This article shows how museums – as places of learning for Education for Sustainable Development (ESD) – can contribute to such processes of social change by means of a special exhibition developed in a participatory manner at the Senckenberg Natural History Museum Frankfurt. To this end, the connections between social transformations and ESD are presented first. This is followed by a brief insight into the special features of (natural history) museums as extracurricular places of learning in relation to ESD. An overview of three future scenarios as the basis for the content of the special exhibition leads into the practical presentation of the project. Afterwards, participatory workshops with young people that are relevant to the development of the exhibition and the exhibition in the narrower sense are presented. This is supplemented by the effects and reception of the formats on the participants. The conclusion summarises the insights gained from the project with regard to ESD in the museum and the support of social transformation processes.

2. Transformation and ESD

How societal changes can emerge or even be specifically stimulated is widely discussed in the context of sustainability. Brunner (2019: 180) distinguishes between approaches that focus on a structural change of social practices (system change) and approaches that address a change in the behaviour of individuals (behaviour change). In the case of system changes, political decision-makers have the responsibility to (co-)steer a transformation in the sense of sustainable development through measures related to social practices (ibid.). This does not necessarily have to go hand in hand with the establishment of new, unknown practices, but can also include the reactivation of marginalised practices with fewer resources (Brunner 2019: 180). Behaviour change, on the other hand, places the attitudes, values and behaviours of individuals at the centre of sustainable development discourse. Thus, it is the responsibility of individuals to adapt and establish sustainable behaviours (ibid.: 181). Brunner (ibid.) sees both perspectives as intertwined. Individual unsustainable behaviours are embedded in social practices, which is why they should always be complemented by a practice-theoretical perspective (ibid.). Accordingly, overcoming unsustainable habits requires not only knowledge transfer and reflection on one's own actions, but also consideration of structural mechanisms for establishing these social practices (ibid.: 180).

ESD is seen as a central driver, giving pace to visions of a great transformation (UNESCO 2020: 18; Rieckmann 2019: 81). In its roadmap, UNESCO writes: "ESD must focus on the big transformation that is needed for sustainable development and provide relevant educational interventions" (ibid.: 18). Here, too, a focus on "changes in individual action" (ibid.) and "reorganization of societal structures" is called for (ibid.). Rieckmann (2020), following UNESCO, formulates the central goal of ESD as the empowerment of people "to participate in societal learning and understanding processes for sustainable development, the implementation of the SDGs and thus the promotion of a 'Great Transformation'" (58). Regarding concrete implementations to achieve this goal, numerous different conceptual interpretations of ESD, as well as content-related and pedagogical approaches, have been established in recent years.

A much-cited approach to make the basic currents of ESD tangible is the distinction between ESD 1 (an instrumental approach) and ESD 2 (an emancipatory approach) (Vare & Scott 2007; Wals 2011; Rieckmann 2020: 59). ESD 1 is understood as a "top-down" approach, in which expert knowledge, as well as values and behaviours considered sustainable, serve as a guideline for the design of ESD (Wals 2011: 177). The aim of the approach is to teach these contents, values and behaviours. A classic example of this is separating waste or saving energy (Rieckmann 2020: 59). This is achieved, for example, by establishing incentive or sanction systems (ibid.). Wals (2011: 178) critically notes that such an ESD approach could lead to "big brother sustainability", which might be sustainable from an ecological perspective, but would not contribute to people's overall satisfaction. ESD 2, on the other hand, does not focus on fixed knowledge or specific behaviours, but sees education as an open-ended, reflexive process (ibid.). "What may appear to be sustainable behaviour today may turn out to be unsustainable later in time" (ibid.: 179). This contrasts the "top-down" approach of ESD 1 and tends to produce "grassroots sustainability" (ibid.: 178) rather than "big brother sustainability". ESD 2 focuses on the empowerment, co-creation and participation of learners in their own education process, through learning content that directly affects them (Wals 2011: 178). However, ESD 1 and ESD 2 are not discussed as opposing each other in the literature, but are considered complementary approaches. Vare and Scott (2007: 195) illustrate the relationship between the two approaches as yin and yang. According to this, profitable ESD is characterised by a balanced relationship between imparting specialised knowledge and emancipatory methods (ibid.). Furthermore, it becomes clear that there cannot be a single, permanently valid ESD that equips learners with an all-encompassing toolkit to drive a major transformation towards sustainable development. Rather, ESD needs to be delivered through a diverse, cross-disciplinary and flexible educational offering across different actors in the education sector. Above all, in the sense of ESD 2, this requires a balance of action-oriented methods that enable learners to shape sustainable development.

Rieckmann (2019: 88) sees participatory formats in particular as an important element of ESD. Participation, along with equity, ecological boundaries and global orientation, is thus a central element of sustainable development in the sense of a societal learning, understanding and design process. Such processes are only possible through participation (Rieckmann 2020: 58). This is in line with the view of the WGBU, which advocates for the earliest possible participation of civil society, enabling a better understanding of problems and ultimately facilitating the legitimisation and acceptance of transformation processes (German Advisory Council on Global Change 2011: 8). Formal educational contexts often allow little freedom for the design of open-ended forms of teaching and learning such as workshops, which is why action-oriented ESD is seen as profitable primarily as a link between formal and informal learning (Rieckmann 2019: 88). This requires partnerships at different geographical levels from local to international (Rieckmann 2020: 69).

3. Museums as ESD-learning Locations

Museums have a special role to play in this context, as they are both places of education but also lived socio-cultural practice. "Museums are perfectly positioned to address and enhance sustainability as they are able to work with communities to raise public awareness, support research and knowledge creation to contribute to the well-being of the planet and societies for future generations" (ICOM 2021: n.d.). In their exhibitions, they contextualise original exhibits, relate them to each other and thus offer inspiration for discussion (Sommer Häller et al. 2016: 9). Educational work in museums is constantly evolving and, in addition to a wide range of methods, picks up on current social impulses such as intensified participation and co-determination (Deutscher Museumsbund & Bundesverband Museumspädagogik 2020: 10). This also applies to relevant discourses, new scientific findings and fundamental values (ibid.). Museums are places of exchange: visitors meet with each other and with experts from the museum. Here, too, direct engagement with objects, collections and research focuses play a central role. The concrete work on objects offers visitors the opportunity to relate their own experiences and perspectives and to emphasise the relevance to everyday life in exhibitions (ibid.: 29). The direct exchange with experts on site, during personal mediation formats such as dialogue tours, workshops or open stations in the exhibition, also promotes the involvement of visitors and their experiences (ibid.: 46). Here, opinions are discussed and facts critically questioned.

Depending on how ESD is conceptually interpreted, it can be assumed that many museums contribute to ESD with their educational formats, but without consciously naming it as such. This is indicated, among other things, by the founding paper[1] of the ESD expert group of the Bundesverband Museumspädagogik e. V. (Federal Association of Museum Education; Ackermann & Rupprecht 2021). Thus, ESD, global citizenship education and the SDGs are points of contact that flow into museum work and orientation, but are not recorded in a structured and systematic way. Currently, it is difficult to state to what extent concepts of ESD are adopted into museum education, as corresponding approaches for indicator-based educational monitoring across all educational sectors have only been developed in recent years (Retsch 2020: 91; Singer-Brodowski et al. 2019: 95).

---

1 https://www.museumspaedagogik.org/fileadmin/Data/Bundesverband/Antrag_Gruendung_FG_BnE.pdf

Singer-Brodowski et al. (2019) conducted initial research on the prevalence of ESD. The aim of the research was to gain insights into the diffusion of ESD as a social innovation and into leverage points for the further dissemination of ESD in individual areas of the German education system, and to elicit the impact of ESD in educational practice (Singer-Brodowski et al. 2019: 97). The area of non-formal and informal education was also taken into account, which Singer-Brodowski and colleagues (2019: 104) define as educational opportunities that are characterised by the aspects of voluntary, demand-oriented, participatory, experimental and open. Places of informal education are thus diverse and range from adult education centres to theatres and concert halls to botanical gardens – and museums (Schwan & Noschka-Roos 2019: 133). According to Schmidt (2009: 17), the latter represents a learning situation that can be visited on a voluntary basis according to need and is open to the public. In the exhibition itself, too, the engagement with content is usually self-directed and guided by personal interests and points of contact (Noschka-Roos & Lewalter 2013: 246). Museums thus offer the possibility of direct, individual exchange with diverse topics and issues and therefore contribute to the self-education of visitors, regardless of age and educational level (ibid.; Sommer Häller et al. 2016: 8).

The expert interviews conducted by Singer-Brodowski (2019) confirm the assumption that the spread of ESD in informal education is difficult to record, especially due to its diversity. Nevertheless, it can be assumed that they represent an important complement to formal ESD. Many of the interviewees see the characteristic aspects of non-formal education, such as flexibility and participation, as added values for anchoring ESD in this sector (ibid.: 293f.). Thus, with their expanded understanding of learning, they offer a critical complement to the formal education sector (ibid.: 299). Non-formal learning is seen as particularly beneficial for those children and young people for whom formal education is too demanding (ibid.). From the interviews with experts, Singer-Brodowski et al. (2019: 301f.) also describe current developments in the non-formal education landscape. According to them, there is an increase in quality and differentiation of educational offerings (ibid.: 301) and stronger networking between formal and non-formal education, whereby the initiative for cooperation can come from both independent educational institutions and schools. This leads to increasingly institutionalized cooperation between formal and non-formal organisations (ibid.: 303). However, concrete statements on how widespread ESD is in the field of non-formal education could hardly be derived from the interview data (ibid.: 324). The reasons for this also coincide with theoretically named challenges such as a lack of systematic surveys and corresponding instruments. In addition, the field of informal and non-formal education is more difficult to narrow down than other areas of the education sector (ibid.) and the focus of the institutions involved in informal education is often not on the design of concrete, transformative formats, but on the change of society itself (ibid.). Accordingly, ESD is part of the work processes of non-formal education providers, without this being specifically stated. The experts interviewed see the effective public communication of ESD as a desideratum and point of leverage to make ESD better known and thus strengthen it (ibid.: 324f.). Structures such as the ESD expert group of the Federal Association of Museum Education can contribute to such targeted communication and strengthening of ESD within non-formal education.

4. The World in 2040: The BioKompass Scenarios

In the following, the possibilities of the museum as a place of learning in the sense of ESD are explained through a practical example in the Senckenberg Natural History Museum Frankfurt. In the context of the BioKompass project, which was funded by the Federal Ministry of Education and Research (BMBF), the museum was a central place for participatory and discursive formats to collect and communicate ideas of sustainable transformations. In the following chapters, these museum formats are presented and discussed with regard to their added value for ESD. In terms of content, the focus was on the opportunities and challenges of the transformation to a sustainable bioeconomy.

"Bioeconomy – the key to sustainable development" (Federal Ministry of Education and Research 2021). This is the title of the online presence of the Science Year 2020/2021, an initiative of the Federal Ministry of Education and Research. An important goal of the bioeconomy is the shift from an economy based on fossil raw materials to an economy based on renewable resources. The approach has become increasingly important in recent years, which is reflected in numerous bioeconomy funding lines and strategies at regional, national and international levels. Broad communication measures such as the Science Year are intended to make the complex and multi-layered approach better known to the public, to highlight its potential as a driver towards a sustainable economic system and to stimulate public discourse. The project BioKompass – Communication and Participation for the Societal Transformation to a Bioeconomy – is also the result of BMBF funding with similar goals. The collaborative project[2] was developed within the context of the 2016 ideas

---

2   The following partners were involved in the project:

ESD in the Museum: The Project BioKompass

competition "New Formats of Communication and Participation in the Bioeconomy". The project is based on alternative visions of the future developed in a participatory manner, which deal with the economic, ecological and social aspects of sustainable development towards a bioeconomy in 2040. They are the starting point for communication and discourse and are brought to the public via different formats. The central platform is the Senckenberg Natural History Museum in Frankfurt with the special exhibition Shaping the Future – How do we want to live? (hereafter: Shaping the Future), which has been on show at the museum since May 2019.

The scenarios and concrete future stories were developed with people from science, economy and society during two future dialogues at the Natural History Museum. In the first discursive format, 60 participants identified focal points from various aspects of everyday life, such as consumption, nutrition, housing and social change, which are to be the focus in the following. Possible future developments in these areas were discussed, always with a special focus on bio-based innovations and processes and their intended added value for sustainability and biodiversity protection. On this basis, the project team, together with other experts, developed different future scenarios[3] based on selected influencing factors, which were filled with life in the second future dialogue. In a storytelling process, young people and representatives from industry and science created concrete stories from everyday life in the respective scenarios. Three of these scenarios are the focus of the special exhibition Shaping the Future. They are intended to encourage people to actively consider possible development paths, different contexts and thus alternative futures. They are subdivided by colour to distinguish them.

4.1 Blue Scenario: High with High-Tech Bioeconomy

In the blue scenario, a high-tech bioeconomy has established itself in Germany in 2040. This change was initiated by industry, politics and society. Central features are the avoidance of petroleum-based products and their substitution with products made from bio-based materials. For

---

- Fraunhofer Institute for Systems and Innovation Research ISI (project management)
- Senckenberg – Leibniz Institution for Biodiversity and Earth System Research (SGN)
- Fraunhofer Institute for Chemical Technology ICT
- Fraunhofer Institute for Computer Graphics Research IGD
- ISOE – Institute for Social-Ecological Research

3   Further information on the scenarios and their development see online: https://museumfrankfurt.senckenberg.de/wp-content/uploads/2019/04/zukunftsbilder_biokompass_langfassung.pdf (accessed: 28.12.2021)

this purpose, agriculture has been intensified, whereby greater environmental pollution is counteracted by the use of modern technologies. Fertilisers and pesticides are only applied as needed, production processes are shifted to multi-storey greenhouses and farmers receive premiums for resource-conserving cultivation of their land. In addition, the relevance of recycling processes and thus the lifespan of products is increased. In this scenario, there is little change in consumer behaviour and the economic model is compared to the present.

4.2 Yellow Scenario: Bioeconomy Through Ecologically Conscious Lifestyles

In this scenario, transformation processes are mainly initiated by people who are willing to accept restrictions for more sustainability. This is ultimately reflected in legislation. Meat is taxed because of its poor ecological balance, and coffee-to-go cups as well as petroleum-based plastics are banned. Although the bioeconomy sector is growing as a result, the slump in other economic sectors is slowing down economic growth overall. People trust regional food more than non-transparent, international certificates and avoiding waste is an important part of consumer behaviour. Agricultural land has been expanded due to increased demand for biomass, and management is more efficient, diverse and sustainable. A combination of different approaches – from permaculture to smart farming – are used for this purpose and biodiversity enhancing measures are an integral part of agriculture.

4.3 Turquoise Scenario: Sustainable Bioeconomy – Made in Germany

In this scenario, sustainable transformation is primarily driven by political decisions, with the principle that climate protection must be in harmony with economic growth as a priority basis for decision-making. Resulting restrictions in private consumption are accepted by the population against the background of a growing environmental awareness. Consumption and behaviour patterns are politically steered through corresponding subsidies and sanctions. But initiatives such as education campaigns on environmental issues or the expansion of public transport networks also contribute to the change. Smart farming reduces the amount of land needed for agriculture, freeing up land for biodiversity conservation and turning it into networked protected areas.

The participants of the future dialogues did not assess any of the future scenarios exclusively positively; there were extensive discussions about the respective advantages and disadvantages, with regard to general

ESD in the Museum: The Project BioKompass 147

sustainability issues. In addition, the relationship between bioeconomy and sustainability was repeatedly addressed in the scenario development process. A pure switch from fossil to renewable raw materials is not automatically sustainable; thus, two of the originally developed scenarios were accompanied by negative consequences for biodiversity. These scenarios are not shown in the exhibition, but their findings are an important means of drawing attention to possible negative impacts and conflicting goals. The aim of communicating the scenarios shown in the exhibition is to demonstrate sustainable living environments in the future in a tangible, real-life way.

The scenarios shown differ significantly with regard to the central drivers of transformation processes. While the yellow scenario is largely characterised by individual rethinking and changes in everyday behaviour and thought patterns, the turquoise scenario is based primarily on political decisions that take precedence over individual impulses. In the blue scenario, it is chiefly industry and business that drive change with high-tech ideas. Due to the different design of the three scenarios, people with diverging attitudes and backgrounds feel addressed by specific scenarios and can discuss their thoughts on them with others. In connection with general topics from the field of bioeconomy and the sustainability discourse, the images of the future served as a basis for the further participatory formats during the project.

5. Participation for Transformation: The BioKompass Activities in the Museum

An important feature of the BioKompass project is the active participation of external actors in all project phases. Against this background, various formats were also developed and implemented for the museum, which enable interested parties to deal with questions and challenges of sustainable transformation processes, but above all to actively participate in the museum's preparation and presentation of the contents. In doing so, formats with different levels of participation were deliberately implemented. According to Nina Simon's model, the concepts of the participatory formats were based on approaches of contribution (the framework is given, the participants provide input) and collaboration (the participants are active partners and play a decisive role in shaping the content) (Simon 2010: n.d.). Two of these formats are examined in more detail below: multi-day workshops with young people (BioKompass Weeks) and the growing special exhibition Shaping the Future. In the project, the formats were accompanied and evaluated in order to find out their effect on the participants and to get their feedback. In addition, this monitoring aimed to examine whether and how formats developed for the topic of sustainable bioeconomy can be used in dealing with other complex topics related to sustainability.

5.1   The BioKompass Weeks

In the workshop format of the BioKompass Weeks, secondary school students actively helped to develop the contents of the exhibition. The aim of the events, which lasted several days, was to encourage the participating pupils to engage in a self-motivated and interest-driven debate and to form opinions regarding a sustainable future (Theiler & Lux 2019: 4). Each week had a specific methodological focus. For example, content for the exhibition and an accompanying AR app were developed and comics were drawn for the different scenarios. The BioKompass Weeks enabled participation in the sense of collaboration (Simon 2010: n.d.). Here, the young people are given the opportunity to independently create content within a museum project as experts of their living environment and active partners. The participants thus have a certain degree of autonomy in the process of creating the exhibition.

Results of the Evaluation

Two of the workshops were evaluated by a written before/after survey and these statements were supplemented by participant observation and informal interviews, as well as a survey of the accompanying teachers. The young people's motivation to participate in the events was very diverse. Many pupils cited their own interest in the topic of sustainability, the opportunity to contribute to it themselves and to communicate the topic of sustainability to others through their participation in the exhibition as reasons for taking part (Theiler & Lux 2019: 10f.). The expectations in terms of content were broad and included topics such as avoiding plastic, energy production or environmental protection (ibid.: 10). At least as often as the topic of sustainability, working on a practical product – in the case of the workshops studied, working on an app and drawing comics – were also mentioned as a reason for participation. The combination of appealing practical products with sustainability topics proved to be very suitable to keep barriers as low as possible and target new groups that were not yet very interested in sustainability topics. This creative and interest-driven work process was also evaluated as positive in retrospect. The pupils particularly remembered the concrete topics that they chose and worked on independently in small groups, such as the use of algae or concrete individual aspects like recycling (ibid.: 10f.).

The scenarios and future stories presented above served as a framework and inspiration during the events. Especially during the creative work on the comics, the students worked intensively with the scenarios (ibid.: 22). They picked up elements and combined different scenarios with each other. Repeatedly, specific questions about life in the year 2040 were integrated into the workshops. In the before/after survey, it was noticeable that the young people's view of a sustainable future changed during the course of the workshops. After the BioKompass Weeks, fewer young people than at the beginning said that they did not yet know how to shape a sustainable future. In addition, fewer students agreed with the statement that the thought of the future of the planet made them very uneasy; most of them appeared more positive about the future than before the week (ibid.: 10f.). The direct confrontation with future ideas and innovations seems to have shaped and changed the attitude of the young people, at least immediately after the workshop.

The two teachers who accompanied the BioKompass Weeks from the school side rated the intrinsic motivation of the students during the workshops as extraordinarily high. Such intensive, self-motivated work is rarely observed in traditional school lessons (Theiler & Lux 2019: 12). Some students even wanted to continue working on their results after the end of the workshop (ibid.). The teachers were of the opinion that this motivation was prompted by two factors (ibid.): (1) the direct involvement in the results of the work, for example, the comics they had worked on were shown in the exhibition and the interest in the technical implementation of their own work in an app motivated the pupils; (2) the pupils acquired the role of active multipliers for a sustainable future and had the ambition to reach other people with their own work.

The extracurricular project weeks without pressure to take grades were conducive to the students' motivated work on content (ibid.: 18). The students acquired content independently and reflected on it against the background of their previous knowledge (ibid.). They found it particularly motivating to create a tangible product, although there was a danger that the ambition to develop a particularly good product (e.g., to draw an exceptionally beautiful comic) overshadowed the content-related examination of the topic of sustainable bioeconomy (ibid.: 22). Challenges of the format can be understood as the limited time for acquiring knowledge and the high level of staff supervision required during preparation and implementation (ibid.: 25). The strength of the format was the extracurricular character of the BioKompass Weeks, which gives pupils freedom in terms of content creation and creativity (ibid.). The intensive work over several consecutive days enables immersion in the task and the simultaneous teaching of content and methodological skills (ibid.).

5.2 The Exhibition Shaping the Future

In contrast to most exhibitions at the Senckenberg Natural History Museum, not curators in collaboration with scientists developed the exhibition Shaping the Future. Instead, the basis is a participatory process involving different formats and groups of actors. It thus reflects the discussions, topics and results of the Future Dialogues and the BioKompass Weeks and is intended to encourage visitors to engage with the content on the one hand and to promote participation during their visit to the exhibition on the other. The exhibition had the following goals:

- Visitors acquire knowledge about bioeconomy and a sustainable future.
- Visitors enter an exchange with each other or with the museum staff, discussions on a sustainable bioeconomy/sustainable future arise.
- Visitors use the participatory elements in the exhibition.
- Visitors are encouraged to reflect on their own everyday behaviour and take away new impulses and options for action.

The main target groups of the exhibition are young people from the age of 15 and adults. However, some of the primarily participatory elements are also aimed at younger visitors. The content of the exhibition focuses on the three BioKompass future scenarios described above. In addition, young people defined the main topics of the exhibition in a first BioKompass Week as 1) sustainable consumption, 2) food with a focus on meat consumption and 3) energy. Following these topics, visitors move through a fictitious day in the year 2040 while visiting the exhibition. The exhibition was also designed to "grow"; little by little, content and modules were added. In this way, current references could be made, new developments could be taken up and the results of the workshops could be integrated. In addition, visitors were encouraged at various stations to contribute their own opinions on the scenarios developed, to discuss them together and to exchange their points of view both with other visitors and in conversation with experts. These results were in turn incorporated into the development of new modules. The final exhibition also offers visitors the opportunity to actively participate and engage with the scenarios. In this way, they are encouraged to engage with the topics and different perspectives. For the evaluation of the exhibition, visitors were surveyed by questionnaire over a period of two months and this data was supplemented by participant observation (Theiler & Lux 2020).

ESD in the Museum: The Project BioKompass

Results of the Evaluation

The special exhibition is part of the general museum tour; only a few people visit the museum specifically because of the special exhibition. Therefore, many visitors simply walk through the room or only briefly look at individual exhibits. People who stay longer in the room and deal intensively with the exhibition are usually interested in the topic of sustainability and have prior knowledge (ibid.: 15). Nevertheless, most visitors stated that they had learnt something new from the exhibition (ibid.). In contrast to the young participants of the BioKompass Weeks, exhibition visitors were not very optimistic about the future after the visit (ibid.). One possible reason for this could be that the current state of many sustainability problems is presented in great detail in the exhibition (ibid.). The scenarios are a central element of the exhibition concept (ibid.: 36). However, the survey showed that although visitors notice the individual innovations and possible developments in the future, the interrelated scenarios and the resulting different options for a sustainable future were not perceived during the visit to the exhibition. However, the scenarios proved to be very suitable starting points for dialogue formats and guided tours (Theiler & Lux 2020: 36). Conversations and discussions about the exhibition and one's own behaviour were seen as a central element for forming opinions with regard to a sustainable future. In addition to the exchange between visitors and museum staff, conversations between adults and children took place in the exhibition (ibid.: 20). In the process, their own behaviour and their own possible contribution to more sustainability were often the topic of discussion.

Two very different elements proved to be beneficial for the acquisition of knowledge. On the one hand, many visitors stated that they did not know the exhibited biobased products before and learnt new things about the use of materials and product production. Here, the means of surprise – through the recognition value of familiar everyday objects in a new form – and an emotional dimension seem to be purposeful (ibid.: 29). On the other hand, visitors were interested in parts of the exhibition that contained numbers and statistics. These were found to be particularly informative, the data given was also often unexpected and thus memorable (ibid.: 29f.).

The strength of the exhibition is the transfer of knowledge on different levels, for example through direct reference to objects and everyday life or through personal contact (Theiler & Lux 2019: 38). When visitors were made aware that young people were involved in the development and conception of the exhibition, they rated this very positively. In the perception of the visitors, the participation of young people increased the relevance of the contents, created identification possibilities and a recognition value (ibid.).

6. Conclusion

The description of the BioKompass workshops and the special exhibition on bioeconomy as well as their reception give an insight into the opportunities and challenges of museums as extracurricular places of learning, and how to deal with complex, multi-layered topics as they are addressed in the field of sustainable development. At the local level, museums can be important actors in shaping innovative and participatory formats of ESD. They open up authentic participation opportunities, which cannot always be achieved in a school context. Without the rather strict curricular framework, museums can create open-ended, action-oriented educational opportunities that do not focus solely on the teaching and acquisition of concrete subject knowledge or specific competences. Learning is understood more as a process of participation in shaping a sustainable future, accompanied by experts. The opinions and positions of the learners are not just heard by experts in the sense of a quasi-participation and then discarded, but actually find their way into a public exhibition. The example of the BioKompass Weeks and the exhibition shows that young people see themselves as multipliers for ESD when they help to determine content and develop museum methods of communication. This increases the impact of children and young people as change agents well beyond their personal environment. Young people have the opportunity to formulate their views and make them heard. Their perspectives thus become part of the social discourse and an active negotiation of different transformation strategies with other actors can emerge from the exhibition.

In order to make full use of the potential with regard to formats for young people, close cooperation between schools and museums is of great importance. In cooperation, an exchange of knowledge, experiences and methods can be optimally promoted. In the museum, school working methods and contents are connected, but these are placed in a different context and structural framework. Here, too, the example of the BioKompass Weeks shows that working in the real context of the museum seems to be an important motivational factor for the students' engagement with the topic of sustainability, which cannot be reproduced in this way in school lessons. At the same time, after the BioKompass Weeks, the exchange of content that started in the museum format was continued in the school environment for several weeks after the workshop. One reason for this successful and long-term discussion of content was the participation of the pupils in the selection of topics even before the workshop format began. This emancipatory approach favoured the selection of content with regard to its connectivity to the participants' existing experiences and values. Furthermore, the participating students seemed to consider the work in the BioKompass Weeks as practicable and useful for them. At the end of the BioKompass Weeks, the young people were more optimistic about the future of the planet than at the beginning.

In the exhibition Shaping the Future, it was above all the way in which the basic content was presented, but also the dialogue-oriented formats, that proved to be very effective. The visitors found the presentation of facts and figures as well as new products or technical innovations particularly impressive. In addition, the participatory and dialogue-oriented concept of the exhibition contributed significantly to visitors reflecting on their own opinions and behaviour in the context of sustainable development. The combination of the different formats and the resulting possibilities for a varied transfer of knowledge offer great value. Due to the conception as a growing special exhibition, it has a high degree of topicality because, in contrast to permanent exhibitions, it is not designed to be "timeless", but rather picks up on current events and discourses and can thus provide further opportunities for personal points of connection.

Across formats, concrete connections to everyday actions on the one hand, and broad references to sustainability from agriculture to new materials and technical innovations on the other hand seem to be important success factors for dealing with sustainable development. In this context, the content-related link to the transformation towards a sustainable bioeconomy proved to be promising, as the complex, multi-layered, but, nevertheless, everyday topics provided exciting aspects for self-directed knowledge acquisition for the workshop formats as well as the exhibition. The multifaceted presentation of a sustainable future via scenarios, options for action and discursive formats can contribute to linking the specialist scientific and systemic approach of ESD on the one hand with the emancipatory and individual approach on the other. The museum pedagogical preparation in the form of different formats such as activating events and appealing exhibitions enables interested people of different ages and educational levels to get involved in the process. The possibility of making different perspectives visible and linking them with scientific foundations and current research results illustrates the enormous innovation potential of museums in the implementation of ESD. As a platform for knowledge transfer and participation, they can therefore contribute significantly to the social transformation process of sustainable development.

Bibliography

Ackermann, Jakob/Rupprecht, Carola (2021): Antrag zur Gründung einer Fachgruppe Bildung für nachhaltige Entwicklung/Global Citizenship Education im Bundesverband Museumspädagogik.

Brunner, Karl-Michael (2019): Sustainable Consumption and the Dynamics of Demand. From individualistic to systemic concepts of transformation. In: Luks, Fred (ed.): Opportunities and Limits of Sustainability Transformation Economic and Sociological Perspectives. 1st edition. Wiesbaden: Springer Gabler, pp. 167-184.

Federal Ministry of Education and Research (2021): Homepage – Science Year 2020: Bioeconomy. Online: https://www.wissenschaftsjahr.de/2020-21/ (accessed: 30.04.2021).

Deutscher Museumsbund/Bundesverband Museumspädagogik (2020): Bildung und Vermittlung im Museum gestalten. Guidelines. Berlin: Deutscher Museumsbund e.V.

German Advisory Council on Global Change (2011): World in Transition. Social Contract for a Great Transformation. Main Report. 2nd edition. Berlin.

ICOM (2021): Sustainability and Local Development – ICOM. Online: https://icom.museum/en/our-actions/museums-society/sustainability-and-local-development/ (accessed: 27.01.2021).

Noschka-Roos, Annette/Lewalter, Doris (2013): Lernort Museum. Tendencies and Findings. In: Hessische Blätter für Volksbildung 03, pp. 243-249.

Retsch, Riccarda (2020): Enabling Education for All. Goal 4 of the Global Sustainability Goals: Quality Education. In: Kminek, Helge/Bank, Franziska/Fuchs, Leon (ed.): Kontroverses Miteinander. Interdisziplinäre und kontroverse Positionen zur Bildung für eine nachhaltige Entwicklung. Frankfurt a. M.: Goethe-Universität, FB04-Dekanat, pp. 87-98.

Rieckmann, Marco (2019): Contributions of Education for Sustainable Development to the Achievement of the Sustainable Development Goals. Perspectives, learning goals and research needs. In: Clemens, Iris/Hornberg, Sabine/Rieckmann, Marco (ed.): Bildung und Erziehung im Kontext globaler Transformationen. Schriftenreihe "Ökologie und Erziehungswissenschaft" der Kommission Bildung für eine nachhaltige Entwicklung der Deutschen Gesellschaft für Erziehungswissenschaft (DGfE). Opladen/Berlin/Toronto: Barbara Budrich, pp. 79-94.

Rieckmann, Marco (2020): Education for Sustainable Development in the Context of the Sustainable Development Goals. In: Kminek, Helge/Bank, Franziska/Fuchs, Leon (ed.): Kontroverses Miteinander. Interdisziplinäre und kontroverse Positionen zur Bildung für eine nachhaltige Entwicklung. Frankfurt a. M.: Goethe-Universität, FB04-Dekanat, pp. 57-86.

Schmidt, Claudia (2009): Complex phenomena and their communicability. An empirical study on climate exhibitions. Accessed: Augsburg, Univ., Diss., 2008. 1st edition. Bad Heilbrunn: Verlag Julius Klinkhardt.
Schwan, Stephan/Noschka-Roos, Annette (2019): Non-formal and informal educational opportunities. In: Köller, Olaf/Hasselhorn, Marcus/Hesse, Friedrich W./Maaz, Kai/Schrader, Josef/Solga, Heike/Spieß, Katharina/Zimmer, Karin (ed.): Das Bildungswesen in Deutschland. Stock and Potentials. utb Pädagogik. Bad Heilbrunn: Verlag Julius Klinkhardt, pp. 131-160.
Simon, Nina (2010): The participatory museum – Read Online. Santa Cruz, California: Museum 2.0.
Singer-Brodowski, Mandy (2019): Education for Sustainable Development in Non-formal and Informal Learning. In: Singer-Brodowski, Mandy/Etzkorn, Nadine/Grapentin-Rimek, Theresa (ed.): Pathways of Transformation. The Dissemination of Education for Sustainable Development in the German Education System. Schriftenreihe "Ökologie und Erziehungswissenschaft" der Kommission Bildung für eine nachhaltige Entwicklung der Deutschen Gesellschaft für Erziehungswissenschaft (DGfE). Opladen/Berlin/Toronto: Barbara Budrich, pp. 291-348.
Singer-Brodowski, Mandy/Etzkorn, Nadine/Brock, Antje/Grapentin-Rimek, Theresa/Seggern, Janne von (2019): Nationales Monitoring BNE. Status and process of dissemination of ESD. In: Clemens, Iris/Hornberg, Sabine/Rieckmann, Marco (ed.): Bildung und Erziehung im Kontext globaler Transformationen. Schriftenreihe "Ökologie und Erziehungswissenschaft" der Kommission Bildung für eine nachhaltige Entwicklung der Deutschen Gesellschaft für Erziehungswissenschaft (DGfE). Opladen/Berlin/Toronto: Barbara Budrich, pp. 95-110.
Singer-Brodowski, Mandy/Etzkorn, Nadine/Grapentin-Rimek, Theresa (2019): Paths of Transformation. The diffusion of Education for Sustainable Development in the German education system. Schriftenreihe "Ökologie und Erziehungswissenschaft" der Kommission Bildung für eine nachhaltige Entwicklung der Deutschen Gesellschaft für Erziehungswissenschaft (DGfE). Opladen/Berlin/Toronto: Barbara Budrich Publishers.
Sommer Häller, Barbara/Brovelli, Dorothee/Fuchs, Karin/Rempfler, Armin (2016): Zur Bedeutung von Museen und Ausstellungen als außerschulische Lernorte. In: Brovelli, Dorothee (ed.): Museen und Ausstellungen als ausserschulische Lernorte. Tagungsband zur 4. Tagung. Ausserschulische Lernorte der PH Luzern vom 22. November 2014. Ausserschulische Lernorte – Beiträge zur Didaktik, Band 4. Zürich/Münster: Lit.
Theiler, Lena/Lux, Alexandra (2019): Evaluation Evolving Lab. Report AP9. Part A: Evaluation Report Exhibition.
Theiler, Lena/Lux, Alexandra (2020): Evaluation Evolving Lab. Report AP9. Part B: Evaluation report Biocompass Weeks.
UNESCO (2020): Education for sustainable development. a roadmap. Paris.
Vare, Paul/Scott, William (2007): Learning for a Change. In: Journal of Education for Sustainable Development 1, 2, pp. 191-198.

Wals, Arjen E. J. (2011): Learning Our Way to Sustainability. In: Journal of Education for Sustainable Development 5, 2, pp. 177-186.

Sustainable Development at Institutions of Higher Education – The Example of Goethe University

Anna Geyer

> Acting is easy, thinking hard;
> acting in accordance with thinking is uncomfortable
> (Goethe 2013: 451).

1. Introduction[1]

Ascribed to the eponym of the university in Frankfurt am Main, Germany, the above quotation expresses a fundamental challenge faced by humankind. Many social, ecological and economic problems could be solved by acting in accordance with our better knowledge. Institutions of higher education and their stakeholders encounter this discrepancy in a special manner: scientists started to *think*, thereby discovering the fatal relationship between the increase of greenhouse gas emissions on the one hand, and the rise in global average temperature on the other. While climate and land-system change are in a "zone of uncertainty" of the planetary boundaries with increasing risk of destabilizing the Earth system, the loss of biodiversity and the global phosphorus and nitrogen cycles are beyond this zone, with high risk to the safe operating space for global societal development (Steffen et al. 2015: 736). Academia disclosed, and is still discovering, the complexity, interconnectedness, as well as vulnerability of ecological and social systems. The public dissemination of these insights provoked the career of the concept of sustainability[2], commonly defined by the Brundtland report: "Sustainable development is development that meets the needs of the present without compromising

---

[1] I would like to thank Helge Kminek, Markus Siewert, Mohammed Salhi, Moritz Schmitthenner and Simone Blandford for the many helpful comments on this article and the thorough editing.
[2] Note that for simplicity I will use *sustainability* and *sustainable development* interchangeably in this article. For a critique of this practice see Vieweg 2019: 91-93.

the ability of future generations to meet their own needs" (World Commission on Environment and Development 1987: 41). While *thinking* about what this means is already hard, *acting in accordance* with it is even more challenging. And, if acting is not only necessary at an individual but also a collective level – as it is in the context of sustainability – the task becomes tremendously difficult.

It is quite indisputable that (the lack of) sustainability is a major challenge to humanity in the 21st century. What it means in theory and what it requires in practice are, however, very controversial. This article builds on the common, broad concept of sustainability integrating ecological, societal and economic issues (Vieweg 2019: 26-32; Grober 2013: 21). While this does not allow to pin down specific goals and means[3], it becomes evident that it requires the engagement of individuals, organizations and countries around the globe to find solutions. Coming from their academic perspective, institutions of higher education (IHE) bear a special responsibility to switch to sustainable paths. Not only are they places of knowledge, research, innovation and education, but they also have a substantial ecological and societal impact. Depending on their size, their ecological footprint is comparable to that of entire towns. Moreover, they usually have vivid connections to local communities, industries and beyond, thereby influencing many people. Hence, actively working on sustainable development and being a role model allows IHE to profoundly contribute to a societal transformation towards sustainability.

Institutions of higher education throughout the world increasingly acknowledge this responsibility and have started transforming themselves to become more sustainable. Thereby, they address the areas of teaching, research, governance, operations and transfer (McCowan et al. 2021). While some IHE like Leuphana University Lüneburg have already taken crucial steps towards realizing climate neutrality (at least from an accounting perspective) and introducing sustainability studies (Brüggen 2020), others like Goethe University (GU) in Frankfurt are only at the outset of this progress. For Germany and beyond, there are comprehensive overviews of flagship projects and institutions.[4] However, for those IHE that jumped on the bandwagon like GU, little has been

---

3 For educational practices compare Kminek, Helge/Wallmeier, Philip (2020): Nicht abschließbare Problemorientierung als Leitprinzip – Zur Bildung für die sozial-ökologische Transformation in polarisierten Zeiten. In: Eicker, Jannis/Eis, Andreas/Holfelder, Anne-Katrin/Jacobs, Sebastian/Yume, Sophie (ed.): Bildung Macht Zukunft. Lernen für die sozial-ökologische Transformation? Frankfurt a. M.: Wochenschau Verlag, pp. 54-63.

4 For an international perspective see for example Mc Cowan et al. (2021); for Germany see the good practice collection of *netzwerk n*. Online: https://www.netzwerk-n.org/angebote/good-practice-sammlung/ (accessed: 03.09.2021); or the sustainability map of the project *Hoch N*. Online: https://www.hochn.uni-hamburg.de/ (accessed: 03.09.2021).

written about the processes of change. This article contributes to filling this gap by taking a closer look at the initiation, development and status quo of sustainable transformation at GU: which actors and events are relevant for the progress? How does it evolve? What successes and/or failures can be reported?

By elaborating on these questions, I stay explicitly limited to my subjective perspective as a student (of political science, economics and business), co-project-initiator, student assistant as well as initiative and committee member. I will not further take up literature on sustainability in IHE but instead focus on the case description – offering practitioner's insights that might be valuable, especially to sustainability actors at other IHE. Moreover, I do not proclaim completeness within the case of Goethe University. There have been and are more sustainability movements, projects and actors than I can include here. Where possible I will refer to them, yet I will focus on the projects and initiatives that I was and am a part of. Thereby, I vary between a dominant, rather descriptive report on the one hand, and a few personal reflections on the other – which I thoroughly try to make distinguishable.

The article proceeds as follows: to illustrate the outset of sustainable development at Goethe University, I begin by introducing the interdisciplinary sustainability QSL-teaching project (2). Then, I present the student initiative *Goethe's Green Office* as one of the most relevant sustainability actors at GU (3). Next, I elaborate on the sustainability institutionalization processes (4) by examining GU's Senate working group (4.1), the sustainability office (4.2) and an initiative on academic air travel (4.3). Finally, I summarize the main points (5).

2. QSL-Teaching Project

At Goethe University there exists a fund for Securing Qualitative Teaching (QSL) which annually supports innovative teaching projects that lecturers can apply for. Working back then at the same chair, Markus Siewert and I agreed about the urgency of a societal transformation towards sustainability and the backwardness of Goethe University not contributing to this. Against this background, we decided to hand in a sustainability teaching project at the fund. While we were already planning the project, we met Helge Kminek at a network meeting on "sustainability at IHE" of *Renn.West*[5], a networking initiative by the German government to promote

---

5 RENN – Regionale Netzstellen Nachhaltigkeitsstrategien / RENN West. Online: https://www.renn-netzwerk.de/west (accessed: 03.09.2021).

communication on sustainability concepts and processes. As he was also planning to submit a sustainability project at the QSL-fund, we decided to combine (I) Helge's idea of a lecture series on Education for Sustainable Development with (II) Markus' and my idea of a networking initiative and (III) a service-learning seminar – which formed the three modules of the project. We entitled the proposal "Education for Sustainable Development through and at Goethe University" (Bildung für nachhaltige Entwicklung durch die und an der Goethe-Universität), underlining the dual focus of transformations *at* GU itself and in society *through* the support of GU. A few months after the submission, the requested project means were affirmed for the period from October 2019 to September 2020. From January 2020 on, the project team was extended by the student assistant Jacqueline Reich.

The QSL-project consisted of the three aforementioned modules. Firstly, an interdisciplinary lecture series on Education for Sustainable Development (ESD) was held in the winter semester 2019/2020. While for the first block of the series invited speakers focused on generally scientific and societal perspectives on sustainable development, the second block was about views from educational science. Speakers came from different contexts and locations, creating a fruitful mix that reflected the controversial and multidimensional discussion on ESD. To provide the sustainability and accessibility of the project, lectures were recorded and are available online.[6]

Meanwhile, the second networking module launched with the goal of bringing sustainability actors of Goethe University together. As there has not yet been a comprehensive sustainability network at GU, a fundamental investigation of relevant actors at different levels and positions was necessary. The result was a list with more than 50 persons which is, however, far from being complete. The difficulty was and is, that a lot of people which are committed to sustainability in one way or another do not identify themselves with this concept – intentionally or not. Considering the breadth and ambiguity of the term, this is no surprise. Yet, the concept of sustainability has its strength exactly in integrating different dimensions and thinking in interdisciplinary trade-offs. Hence, it was our goal to reach both intentional and unintentional sustainability actors and bring them together to reap the benefits of a sustainability approach. Together with the *user-sensibilization-project* of the energy management of GU led by Patrizia Neuhofer, we arranged the first comprehensive networking meeting on sustainability at Goethe University in November 2019. According to the motto "Research and Teaching for Sustainable

---

6 Ringvorlesung BNE (ESD Lecture Series). Online: https://video.uni-frankfurt.de/Mediasite/Channel/76c9df63b71b459189bfa0440145ec505f (accessed: 03.09.2021).

Development", sixteen professors, academic assistants and doctoral candidates from different departments connected, discussed the status quo, and affirmed the need for further teaching, research and project intentions. Next to the amplified visibility between the actors and a broad collection of ideas, concrete projects and initiatives did not evolve directly from the meeting as we had hoped. This must be seen, however, in the context of the upcoming Coronavirus pandemic and the installed Senate working group for sustainability, which I will discuss below. Still, a mailing list was set up which is currently planned to live up to a regular newsletter on sustainability issues at GU. In February 2020, a second networking meeting only for non-professorial academics took place for launching a project proposal on the topic "sustainable city", which also has no concrete results yet. The last intended network meeting addressed sustainability actors within the city of Frankfurt in the spirit of GU's third mission. Dated for the end of March 2020, it had to be cancelled due to the ever-evolving pandemic and was not caught up on to date. We discarded the option of conducting it online because we believed that it would not allow the same depth of networking and because back then the temporal extent of the pandemic was not yet conceivable. Instead, we conducted a survey on sustainability issues among the invited actors which revealed the wish for further networking, a chance to exchange knowledge and experiences and an interest in cooperating with GU. Finally, together with the *user-sensibilization project* we launched an official university website on sustainability as part of the networking module.[7] Structured by the *Sustainable Development Goals* of the United Nations, it gives an overview of sustainability experts, projects and organizations at GU, thereby aiming to facilitate the networking between sustainability actors within and beyond GU.

The third module of the QSL-project consisted of the service-learning seminar "Sustainability at and through Goethe University" (Nachhaltigkeit an der und durch die Goethe-Universität) in the summer semester 2020. It was open to different disciplines but mainly attracted students of educational science and sociology. Our aim was to live up to the pedagogical concept of service-learning by letting the students develop projects that would be a service to the community of Frankfurt while allowing practical insights for the students (Aretz 2020: 16). This was only unsatisfactorily achieved, again due to the Coronavirus situation. Nevertheless, through online meetings, the different student groups developed interesting projects spanning from art installations criticizing

---

7   Goethe-Universität Frankfurt am Main (2021): Sustainability at Goethe-Universität. Online: https://www.goethe-university-frankfurt.de/96114502/Sustainability_at_Goethe_Universität (accessed: 03.09.2021).

"Amazon's ordering culture" to Instagram workshops on plastic waste. One of these projects, the free shop *Drehscheibe*[8], was before and still is active in the framework of the student initiative *Goethe's Green Office* that I will introduce next.

All in all, the QSL-teaching projects allowed students to encounter the topic of sustainability within their curriculum and to get credits for their engagement. The lecture and seminar were among the pioneering sustainability courses at GU, which since then offers an increasing number of related courses. Furthermore, the initiation of the QSL-project itself and its activities underline the importance of networking for sustainability at IHE. Even if initiatives were not directly influenced by the networking meetings, they have contributed to the overall dynamic of sustainable transformation at GU, as depicted below.

3. Student Engagement: "Goethe's Green Office"-initiative

Goethe's Green Office (GGO) is a student led initiative founded at the end of 2018 by a group of students of sociology, political science and anthropogeography who were also politically active at Goethe University. They participated in an online workshop of the *green office movement*[9] originating from the Netherlands and decided to initiate a *green office*[10] at GU that would guide its transformation towards sustainability. With public actions like campus clean-ups, posters and participation in university events, they were successfully recruiting people (like me) to join their cause. In summer 2019, Goethe's Green Office officially registered as a student initiative at GU. Before the onset of the Coronavirus pandemic, there were over twenty members, from which about half are still actively participating to date.

The inner structure of the initiative was revised a few times before it reached its current state during a *Wandercoaching* weekend of the Germany-

---

8 Goethe's Green Office (2021): Umsonstladen "Drehscheibe". Online: http://goethesgreenoffice.org/umsonstladen-drehscheibe/ (accessed: 03.09.2021).
9 Students Organizing for Sustainability International & Leuphana University Lüneburg (2021): Das Green Office Modell. Online: https://www.greenofficemovement.org/de/ (accessed: 03.09.2021).
10 A green office is a special form of a sustainability office at an IHE. Further explanation follows in chapter 4.2.

wide student sustainability organization *netzwerk n*[11]. There are four subgroups: coordination, public relations, projects and institutionalization. While the coordination group is responsible for the inner organization of the initiative, the public relations group organises the online and offline publicity like (ecological) flyers or the website[12]. The project group is itself an agglomerate of subgroups: the campus garden[13] and the above-mentioned free shop project. Finally, the institutionalization group is responsible for the core aim of the initiative, that is to institutionalize a green office at GU. As their work is related most closely to sustainable development at GU and as I was mostly involved in this subgroup, I will focus on its perspective.

Throughout 2019, the institutionalization group developed a concept for its vision of a green office at GU. Being a piece of ongoing discussions, it sums up the initiative's comprehension of sustainability, its goals and the envisioned sustainability structures. Common values are the interdependency of social and ecological topics, as well as a participatory approach. This is reflected by the separation of the sustainability structure into two main elements: a sustainability *office* and a sustainability *committee*. While the office should have salaried employees and is supposed to take a coordinative and operative part (e.g., developing a sustainability report), the committee should work discursively by elaborating on common sustainability goals. To ensure participation, the committee should consist of members of all status groups of the university and work transparently. The idea is that the committee legitimizes and monitors the goals and measures the office implements, functioning as checks and balances. A third, additional element is the idea of a sustainability *convention*. It should be an annual event where all university members are invited to debate, elaborate on and grapple with sustainability issues at GU in workshops and discussion rounds. It should guarantee low-level access for all university members to participate in the sustainable transformation of GU.[14]

---

11   netzwerk n e.V. (2021): Wandercoaching. Mit diesem Projekt unterstützen wir Eure Nachhaltigkeitsinitiative. Online: https://www.netzwerk-n.org/angebote/formate/wandercoaching/ (accessed: 03.09.2021).
12   Goethe's Green Office (2021): Goethe's Green Office – Zusammen. Zukunftsfähig. Online: http://goethesgreenoffice.org/ (accessed: 03.09.2021).
13   Two permaculture campus gardens were launched in spring 2021 in cooperation with the student union executive committee (AStA) of GU and the local permaculture initiative "vegetable heroes" (GemüseheldInnen). For an article on the projects see online: https://aktuelles.uni-frankfurt.de/campus/campusgaerten-permakulturinseln-der-goethe-uni-als-begegnungsorte-der-stadt/ (accessed: 03.09.2021); for the GemüseheldInnen see online: https://gemueseheldinnen-frankfurt.de/ (accessed: 03.09.2021).
14   Goethe's Green Office (09.06.2019): Green Office Konzept. Online: http://goethesgreenoffice.org/2019/06/09/green-office-konzept/ (accessed: 03.09.2021).

Parallel to this conceptualization process, the institutionalization group networked with actors and organizations within and beyond GU to lobby for its goals and gain support. Among these were professors, the executive board of GU, initiatives and green offices at other IHE, the environmental department of the city of Frankfurt and NGOs like the "Development Policy Network Hesse" (Entwicklungspolitisches Netzwerk Hessen e.V.)[15]. These contacts were and continuously are crucial for the progress of building a sustainability structure at GU. By request of the former president of GU, the institutionalization group was invited to several meetings with the university's chancellor, Albrecht Fester, throughout summer 2019. This alone was, however, not very fruitful and it was only until the GGO-initiative heard about a Senate[16] proposal of the law professor and Senate member Cornelius Prittwitz that the situation changed substantially. As his proposal was entitled, he wanted Goethe University to react to the dangerous effects of climate change. Before its introduction in the Senate, the GGO institutionalization group contacted Prittwitz who was open to meet and involve them. Thereupon, on November 20th, 2019, the Senate of GU resolved the following three main points: firstly, institutions of GU are requested to name and consider, to the greatest possible extent, climate relevant aspects of their activities and decisions. Secondly, sustainable development should be incorporated into the "university development plan" (Hochschulentwicklungsplan) and the mission statement of GU. Thirdly, an open Senate working group is established which collects and discusses climate relevant activities of GU and compiles recommendations for their reduction. It should collaborate with the executive board and administration of GU and be intertwined with the initiative "Green Office" (Goethe-Universität 2019: 9).

This resolution was a milestone for the sustainability process at GU and the GGO-initiative. While the first two points are not yet fully implemented to date, there is no way around the topic anymore. It is especially the working group established through the third point that grew beyond its expected potential and gave a valued voice to sustainability actors and initiatives like the GGO at a top level of GU.

---

15 EPN Hessen e.V. (2021): Gemeinsam und vernetzt für globale Gerechtigkeit und Entwicklung in der Einen Welt!. Online: https://www.epn-hessen.de/ (accessed: 03.09.2021).

16 The Senate is one of four organs of Goethe University and contains members of all status groups (professors, students, academic and technical-administrative staff). It discusses central topics in line with GU's functional self-government and has a say in many principal affairs at GU. Online: https://www.uni-frankfurt.de/senat (accessed: 03.09.2021).

4. Institutionalization of Sustainability

4.1 Senate Working Group

In March 2020, the "Senate working group on sustainability" (Senats-AG Nachhaltigkeit) met for the first (and to date the only offline) time. Among the regular participants are the chancellor of GU, members of the Senate, academic and technical-administrative staff, members of *Students for Future* (SFF) and the *Goethe's Green Office* initiative. At the second meeting in May 2020, the purpose of the group originating from Prittwitz' Senate resolution was reflected and an agenda with sustainability topics was set for the remainder of the year. Since then, monthly meetings have taken place, each focusing on a special subject addressing structures as well as concrete projects. The meeting agenda, protocols, the mailing list and supplementary tasks like surveys among the participants are organised by the GGO-initiative. So far, the working group has discussed topics such as: a sustainability office, alimentation, academic air travel, sustainability reporting, waste, buildings and construction, energy, mobility and infrastructure, sustainability networks and organizations and a sustainability strategy. Future topics are the investment of university funds, green spaces, teaching and education, campus life and sensibilization and research. The main outcomes of these meetings are summarized in protocols that should guide the activities of the newly established sustainability office that I will come to below. The protocols reflect the status quo concerning a particular topic, depict different perspectives and propose further actions. Generally, the working group does not get active beyond this stage due to scarce capacities and its voluntary character. However, in the case of the sustainability office and academic air travel, concrete actions were initiated which I introduce in the following section.

4.2 Sustainability Office

The relevance of the sustainability office is illustrated by the fact that it was ranked as the most important topic by the participants of the working group. Therefore, it was discussed in the first regular meeting in June 2020 where the GGO-initiative gave an input on the "Hessian Pact of Higher Education" (Hessischer Hochschulpakt) for 2021-2025.[17] This political

---

17 Hessischer Hochschulpakt 2021-2025. Online: https://wissenschaft.hessen.de/sites/default/files/media/hmwk/200310_hhsp_2021-2025.pdf (accessed: 03.09.2021).

paper sets the guiding principles for Hessian universities like GU and dedicates a chapter to sustainability. Among important guidelines concerning research, teaching and administration, it explicitly requires universities to install central sustainability structures like "Green Offices" referring to the aforementioned green office movement. This and other demands are part of the pact thanks to a progressive initiative of Hessian student union executive committees that is closely connected to the GGO-initiative. With a second input the GGO-initiative introduced the main elements of the green office concept: a green office is a special form of sustainability office which is collectively led by university employees and students and is financed through the university. It is integrated into the university structures as an official department and its mandate is to coordinate sustainability issues, for which it cooperates with all university divisions (governance, operations, research, education and student organizations). The green office is responsible for a common sustainability strategy and a report which provides transparency. Compared to other sustainability structures like commissions or coordinators, a green office has the advantage of actively involving different status groups, increasing its outreach and bearing less risk to disappear in bureaucracy. It allows for the coordination and/or incorporation of existing engagement and functions as a central contact point for sustainability issues at IHE.[18] There is a growing movement of IHE around the globe to build such green offices which underlines the success of the concept. To date, there are 65 officially established green offices and about 750 green office projects worldwide.[19]

After these inputs, the Senate working group discussed financing, integration into the university structures, areas of responsibility, staff and a permanent office space for the future. Based on this debate, a joint concept paper on a sustainability office at GU was composed. It stipulates two permanent full-time positions and six student assistants from different disciplinary backgrounds, a yearly budget of €250,000 coming from university funds, a tie with the executive board of GU and viewing sustainability as a cross-sectional task that cannot be limited to the administration department. The tasks of the office should be the coordination of existing projects and initiatives, the sensibilization of GU members, cooperation with research and teaching, further developing sustainability structures, planning and realizing new projects, having an

---

18 Green Office Movement (20.11.2013): The Green Office Model: A student-led sustainability office to create more sustainable universities. Online: https://www.youtube.com/watch?v=0cOI8S-e5CI&t=131s (accessed: 03.09.2021).
19 Students Organizing for Sustainability International & Leuphana University Lüneburg (2021): Das Green Office Modell. Online: https://www.greenofficemovement.org/de/ (accessed: 03.09.2021).

impact towards society and implementing a sustainability strategy and report. This concept paper was consigned to the executive board of GU.

In July 2020, Enrico Schleiff was elected as the new president of GU, leading to an acceleration of sustainable development at the university. Before his presidency started in January 2021, Schleiff participated a few times in the Senate working group. Here he showed interest in different sustainability projects and promised to promote a sustainable transformation at GU. In December 2020, he and the chancellor summoned an extraordinary meeting on the personnel of the sustainability office. They proposed Norbert Dichter, a union member of the Senate who was a member of the working group from the beginning, as sustainability coordinator. As Dichter is known for his long-term civil engagement for sustainability issues and his comprehensive knowledge on the structures and processes of GU, the working group affirmed this proposal with unanimity. Parallel to the approval of an adequate budget for sustainability within the university's financial plan for the year 2021, Dichter took up his position. Until his prospective retirement after the first quarter of 2022, his tasks will be to coordinate the Senate working group, to support promising ideas and projects in the context of sustainability and to network with relevant actors of GU and beyond. In particular, he will promote the institutionalization of the sustainability office. To support this, four student assistants will be employed in October 2021. Furthermore, the executive board is currently applying for means from a Hessian budget to support sustainability structures at IHE, with which it wants to fund five full-time positions to complete the sustainability office. In addition to this, for 2022 and the upcoming years, it is intended to further raise the internal sustainability budget of GU. Hence, the course is set for a long-term institutionalization of sustainability at GU.

With the institutionalization of this office, the second element of a sustainability structure which the GGO-initiative envisioned is still open to debate – that is the sustainability committee. To date, the Senate working group has taken the role of an advisory committee that sets priorities and elaborates on the next steps. While this works very well in practice, in my view there is a legitimacy problem that must be addressed in the future. As the Senate resolved in its convocation, the working group is open to all university members. This lack of a defined member group makes it difficult to find a voting procedure to take binding decisions. As the office further consolidates, this will become increasingly important. There are different possibilities to solve this which are intertwined with the future of the working group. Firstly, the Senate working group could be separated into a core group that is legitimized to make decisions and a supplemental, open group that participates in the meetings. This could guarantee a fair voting procedure as well as open access. A second option is that the working group keeps operating as before and official decisions go through the Senate. The problem with this option is that the Senate presumably does not have the capacities to go through relatively minor yet important questions on sustainability. This option could therefore miss the aim of functioning as a counterweight to the sustainability office. Thirdly, a new sustainability committee could be convoked that consists of representatives of all status groups of GU. The working group then would either do the preliminary work for this committee or dissolve. Other models combining these elements are conceivable. It must be left open to which solution GU will converge and which role the Senate working group will play in the future. Yet, I personally hope (and the GGO-initiative will advocate) that GU implements a solution that allows for the participation of all university members – as a sustainable transformation can only be successful on a societal level working *with* the people and not through top-down methods.

4.3   Initiative on Academic Air Travel

The second case in which the Senate working group got active beyond its usual scope is the initiative for a Senate recommendation on academic air travel. The topic was first discussed in a working group meeting in August 2020. The chancellor informed the working group on the basic facts around air travel at GU. Since 2018, flight kilometres of GU members are reported to the federal Hessian government which compensates them through the German non-profit corporation *atmosfair*[20]. Joachim Curtius, professor of experimental atmospheric research at GU and member of the working group, gave an input on air travel and its importance for the CO_2-account of IHE. Measured in CO_2-equivalents (CO_2e), air travel is the most climate damaging means of transport. While air travel only accounts for about 2.8% of global CO_2-emissions in 2019 (International Aviation Agency 2021), its climate effectiveness is about three times higher, summing up to a share of more than eight percent (Niklaß et al. 2019). Moreover, the latest forecast of the International Civil Aviation Organization (2021), using 2018 as a baseline, expects global passenger traffic to double until 2035 and global freight traffic until 2038. Even with a potential reduction due to the Coronavirus pandemic, this trend is unambiguous. While some innovative aviation technology, especially for short-distance flights, might gain importance in the future, relevant

---

20   atmosfair gGmbH (2021): nachdenken – klimabewusst reisen. atmosfair. Online: https://www.atmosfair.de/ (accessed: 03.09.2021).

alternatives to kerosene and predominant aviation technology are not in sight (Bopst et al. 2019: 24). At ETH Zurich, greenhouse gas emissions caused by air travel make up more than half of its CO_2e-account (Kassab 2019: 64). While ETH Zurich is a very internationalized university, it must be expected that emissions from air travel make up a significant share at GU and other IHE as well.

Based on Curtius' arguments and his proposal of reduction measures, the subsequent discussion focused on short-distance flights, digital alternatives especially to conferences[21], the motivation of university departments to engage and rail travel. All members of the working group agreed that measures to reduce academic air travel were necessary, and the momentum of the Coronavirus pandemic was a good opportunity to implement these due to the increased experience of academic staff with digital alternatives. Therefore, the Senate working group agreed upon founding an initiative that would formulate a Senate recommendation on air travel at GU. With the turn to 2021, a subgroup of the working group started to meet outside of the regulatory schedule. In January, the official flights record of Goethe University which was annually reported to the federal government was presented for 2019. While the air travel in 2019 caused an enormous amount of CO_2-emissions, it is relatively small in relation to comparable universities. However, this is probably less due to the actual flying behaviour of GU members but more to the incompleteness of the data. As the record only encompasses flights that were settled with the traveling costs, and that were booked and prefinanced by the traveller, flights that were provided by the organization and flights that were not settled with the traveling costs are neglected. At the insistence of the working group, a process to fill this data gap was initiated by the chancellor. First insights of this confirm that the real scope of air travel at GU is significantly higher, yet exact numbers must be awaited. As they were not expected before the second half of 2021, the initiative decided to introduce its recommendation to the Senate without them, referring to the ongoing process and the substantial extent of the already known numbers.

Alongside interesting debates within the initiative, a joint recommendation document was composed, mainly formulated by Curtius and the GGO-initiative. In February 2021, the plan of the initiative was announced in the Senate and its members were invited for the next meeting of the initiative. While the feedback of the Senate members was predominantly positive, a surprise occurred the morning of the crucial

---

21 The immense amount of CO_2-emissions from international academic conferences is for example calculated by Sebastian Jäckle (2019). Online: https://link.springer.com/article/10.1057/s41304-019-00220-6 (accessed: 03.09.2021); or by Milan Klöwer et al. (2020). Online: https://www.nature.com/articles/d41586-020-02057-2 (accessed: 03.09.2021).

Senate meeting on May 19th. Instead of searching an open debate with the working group, the Senate list UNIVERSITAS[22] handed in a counter recommendation the evening before the respective Senate meeting. Thereupon, the working group initiative was able to spontaneously formulate an updated proposal, highlighting a few adjustments and arguing why the alternatives proposed by UNIVERSITAS were rejected. In the Senate meeting, the initiative's and UNIVERSITAS' recommendations were presented. An extensive debate evolved, and as the Senate was already behind its schedule and as there was a large number of requests to speak, the Senate decided to delay the topic.

Consequently, on May 27th an extraordinary Senate meeting on the reduction of air travel took place. After a heated debate, the Senate resolved to recommend that it is the goal of Goethe University to reduce its CO_2-emissions due to air travel by at least 25 percentage points by 2025 compared to 2019, excluding the compensation of emissions. To reach this goal, the university institutions are supposed to develop appropriate reduction plans that are monitored annually. Firstly, further recommendations are that short-distance flights should generally be replaced by rail travel, but justified exceptions remain possible. Secondly, on top of the reduction due to fewer short-distance flights, GU aims at reducing the remaining CO_2-emissions due to flying by at least 3% per year. Thirdly, the business travel application form should be supplemented by the specification of the caused CO_2e-emissions which have to be filled in by the applicant (e.g., via the provider *atmosfair* or *ecopassenger*). To facilitate the calculations a cooperation with a provider should be established. Fourthly, air travel costs should only be recoverable when a business travel application form was submitted to allow exhaustive data collection. Fifthly, the remaining air travel should be completely compensated. And finally, the flight data of GU should be collected and published annually. It should be the task of the Senate to annually occupy itself with the data and discuss further reduction potentials and goals. While a major part of these recommendations comes from the working group's proposal, parts of the UNIVERSITAS' elaboration were also accepted. In the end, the Senate unanimously recommended to the executive board to develop appropriate measures at the latest by June 2022 to reach its goals (Goethe-Universität 2021: 3-6). The responsibility to implement these recommendations is now in the hands of the executive board and the institutions of GU.

All things considered, the resolution of this recommendation can be seen as an important success in the sustainability transformation at GU. It

---

22 Goethe-Universität Frankfurt am Main (2021): UNIVERSITAS. Online: https://www.uni-frankfurt.de/44336301/UNIVERSITAS (accessed: 03.09.2021).

is the first time that the university has decided to restrict itself for ecological reasons. Even though conflicts will be inevitable in practice, the necessary direction seems indisputable. This example underlines the relevance of the GGO-initiative and the Senate working group as agents of change. Without them, this resolution would probably not have been possible. Yet, it also shows the interest of other, less sustainability-related groups like UNIVERSITAS and the necessity for open forms of collaboration to push more effectively for the common goals.

5. Conclusion

Much has been written about the flagship projects of sustainable development at institutions of higher education. However, there are few practical insights on the progress of the IHE that jumped on the bandwagon. To get an overview of the initiation, development and status quo of the sustainable transformation at Goethe University, I introduced the QSL-teaching project, the student initiative Goethe's Green Office, the Senate working group on sustainability, the sustainability office and the initiative on academic air travel. With this descriptive and rather subjective article, I offer practical insights that mainly aim at sustainability actors at IHE – to share experiences, inspire action and contribute to the global transformation towards sustainability.

The relevant actors of sustainable development at GU can be located at different levels, underlining the importance of parallel bottom-up and top-down processes. Foremost, the student initiative Goethe's Green Office, especially its members David Delto, Moritz Schmitthenner and Emil Unkrig, must be named as a crucial actor, pushing for change and voluntarily taking over conceptional and operational tasks for which no responsibilities were/are yet established. However, their engagement was only fruitful due to the increasing openness of the executive board to support sustainability structures at GU. The initiation of the Senate working group can be seen as a catalyst for the process as it allows the different actors (technical-administrative and academic staff, especially Norbert Dichter and Joachim Curtius, as well as students) to reliably participate in the sustainability transformation. There are many more actors, groups and projects like the QSL-project that contribute to the change at GU – representing the diversity and complexity of the issue.

Around the world, the challenge to *act in accordance with thinking* is increasingly approached through establishing sustainability structures like green offices or sustainability reporting – in some cases for more than a decade. Goethe University is rather a latecomer in this transformation. Ideas must be enhanced, and processes accelerated to switch to a sustainable path. Now that an institutionalization is taking place, maintaining transparency and participation will become a particular challenge. Only the future will show whether the initiated sustainability process at Goethe University is enough to meet its societal responsibility.

Bibliography

Aretz, Hans-Juergen (2020): After Humboldt? Hochschule und Service Learning. In: Rosenkranz, Doris/Roderus, Silvia/Oberbeck, Niels (ed.): Service Learning an Hochschulen. Konzeptionelle Überlegungen und innovative Beispiele. 1st edition. Weinheim/Basel: Beltz Juventa, pp. 16-24.

Bopst, Juliane/Herbener, Reinhard/Hölzer-Schopohl, Olaf/Lindmaier, Jörn/Myck, Thomas/Weiß, Jan (2019): Umweltschonender Luftverkehr lokal – national – international. Dessau-Roßlau: Umweltbundesamt.

Brüggen, Irmhild (07.12.2020): Nachhaltige Universität. Online: https://www.leuphana.de/universitaet/entwicklung/nachhaltig.html (accessed: 03.09.2021).

Goethe, Johann W. von (2013 [1796]): Wilhelm Meisters Lehrjahre. Hamburg: Zeitverlag Gerd Bucerius Gmbh & Co. KG.

Goethe-Universität (2021): Protokoll der Sondersitzung des Senats der Goethe-Universität am 27.05.2021. Vom Senat am 16.06.2021 genehmigte Fassung (unpubl.).

Goethe-Universität (2019): Protokoll der Sitzung des Senats am 20. November 2019. Vom Senat am 18.12.2019 genehmigt (unpubl.).

Grober, Ulrich (2013): Die Entdeckung der Nachhaltigkeit. Kulturgeschichte eines Begriffs. München: Kunstmann.

International Civil Aviation Organization (2021): Economic Development of Air Transport. Forecasts of Scheduled Passenger and Freight Traffic. Online: https://www.icao.int/sustainability/Pages/eap-fp-forecast-scheduled-passenger-traffic.aspx (accessed: 03.09.2021).

International Energy Agency (2021): Aviation. Online: https://www.iea.org/reports/aviation (accessed: 03.09.2021).

Kassab, Omar/Bratrich, Christine/Guggenheim, Carole/Knutti, Reto (2019): ETH Zurich. Sustainability Report 2017/2018. Online: https://ethz.ch/content/dam/ethz/main/eth-zurich/nachhaltigkeit/Berichte/Nachhaltigkeitsbericht/ETHzurich_Sustainability_Report_2017_2018_web.pdf (accessed: 03.09.2021).

Kminek, Helge/Wallmeier, Philip (2020): Nicht abschließbare Problemorientierung als Leitprinzip – Zur Bildung für die sozial-ökologische Transformation in polarisierten Zeiten. In: Eicker, Jannis/Eis,

Andreas/Holfelder, Anne-Katrin/Jacobs, Sebastian/Yume, Sophie (ed.): Bildung Macht Zukunft. Lernen für die sozial-ökologische Transformation? Frankfurt a. M.: Wochenschau Verlag, pp. 54-63.

McCowan, Tristan/Leal Filho, Walter/Brandli, Luciana (2021): Universities facing Climate Change and Sustainability. Hamburg: Körber-Stiftung.

Niklaß, Malte/Dahlmann, Katrin/Grewe, Volker/Maertens, Sven/Plohr, Martin/Scheelhaase, Janina/Schwieger, Jonathan/Brodmann, Urs/Kurzböck, Claudia/Repmann, Mischa/ Schweizer, Nina/Unger, Moritz von (2019): Integration of Non-CO2 Effects of Aviation in the EU ETS and under CORSIA. Final Report. Hamburg/Oberpfaffenhofen/Köln: Deutsches Zentrum für Luft- und Raumfahrt e.V.; Zürich: First Climate (Switzerland) AG; San Francisco: Coastland Climate Policy LLC.

Steffen, Will/Richardson, Katherine/Rockström, Johan/Cornell, Sarah E./Fetzer, Ingo/Bennett, Elena M./Biggs, Reinette/Carpenter, Stephen R./de Vries, Wim/de Wit, Cynthia A./Folke, Carl/Gerten, Dieter/Heinke, Jens/Mace, Georgina M./Persson, Linn M./Ramanathan, Veerabhadran/Reyers, Belinda/Sörlin, Sverker (2015): Planetary boundaries: Guiding human development on a changing planet. In: Science 347, 6223, pp. 736-746.

Vieweg, Wolfgang (2019): Nachhaltige Marktwirtschaft. Eine Erweiterung der Sozialen Marktwirtschaft. 2nd, updated edition. Wiesbaden: Springer Gabler.

World Commission on Environment and Development (1987): Our Common Future. Online: https://sustainabledevelopment.un.org/content/documents/5987our-common-future.pdf (accessed: 03.09.2021).

Reports on Climate Change

Georg Ehring

1. Introduction

"When a dog bites a man, that is not news. When a man bites a dog, that is news." – Since the 19th century, this saying has been used to show which events are newsworthy and which are not: the extraordinary is newsworthy. When events go their normal course, this tends not to be worth mentioning in the media. Perhaps this also offers an explanation for why the topic of global warming has such a hard time in the media despite its dramatic consequences: Since the beginning of industrialisation, the CO_2 content of the earth's atmosphere has been rising, and the increase has been extraordinarily steady for decades. The rise itself is gradually accelerating because more and more greenhouse gases are being released into the atmosphere, but even this acceleration knows no leaps or interruptions. The climate catastrophe is taking its course, seemingly unimpressed by political decisions, climate conferences or scientific findings.

In other words, the logic of global warming, for all its drama, does not fit the logic of journalism. Journalists report on the unexpected, on political decisions, disasters and accidents or spectacular debates. Although global warming has drastic consequences for our lives, it offers little that is surprising at first glance: There has been near unanimity about it in the scientific community for a long time. It has been known for decades that the heating of the atmosphere leads to disaster – and devastating forest fires, extreme hurricanes, heat waves and droughts are for science the occurrence of the predicted. And the extremely hesitant countermeasures taken by the world community so far offer little reason to report – after all, nothing is happening. But that is precisely the problem.

Admittedly, this comparison is somewhat exaggerated. But there is a lot of truth in it. Especially when it comes to the science of global warming, even new findings rarely change the overall picture. For example, when the Intergovernmental Panel on Climate Change (IPCC) publishes a new assessment report – it does so about every six to seven years. Headlines then go along the lines of "Global warming threatens our existence, or at least our prosperity", "Deserts are spreading", or "Sea levels are rising faster and faster". These are worrying developments, but they are not new. This diminishes attention, even though the findings are existentially important for us humans. And, worse, when climate change deniers spread the view that the scientists' reports are wrong or at least exaggerated, this became news far too quickly for a long time: as a counterpoint to the "previous" view of science – even though climate change deniers usually cannot even begin to base themselves on a factual basis.

The challenge for journalism: to distil current topics for reporting from a steady and slow development, to report news and to make the connections comprehensible. Topics include climate science, weather events related to warming, climate policy as well as economics and technology, i.e., new technologies that make it possible to phase out climate-damaging economic practices and their economic implementation. This paper is mainly about the issues related to warming that I deal with in my work.

2. IPCC Reports and Scientific Studies

In science, there is a body that regularly compiles the state of knowledge on global warming: it is the Intergovernmental Panel on Climate Change (IPCC). It has a special position between science and politics: on the one hand, as an institution of the United Nations: It was founded by the UN Environment Programme UNEP together with the World Meteorological Organisation WMO and confirmed by the UN General Assembly with the mandate to compile the findings of science on global warming and to report on them regularly. Its reports are intended to be relevant to policy without attempting to prescribe a particular course of action for policymakers – a difficult balancing act. On the other hand, the IPCC is a body of scientists working on a voluntary basis. It does not conduct research itself, but compiles reports on the state of global warming by evaluating scientific publications. The summaries for decision-makers are discussed and approved line by line by representatives of the member states.

IPCC Assessment Reports attract a lot of attention in the media worldwide. For Deutschlandfunk, I followed the presentation of the 5th

Assessment Report particularly closely: The summary for decision-makers is regarded as an official diagnosis, so to speak, of how the climate is developing. However, it is also the result of political debates and quite controversial among the scientists involved. Especially representatives of countries that put the brakes on climate protection politically try to water down scientific statements, add reservations or complicate the wording in the hope that the message will not sound quite so alarming – this is what participating scientists repeatedly complain about in personal conversations.

The IPCC's findings have tended to be the same each time so far. From report to report, however, the certainty with which catastrophic warming and its causes are diagnosed – and the richness of detail regarding the consequences – grows. In the meantime, scientists dare to make medium-term forecasts for the temperature development of the next few years – in addition to the general increase in the content of greenhouse gases in the atmosphere, they also take into account natural fluctuations that are more difficult to predict. And individual events are linked to warming – such as extreme precipitation or hurricanes. On the other hand, major uncertainties remain. For example, one central variable is still only very vaguely determined: Will a doubling of the CO_2 content in the atmosphere increase the average earth temperature by 4.5 degrees or only by 1.5 degrees? We don't know, and forecasts are often based on a value in the middle, i.e., about three degrees.

In media coverage, the content of an IPCC report is often summarised and treated as news. In the process, the findings mainly confirm what was already known to experts and also widely covered in the media on earlier occasions. Presumably, the assumption behind this is correct: many who hear, read or see the publications know relatively little about the subject, even basic facts are hardly known. Therefore, the findings are new to the audience as a whole. On the Deutschlandfunk website, the headline read "With almost complete certainty responsible" and the subtitle "Intergovernmental Panel on Climate Change on the role of humans in climate change". It is an attempt to place a new finding prominently in the report. In 2008, in the Fourth Assessment Report on Global Warming, the IPCC had only described it as "very likely" that humans were responsible for most of the warming observed since the mid-20th century. This time the wording was "extremely likely", so the certainty has increased.

It is not only the IPCC that comments on climate science. Time and again there are publications on individual aspects. Deutschlandfunk reports on these mainly in the programmes "Umwelt und Verbraucher" (Environment and Consumers) and "Forschung aktuell" (Research News), but also in other formats. A publication attracts attention above all when it comes from recognised scientists and is published in recognised scientific journals.

The media often rightly strive to "let both sides have their say" on controversial issues so that recipients can form their own opinions. In science reporting – and this includes the climate issue – this is also correct in principle. However, this is only the case if both sides can justifiably refer to science, and this is not the case with climate change deniers. On Deutschlandfunk, there have been repeated contributions dealing with this side, but from the point of view of science and without offering a platform for scientifically refuted positions. "There is no more room for deniers" was a headline of the media programme "@mediasres" in 2018. So we refrain from "revelations" that predict a new ice age or suddenly attribute warming to natural causes and not to humans after all.

Deniers and downplayers of human-made climate change try time and again to use the media for their own purposes. For Deutschlandfunk, the bar is high when it comes to reporting on such actions. In 2012, the two authors Fritz Vahrenholt and Sebastian Lüning jumped over it with their book "Die kalte Sonne" (The Cold Sun) – and they did so because public attention was high and the topic was therefore under discussion. The authors argued that a cooling of the sun in the coming years and decades would slow down global warming and make resolute climate protection superfluous. Their book was publicised with a press conference and elaborate advance notice, but contrary to custom, the text of the work was not released in advance under embargo. So it took several days after publication before scientists could point out errors and the untenability of their theses became apparent. This was apparently the point – for days, many media participated in sowing doubts about the results of science. A few days after the book was published, Deutschlandfunk published a detailed review by me with the conclusion: "The book does not offer a serious examination of the subject, but a preconceived opinion full of conspiracy theories, blinkers and prejudices – and that, moreover, with many errors and misleading details."

3. International Climate Conferences – For a Short Time, the Future of the Planet Takes Centre Stage

Once a year in November or December, the UN Climate Change Conference convenes, formally as the General Assembly of the UN Framework Convention on Climate Change (UNFCCC) and as a meeting of the signatory states to the Paris Agreement. I follow the climate conferences closely – I have been to every climate summit since 2009 in Copenhagen.

The summit in Copenhagen was particularly instructive for me – precisely because it failed spectacularly. The UN Climate Secretariat, many participating countries and environmental associations had presented the event in advance as crucial for future climate protection: An international treaty on limiting greenhouse gas emissions must be reached at this meeting. If this did not succeed, climate protection would have failed. The summit itself was highly dramatic and only ended with a meagre declaration of intent to limit global warming to a maximum of two degrees. The international community was unable to agree on the crucial question of how this could be achieved.

Many media representatives, including myself, adopted the view of a last chance that had to be used. It was already clear in the run-up that the positions of industrialised and developing countries in particular were far apart. My personal conclusion: more critical distance would have been necessary. On the one hand, it is necessary to be close to decision-makers, but on the other hand, it is also necessary to have an independent judgement so as not to be carried away by moods.

In the following years, the climate issue lost attention. In the years that followed, the international community made a new attempt to forge an international agreement. The annual climate conferences were about preliminary decisions on what it could look like and finally it came to pass in Paris in 2015.

For journalists, climate conferences are an opportunity to illuminate the topic from almost every perspective: Governments and groups of states represent their interests and put their activities in the field in the spotlight, non-governmental organisations and business associations make demands and the scientific community presents new research results. Public attention is high, especially at the beginning and at the end: many hours, often more than a day later than originally scheduled, the summit agrees on a final paper that has to be adopted unanimously. In the first week, the negotiations are the responsibility of the diplomats and experts, then the political leaders, environment ministers or heads of state and government take over. In the end, it is usually a matter of formulating details, which, however, point to fundamental differences of interests.

Where do we get the information at climate conferences? The participating states and interest groups address the press every day – there are press conferences in two conference rooms every half hour. And there are plenary sessions and, in some cases, working groups that are open to the public. In addition, there are talks with observers. Non-governmental organisations are sometimes very well informed and they sometimes have access to meetings to which the press is not admitted. The delegations of many states inform the media of their country. It is important to also talk to representatives of other countries and various interest groups in order to get an overall picture.

The importance of climate conferences is not only reflected in the final documents, which often record little progress. For a fortnight a year, the climate issue is at the centre of attention in many countries, which is where it belongs. For poor countries in particular, it is one of the few opportunities to make clear how they are affected by the climate crisis and to attract public attention.

And: International treaties are of paramount importance in climate protection. Because in the short-term it is expensive for an economy to put part of its resources at the service of the general public – i.e., to reduce CO_2 emissions. For example, by making energy more expensive through initial investments in renewable energies. Nevertheless, the willingness of countries to focus on climate protection depends very much on the trust that other countries will do the same. Treaties make an important contribution to this.

However, what is ultimately decisive for the climate is what happens on the ground – in Germany, for example. That is why we are intensively following the energy transition, reporting on renewable energies, the expansion of electricity grids or the price of CO_2 emissions. What is happening is strongly influenced by economic interests, many of them with the aim of continuing to use fossil energy sources and delaying climate protection – even if hardly anyone openly admits this today. But energy suppliers, for example, present coal and gas as the guarantors of a reliable and economical power supply and for a long time sowed doubts that this could also be achieved with renewables. And car manufacturers rely on ever larger and heavier vehicles with petrol or diesel engines that hardly consume less than their lighter and smaller predecessor models.

I see the energy transition as a success story. Just 15 years ago, in 2006, the German government's target for the expansion of renewables in electricity generation was 20% by 2020. "It will hardly be possible to achieve more," Stephan Kohler, head of the German Energy Agency at the time, told me at the time. The target was far exceeded, with net electricity generation reaching 50.5% in 2020. Climate activists who called early on for such shares to be achieved were criticised by representatives of the established energy industry as fantasists; on Deutschlandfunk we let both sides have their say, along with scientists, environmentalists and politicians. The focus of many actors was to emphasise the high costs of the switch. Researchers, on the other hand, point to the high costs of not switching in the form of health damage from poor air quality and climate damage from heat waves and extreme weather events. The shift towards solar and wind renewables came much faster than expected, perhaps a blueprint for the transition to electric mobility in the decade that has begun. The lesson for me as a journalist from this: Don't be too quick to label ambitious expectations as unrealistic. Change is easily underestimated, as also the triumph of mobile communication has shown in recent years. Other things happen agonisingly slowly, the expansion of the electricity grid is an example of this.

Civil society organisations are among the most important drivers of climate protection. For a long time, traditional environmental associations have been among them, and since 2018, the student movement "Fridays for Future", initiated by Greta Thunberg. It has ensured that the mood in Europe in particular has turned pro-climate protection – with the simple demand to listen to science and comply with the Paris Agreement. Knowing full well that this requires a drastic change of course. On Deutschlandfunk, we reported extensively on the protests and their background, including an "Interview of the Week" with Luisa Neubauer, one of the voices of "Fridays for Future" in Germany. "Fridays for Future" and new movements like "Extinction Rebellion" describe the dangers for humanity in a drastic way, but in my impression close to reality and oriented towards science. The sense that our livelihoods are threatened has also recently led to the demand that we journalists become actors in climate policy. If the danger is so blatantly ignored and talked down, journalism cannot remain neutral.

I find this tendency problematic. The means of journalism: researching, reporting based on the facts and evaluating in commentary are the tried and tested forms that ensure trust in reporting – regardless of the political tendency. Journalism that thinks politically and pedagogically about how best to persuade people and aligns its reporting with that becomes activism. Activism is one important task, but that of journalists is another. But the calls for us journalists to approach warming differently than before are more than justified in another respect:

I am convinced that the topic of climate change and climate protection is not given the importance it deserves. After all, it is about a development that threatens the future of humanity as a whole. In politics, short-term interests such as those of the energy industry and the car industry are often taken more seriously than the future habitability of the planet, or the points of view are set against each other. Politicians do the same and the media coverage goes along with it. Should we cut CO_2 emissions to secure the future of humanity – even though this might make electricity a little more expensive? For many journalists, this is an open question where the arguments on both sides have merit. It is the task of journalists to let the different views from politics, business and society have their say. In commentary, it is to take a clear position, but in reporting, the different views should be allowed to have their say. After all, they also carry weight in the decision-making process.

Global warming is currently the most important topic of all with regard to our future – at best in competition with other aspects of the overuse of the planet, such as the destruction of nature and loss of biodiversity. Therefore, reporting belongs much more on the front pages and in the lead positions of news and magazines. This is not a contradiction to the imperative of journalistic distance, but the result of the considerations that we as media makers have as our task.

In the past few years, the preoccupation with global warming has intensified in many areas. Science is producing new findings almost daily, in technology there is progress in CO_2-neutral energy sources and in business the realisation is spreading that ignoring the climate crisis would be expensive. The number of news worth reporting is growing – even if the Corona crisis is currently occupying public attention as rarely before. I expect this to continue in this decade and it is up to us journalists to intensify the coverage as much as possible. The future of all of us depends on how we tackle the climate crisis. Giving it more space is not activism, but the result of sober consideration of relevance.

List of Authors

BEER ALBERS studies Philosophy and German Literature at Goethe University Frankfurt am Main. His interests include the philosophy of German idealism, postanalytic philosophy and ancient Greek philosophy.

ANNA GEYER is a student of Political Science, Economics and Business Administration at Goethe University Frankfurt am Main. She was co-initiator of the QSL-Teaching project on Education for Sustainable Development and worked in this context from October 2019 to September 2020 as a student assistant. Since June 2019 she has been participating in the student initiative "Goethe's Green Office" and since March 2020 she has been a part of the Senate working group on sustainability at Goethe University.

GEORG EHRING is editor at *Deutschlandfunk* in Cologne. He is head of the editorial department for environmental and consumer affairs. He covers climate policy and international climate negotiations for *Deutschlandfunk*.

LEON FUCHS studied Geography and Chemistry for a teaching degree in Frankfurt (Main). His thesis is about challenges in geographic education brought forth by algorithmic cultures. During his studies, he initiated several student projects that focused on innovational eLearning technologies and Education for Sustainable Development. Furthermore, he was a student assistant in the BioKompass project at the Senckenberg Natural History Museum in Frankfurt (Main), which aimed to promote discussions on the role of the bioeconomy for sustainable futures.

CHRISTINA HÖFLING studied Life Sciences. Since 2013 she has been part of the education department of the Senckenberg Natural History Museum in Frankfurt (Main). Her current work focuses on participation and Education for Sustainable Development. She is particularly interested in involving young people in these processes. Within the BioKompass project, she developed an exhibition as well as educational activities at the museum.

DIANA HUMMEL, a political scientist, is a senior scientist at ISOE - Institute for Social-Ecological Research in Frankfurt/Main and has been a member of the executive board since 2014. She is also a research scientist at Senckenberg Biodiversity and Climate Research Centre (SBiK-F) in Frankfurt (Main). Her scientific interests focus on population dynamics and sustainable development, biodiversity conflicts, gender and environment, as well as theories and concepts of societal relations to nature in the Anthropocene.

RENATE HÜBNER, studied for an Economics and Sports doctorate at the Vienna University of Economics and Business. Since 2005, she has worked independently in sustainability consulting and research at the Alpen-Adria-Universität Klagenfurt. Current research focuses: Intervention-oriented sustainability, sustainable consumption, Education for Sustainable Development, sustainability in economic education. She conceived of, implemented and now leads the special field of study Sustainability at the University of Klagenfurt and is the co-founder of the book series of "Kritische Verbraucherforschung" (Springer VS). Affiliation: Institute for Teaching and School Development of the IFF Faculty for Interdisciplinary Research and Further Education.

HELGE KMINEK studied Education (diploma – equivalent to a master's degree) and the subjects Philosophy, Ethics and Politics and Economics for the state examination for the teaching profession at grammar schools. Since October 2013, he has been a research assistant at the Goethe University Frankfurt am Main's Department of Education. In his dissertation, he reconstructed philosophy teaching at secondary schools. Since his dissertation, his work and research focus has been on Education for Sustainable Development. He also works on reconstructive school and classroom research, Professionalisation and Didactics of Philosophy.

JONATHAN MASKIT is Associate Professor of Philosophy and Environmental Studies, Denison University (USA). His work on environmental philosophy, environmental aesthetics, and urban aesthetics has appeared in journals such as *Aesthetic Pathways* (now *Journal of Aesthetics and Phenomenology*), the *European Journal of Geography*, *Research in Philosophy and Technology*, *Philosophy & Geography* as well as in a number of edited volumes. He is currently completing a manuscript on cycling for Bloomsbury.

GUENTHER PFAFFENWIMMER is the retired head of the former Sub-Department for Environmental Education in the Austrian Federal Ministry of Education, Science and Research. He holds a master's degree in Biology and Environmental Sciences (teaching certification) and a PhD in Limnology from the University of Vienna. In his ministerial function, he was responsible for the development of all EE projects and programmes in the Austrian education system since 1986. He has served as the Austrian representative at the ENSI International board, co-ordinated the Austrian ENSI-Team and was involved in the programmes of OECD/CERI, UNECE-ESD and UNESCO.

FRANZ RAUCH is a Professor at the Institute of Instructional and School Development (IUS) at the Alpen-Adria University Klagenfurt (Austria). He holds a master's degree in Natural Sciences (teaching certification), a PhD in Education at Graz University and a Habilitation in Education (with a focus in Environmental Education). He has been involved in research and development projects nationally and internationally for many years. He served as visiting scholar in Newcastle upon Tyne, England, and as Fulbright scholar in St. Louis, USA. He is one of the editors of *Educational Action Research Journal* and of the journal *ARISE* and serves on editorial boards of other journals (like *The Journal of Environmental Education* and *The Journal of Work-Applied Management*). His areas of research, teaching and publication are Education for Sustainable Development, networks in education, school development, science education, continuing education for teachers and action research.

MARKUS B. SIEWERT is lecturer in comparative public policy at the Bavarian School of Public Policy Munich and the TUM School of Social Science & Technology. He received his doctoral degree in Political Science (Dr. phil.) in 2017 from the Goethe University Frankfurt. His research lies at the intersection of comparative politics, public policy and democracy studies. Lately, he works on the governance of the digital transformation and technologies using so-called Artificial Intelligence, concentrating, inter alia, on the connection between digitalization and sustainability from the perspective of policymakers and citizens. Recent work has been published, among others, in Big Data & Society, Comparative Political Studies, European Political Science Review, International Political Science Review, Policy & Politics, or PS: Political Science & Politics.

CHRISTIAN STACHE is an independent scholar who earned his PhD in social and economic history from the University of Hamburg, Germany. His first book *Kapitalismus und Naturzerstörung. Zur kritischen Theorie des gesellschaftlichen Naturverhältnisses* (*Capitalism and the Destruction of Nature: Towards a Critical Theory of the Relation between Society and Nature*, Budrich UniPress Ltd. 2017) was published in 2017. His fields of interest are Marxism, ecology, ecosocialism and human-animal relations.

LENA THEILER is a sociologist and research scientist at ISOE - Institute for Social-Ecological Research in Frankfurt (Main). She works on projects pertaining to the societal and scientific effects of transdisciplinarity. Within the BioKompass project, she conducted a formative evaluation on participatory formats to support societal transformation processes. She is also writing her doctoral thesis on science communication at the University of Hamburg.

Index

A
accessibility, 19, 160
aesthetics, 13-18, 21, 23-24, 27
autonomy, 21, 27, 56, 61-64, 91-96, 98, 101-105, 108-110, 118, 131, 148

B
Bildung, 73, 85, 98-100, 108, 128, 160
bioeconomy, 144-153

C
conditioning 91-96, 98-99, 104-105, 108, 110

D
difference, 13, 19-20, 23, 27, 39, 56, 58-60, 62, 69, 71, 86, 121, 179

E
Education for Sustainable Development (ESD), 51-52, 66, 69-87, 91-98, 108-110, 116-117, 120-132, 139-144, 152-153, 160
Enlightenment, 55, 76, 86, 91, 94-99, 109
everyday aesthetics, 14-16
experience, 13-21, 23-28, 47, 51, 118-119, 121, 129-131, 142, 152-153, 161, 169, 171

F
freedom, 76, 99, 101, 106-107, 109-111, 141, 149

G
Green Office, 159, 162-166, 171-172

H
habit, 102, 104, 106, 106-110, 140
habitus, 92, 95-98

L
liberation, 92, 104, 107-109

M
Marx, Karl 52-54, 59, 60-65
museum education, 142, 144

P
participation, 46, 118, 122, 141-145, 147-148, 150-153, 162-163, 168, 172
phenomenological aesthetics, 13, 17, 27
phenomenology, 14, 23, 27
philosophy of education, 9, 72
philosophy of science, 70, 72, 74, 78, 86-87

S
Schütz, Alfred, 14
second nature, 91-92, 96-97, 99-100, 104-110
Senckenberg Natural History Museum, 139, 144-145, 150
Senate Working Group, 159, 161, 164-171
sustainable future 148-153
social transformation 52, 92, 96, 139, 154

T
transportation (also private versus public transportation), 14-16, 18-28

U
urban mobility, 13-14, 18, 23

W
Weber, Max, 74, 77